EVERYDAY COURAGE

QUALITATIVE STUDIES IN PSYCHOLOGY

GENERAL EDITORS
Michelle Fine and Jeanne Marecek

Everyday Courage:
The Lives and Stories of Urban Teenagers
by Niobe Way

EVERYDAY COURAGE

The Lives and Stories of Urban Teenagers

NIOBE WAY

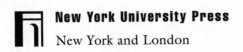
New York University Press
New York and London

NEW YORK UNIVERSITY PRESS
New York and London

© 1998 by New York University

Library of Congress Cataloging-in-Publication Data
Way, Niobe, 1963–
Everyday courage : the lives and stories of urban teenagers /
Niobe Way.
p.   cm. — (Qualitative studies in psychology)
Includes bibliographical references and index.
ISBN 0-8147-9320-7 (cloth : acid-free paper). — ISBN
0-8147-9339-8 (pbk. : acid-free paper)
1. Urban youth—United States—Case studies. 2. Urban youth—
United States—Longitudinal studies. 3. Socially handicapped
teenagers—United States—Case studies. 4. Socially handicapped
teenagers—United States—Longitudinal studies. 5. Adolescence—
United States. I. Title. II. Series.
HQ796.W325   1998
305.235'0973'091732—dc21   97-45296
                                    CIP

New York University Press books are printed on acid-free paper,
and their binding materials are chosen for strength and durability.

Manufactured in the United States of America

10   9   8   7   6   5   4   3

■ ■ ■ ■ ■ ■ ■ ■

To "Malcolm" and "Eva"

Contents

■ ■ ■   ■

■ ■ ■ ■ ■ ■ ■ ■ ■

Acknowledgments

First and foremost, I wish to express my gratitude to the adolescents who were willing to share their stories with me and my colleagues. Without their patience, cooperation, and wisdom, this book would not have been written. I am also grateful to the Henry Murray Research Center at Radcliffe College for financial support of this project.

My deepest appreciation extends to my graduate school mentor and friend Carol Gilligan, whose teachings are the inspiration for my research. Carol's intellectual guidance and vision have provided me with the essential tools with which to pursue my own research questions. There have also been numerous friends, colleagues, former teachers, and students who have graciously read this book and provided me with constructive criticism, wonderful insights, and much encouragement. These people include Elizabeth Abrams, Charles Baraw, Elizabeth Chin, Michelle Fine, JoEllen Fisherkeller, Monica Garcia, Patricia Harmon, Stuart Hauser, Laura Maciuika, Allison Morell, Meg Turner, and Janie Ward. Charles Baraw's extremely close reading of this book was especially helpful. I also want to extend a special thanks to Helena Stauber and Michael Nakkula for interviewing many of the adolescents and for their years of support and intellectual challenge. The project would not have been possible without them. Thank you as well to Jamie Aronson and Stacy Scott for helping to conduct the interviews, to Madeline Alers for taking the photos that grace the cover of this book, and to Annie Rogers whose remarkable work on "ordinary courage" among girls was the inspiration for the title of this book and for the substance of some of the chapters.

Tim Bartlett, my editor at New York University Press, made astute suggestions and was consistently enthusiastic. I thank him for both. I also thank Kelly Washburn for helping me put the manuscript together and for doing an excellent job of editing it page by page.

I am also grateful to my mother, father, and stepfather (Brenda, Peter, and Henry) for their keen observations on this project and for raising me to be a critical thinker and a believer in social justice. My mother's editorial feedback, in particular, has greatly influenced the form and content of this book. Thank you mom!

And, finally, I wish to thank my husband Ulrich, who has not only been a tremendous source of support throughout the many years of this project, but who has also provided constant, thorough, and important feedback at each and every step of the process. His insights and humor were critical to the completion of this book.

Introduction

A feared and seemingly ineradicable stereotype, the urban teen—
pregnant, drug-addicted, violent, fatherless, welfare dependent, poor,
black, and uneducated—is alive and well in the public's mind. The oppo-
site side of this cliché is the somewhat rare though equally reductive urban
teen who has risen up against the greatest of odds to become a highly successful entertainer, athlete, doctor, or lawyer. These contrasting images reside in our imagination, our daily newspapers, weekly magazines, popular
books, and professional journals, and are accepted as the totality of urban
teenage experience. This book, however, is about neither of these stark images. It is neither about adolescents who kill for cash, smoke crack, roam
the streets, and wreak havoc on the world, nor about those who have *overcome* tremendous adversity to reach great heights of success. Instead, this
book is about the urban poor and urban working-class adolescents[1] we
rarely hear about—those who live under oppressive conditions yet do not
necessarily provide titillating stories for fiction writers or journalists. These
teenagers do, however, offer us critical insights into what it means to be an
adolescent in the 1990s. This book is about the 95 to 98 percent of urban
teens who are neither murderers nor superheroes, and are not typically fea-
tured on the evening news.

Among the adolescents described in this book, some do eventually drop out of school or become teenage parents, while others are honor students or stars on the high school basketball team. All of them, however, are persevering, striving, trying to make the best of their difficult circumstances. They are not necessarily invulnerable or particularly remarkable—they are ordinary and courageous teenagers growing up in urban areas of America, and they have a lot to tell us.

This book is about the everyday courage of girls like Eva, an African American girl, who says in her sophomore year in high school:

> I'm not like normal people. If you see a pencil—if you put this pencil on the table, you'll see a pencil and accept it. I'll go around and say, "Yeah, I see a pencil, but why is the pencil there and who put it there." Most people would just see a pencil: "So what? A pencil," like that. That's how I go about solving problems, too. You know, that's it.

This book is about the stories that urban teens tell about themselves and about their relationships, beliefs, values, experiences, and lives. It is about the mundane as well as the exciting. It is about adopting Eva's curiosity about the world and investigating what it is like to be a poor or working-class teenager growing up in urban America in the 1990s.

This book is also about Sonia, a Puerto Rican girl, who reflects as follows in her junior year of high school:

> I feel I always have an image to put up because I think a lot of people have talked so bad about Spanish people. You know, that they get pregnant too soon, they're all on welfare . . . and that's where I come in. It's like I don't want people to think that about me. 'Cause, you know, I am gonna make it far and I'm not gonna let anything stop me. 'Cause if I do, then I'd get, "Oh look, what we all talked about was true." I'm gonna go to college. I'm gonna have a career set for myself and then I'll think about making a family.

It is about the oppression that ethnic minority youth face on a daily basis, the stereotypes that pervade their lives, and their motivation and persistence to overcome such obstacles.

But haven't we heard enough about urban teens? From Jonathan Kozol's acclaimed *Amazing Grace* to Alex Kotlowitz's *There Are No Children Here*, there has been an outpouring of journalistic accounts of the lives of urban children and adolescents.[2] Michael Massing noted this phenomenon recently in the *New Yorker*:

> The inner city, a subject long neglected by journalists, is suddenly in vogue. So many writers, photographers, and documentary film makers are heading out to housing projects and street corners that it's a wonder they don't trip over one another. Their output from the last year alone would fill a small depository.[3]

These reports "from the front" have documented the trials of growing up poor in desolate, devastated, urban neighborhoods, and of being an ethnic minority in a racist, classist, and uncaring society. Such accounts powerfully reveal the traumas experienced by urban youth. However, by focusing on the harrowing and the shocking, they commonly ignore or downplay the regularity of these teens' daily lives. These accounts are not concerned with how urban poor or working-class adolescents understand their worlds over time: how they perceive themselves, their relationships with parents and peers, their futures, their school, and the larger society, and how these perceptions change or stay the same as they go through adolescence. The research upon which this book is based addresses these gaps in our knowledge of urban teenagers. I sought to learn about *adolescence* by listening to urban youth speak about their lives.

As a developmental psychologist counseling and conducting research with urban teenagers in the Boston and New York City public schools over the past eleven years, I have listened to hundreds of adolescents from poor or working-class families speak about their worlds. As I listened, it became clear that their perspectives cannot be neatly summarized in the ways offered by either journalists or academics. Adjectives or categories like "hopeless," "optimistic," "present oriented," "violent," or "impulsive" simply do not suffice. As Eva suggests, the lives of urban teens are intricate, subtle, and rich, filled with contradictions, ambiguities, and continuities. Their stories, like all of our stories, are messy and out of control, and, at the same time, carefully gauged, in control, passionate, and provocative. There are no definitive boundaries within which their perspectives or stories neatly fit. I also began to understand, while listening to these teens, that they do not spend every waking minute confronting violence, drugs, teenage pregnancy, welfare, gangs, and single-headed households. Their lives are as complex and multilayered as their views. Their biggest concern on a given day may be, as it is perhaps for their suburban counterparts, whether they will go to the prom, or whether their math test will be difficult. Finally, and perhaps most importantly, I began to understand that, in contrast to what many developmental psychologists have suggested, the stories of urban adolescents are as important to our theories of adolescence as are the stories from their mostly white, middle-class, suburban peers. There are few studies, however, that elicit from urban teens their personal worldviews, and rarely have researchers examined their perspectives over time. This book presents findings from a three-year longitudinal research study of twenty-four urban adolescents from low-income families. During this period, I systematically investigated how they perceived their worlds over time—in their own words and on their own terms.

More than a decade after Carol Gilligan noted in *In a Different Voice* that girls and women had been excluded from studies of human development,[4] social scientists are now beginning to take note that urban poor and working-class and ethnic-minority adolescents have also been excluded from developmental studies. Almost 40 percent of all adolescents are from poor or working-class families,[5] one-fifth live below the poverty line,[6] and the majority of these poor or working-class youth live in urban areas. It is clear from these numbers that the worldview of this population will have a significant impact on our collective future. Yet as a recent article in the *American Psychologist* noted: "Neither research nor theory in the adolescent field has had much to say about young people growing up in poverty."[7] And the editors of a comprehensive book on adolescent development remarked: "Perhaps the most striking observation across all the chapters in this volume is the degree to which research on normal development has been restricted to middle-class whites."[8] Anthropologist Linda Burton and her colleagues likewise deplore that "a systematic exploration of what constitutes normal development among inner-city, economically disadvantaged, ethnic/racial minority teens has yet to appear in the adolescent development literature."[9] While interest in and research on adolescent development began at the beginning of the twentieth century, we are approaching the new millennium with little understanding of a large portion of the adolescent population.

The research on urban adolescents over the past two decades has focused almost exclusively on high-risk behavior such as teen pregnancy, school dropouts, drug use, gangs, violent and criminal behavior, or on related issues such as sexual attitudes or behaviors (e.g., contraceptive use or frequency of sexual activity). As with most of the research on ethnic-minority adolescents,[10] the research examining urban adolescents has centered almost exclusively on individual deviancy or social problems. Urban poor and working-class, and ethnic-minority adolescents have been and continue to be described as "deprived, disadvantaged, deviant, disturbed, [and] or dumb."[11]

Over the past decade, however, psychologists and educators have begun challenging these pathological representations of low-income populations,[12] ethnic-minority children and adolescents,[13] and of urban adolescents.[14] Disputing the negative images of black adolescents, Patricia Bell-Scott and Ronald L. Taylor point out that "the majority of black youth stay in school, avoid drugs, premature marriage, childbearing, are not involved in crime or other forms of self-destructive behavior and grow up to lead normal and productive lives, in spite of social and economic disadvantages."[15] A similar assertion can be made about urban poor or working-class youth. The statistics repeatedly indicate that the majority of urban adolescents are *not* involved in high-risk behavior. Nationwide surveys compiled by the Children's Defense Fund indicate that approximately 70 percent of twenty to twenty-five-year-olds from poor families (of various ethnicities) graduate from high school.[16] This percentage is much higher than what many imagine after reading the many newspaper articles on urban dropouts. The percentage of those who are poor and who drop out of school is almost exactly the same as the percentage of poor adolescents who go on to college: in 1987, it was 27.7 percent and 27.6 percent, respectively.[17] Yet we hear much about the former and little about the latter. If we do hear about the latter, they are described as the exceptions to the norm—the dropouts are never given such descriptions. These surveys also indicate that fewer than 20 percent of white, black, *or* Latino adolescents[18] under the age of eighteen report using marijuana (white females report the highest and black females report the lowest percentage of use); fewer than 5 percent of white, black, *or* Latino youth report using cocaine (Latinos report the highest and blacks report the lowest percentage of use); fewer than 30 percent of white, black, *or* Latinos report using alcohol (whites report the highest and blacks, particularly black females, report the lowest percentage of use); and fewer than 3 percent of white, black, *or* Latino adolescents reported "serious" alcohol use (five or more drinks per occasion on five or more days in the past month).[19] Furthermore, the 1990 national birthrate statistics for fifteen- to seventeen-year-old girls indicate that twenty-three in one thousand whites, eighty-four in one thousand blacks, and sixty-five in one thousand Hispanics gave birth.[20] In other words, for every thousand girls in this age group, 977 white, 916 blacks, and 935 Hispanics did *not* become adolescent mothers. And yet the experiences of those nine out of ten girls are not reflected in the developmental research. High-risk behaviors, furthermore, frequently overlap: an illicit drug user is more likely to drop out of school than her or his non-using peers, just as a young mother is more likely to drop out of school than a girl who does not get pregnant.[21] These percentages and the overlap between them suggest that far fewer than half of the entire inner-city poor and working-class, or black, Hispanic, or white adolescent population, are actively involved in high-risk behavior.[22] In focusing almost exclusively on high-risk behavior, then, social scientists neglect the lives of over half of the adolescent population. While the research on high-risk behavior is undoubtedly important, there is a dearth of research on normative issues such as parent and peer relationships among urban youth—including those who are and those who are not involved in high risk behaviors.[23] If we are truly interested in understanding adolescents, improving their lives, and helping them grow into productive and healthy adults, as the multitude of books and articles on teenagers suggest we are, then we must not only continue to examine the lives of middle-class adolescents from the suburbs but also begin to investigate the wide-ranging and disparate experiences of ethnically diverse, poor and working-class urban youth.

An additional limitation of the research on urban adolescents, and in fact on all adolescents, springs from the dominant methodology used to gather it. Research projects on adolescents have not, for the most part, asked their participants to describe their experiences in their own words. There has been an overreliance on methods that impose predetermined definitions and categories. True/false or multiple-choice questionnaires are useful in obtaining information as to how well the respondents fit into the categories set up by the scale; they are of less use in exploring the intricacies and subtleties of how individuals perceive, assign value to, and speak about different parts of their lives. Renowned developmental psychologists Urie Bronfenbrenner and Kurt Lewin assert that what matters in development is not only what exists in "objective reality" (i.e., concrete material and environmental conditions), but also how the environment is perceived and constructed by the individuals in that environment.[24] Although researchers may presume to know how urban adolescents perceive their worlds given the "objective reality" (e.g., a high crime, violence, and poverty rate) or developmental phase (i.e., adolescence), our assumptions may not reflect how this reality is actually perceived by the adolescents themselves. Certain assumptions about adolescents and "the adolescent experience" (e.g., the desire for separation from parents) pervade both the media and more academic representations of them. Yet, for the most part, we have neglected to check out many of these assumptions and, consequently, continue to perpetuate what may be myths about adolescents rather than knowledge based on their lived experiences. Listening to adolescents provides an essential window into their experience and allows us to build theories that are more reflective of their lives. Once we begin listening, our theories about adolescents—all adolescents—will likely be challenged and we will be forced to revise and expand what we think we know about them.

Recognizing the limitations in more quantitative approaches to research, anthropologists, sociologists, and psychologists have recently been listening to adolescents, including those who are poor or working class.[25] These qualitative researchers have gone to great lengths to avoid overly simplistic or reductionist portraits of the adolescents they study. Nevertheless, like the more quantitative studies, the majority of the qualitative studies on urban poor or working-class adolescents have concentrated either primarily or exclusively on populations involved in high-risk behavior or have focused on only one or two components of an adolescent's world. Furthermore, few have taken a developmental approach.[26] Studies such as Anne Campbell's compelling exploration of gangs among adolescent girls, or Jay MacLeod's wonderfully descriptive account of two groups of working-class boys, provide us with much-needed information about the thoughts, feelings, and behaviors of their participants and about the structural barriers that prevent them from reaching their dreams.[27] These studies, however, do not provide us with an account of how adolescents perceive their worlds as they grow older, or of the nature of their intellectual and emotional evolution. Listening to a wide spectrum of adolescent girls and boys, as well as discerning how they perceive a wide variety of topics relevant to their daily lives (e.g., themselves, their relationships, their school, the larger society, etc.) over time, is critical for a rich and full understanding of adolescence.

In my three-year longitudinal, qualitative study of twenty-four urban adolescents, I sought to explore their perspectives about many different aspects of their lives, to reveal the multifaceted nature of their lives, and to add their diverse voices to the research literature on adolescents. My questions were threefold: (1) What are the various ways in which urban adolescents perceive their worlds? (2) How do their perceptions change as they go through adolescence? and (3) How do their voices affect our understanding of adolescence as a critical phase in human development? I was intent on exploring areas that have rarely been examined by researchers studying urban youth in particular, and human psychological development in general.

Bronfenbrenner's idea of what constitutes one's world (one's "ecological environment") includes not only the home, school, and workplace, but also the larger society (the "overarching institutional patterns of the culture") in which a person lives.[28] I have incorporated this definition into my understanding of what makes up an adolescent's world. I also owe a debt to Karsten Harries's interpretation of Martin Heidegger's conception of "world":

> "World" cannot mean the totality of facts. Think rather what we mean when we speak of the "world of the baseball player." "World" here means not just bases and balls, ball parks and hotels, players and umpires . . . but first of all a mode of existing, a way in which the baseball player relates to things and persons and to himself.[29]

I aimed to listen to urban adolescents' perceptions of how they relate to themselves, to family members, to peers, to important others, to institutions (such as school), and to the larger culture. I was less interested in the actual existence of certain conditions such as urban violence or poverty (which are the "totality of facts") as I was in the adolescents' "mode of existing" or "ways of relating" within these structural constraints. I investigated the ways in which a group of adolescents speak about their values; about what makes their lives worth living; about their futures; and, finally, about how they experience school and the society at large.[30] I did not attempt to produce separate findings with respect to each of these topics, but rather to detect themes that arose when these adolescents spoke about a range of their experiences.

My research was driven by my desire to go beyond what Toni Morrison has called "the panoramic view"[31]—the view put forth by the media and social science research. I wanted to learn more than what I had seen and been taught (e.g., that living in the inner city is dangerous and depressing). I wanted to listen to the voices and hear the experiences of adolescents growing up in poor, urban areas so that I might come to understand what their worlds "feel like and what they mean personally."[32] With this understanding, I hoped I would be better equipped to help these teenagers thrive.

The book is organized into eleven chapters. The first chapter, divided into two parts, presents the theories that inform my study. The first part focuses on the various philosophical, psychological, and feminist theories that have shaped both the research process and the outcomes of my study. The second part of the chapter discusses how these theories have created a practice of research. It is this practice of research that I have adopted in my own work. The second chapter provides details of the study: the teens involved in the study, the setting of the study, and the data-analytic techniques used to detect themes in their interviews. In the third chapter, I open the discussion of my findings with a case study of Malcolm, an adolescent boy. I devote a full chapter to Malcolm to establish and emphasize the individuality of the adolescents in the study before I discuss, in the later chapters, the common themes heard among them. In the following six chapters, I present common themes that I detected in the teens' interviews. These themes are not always present across or within their stories; they surfaced in some interviews and were notably absent in others. Tracing each theme and its absence led me to identify smaller subthemes, tributaries that further complicated the overarching themes. These themes and subthemes are discussed at length in these six chapters. In the tenth chapter, I offer another story of a life in progress. This case study is of Eva, an adolescent girl. Once again, I attempt to underscore the singularity of the stories that the adolescents told me and my colleagues. In the epilogue, I discuss how the themes intersect and what questions they raise for our understanding of urban adolescents, adolescence, and more generally for the field of social science as a whole.

Before continuing, I want briefly to note what my book will not address. It does not provide an overview of the growing body of research on urban poor, working-class, or ethnic-minority adolescents or any other group of adolescents. Numerous books and research reports have been written over the past decade that have summarized the research findings on these populations.[33] I only make references to previous research when it relates directly to the themes that I detected in the interviews. Furthermore, my book does not present an overview of the cultural beliefs and attitudes among different ethnic groups except as they relate to the themes detected in the data. A problem with inserting homogenizing statements about "Puerto Rican families" or "African Americans" is that such assertions typically ignore the tremendous variations within ethnic and cultural groups. The history, immigrant status, family structure, economic opportunities, political orientation, and even individual personalities within the family will likely influence, for example, the cultural values of a Puerto Rican family. Yet the current fashion in the social sciences is to present global, undifferentiated statements about "Hispanic families" or "black families." I will cautiously draw on such cultural stereotypes, for that is what they are, when I believe they add insight to a particular theme being discussed. In addition, due to the small number of teens from each ethnic group (e.g., only two Irish American students), I do not attempt to locate ethnic/race differences in the interviews. While ethnic/race differences were rarely suggested, it is impossible to determine whether that was the result of small numbers or a reflection of broader patterns. Also, I focus only on the *adolescents'* perceptions. My study is not an ethnography of urban adolescent life.[34] It simply explores the narratives of a group of urban youth over time. Finally, not all topics discussed in the interviews are presented in the book. While the adolescents spoke about their siblings, for example, these relationships are discussed only when they relate to the central themes. This book presents the themes that I discerned in the interview data rather than all the components of an adolescent's life that may be important. Undoubtedly, the reader will note additional omissions or topics that are not adequately addressed in this book. However, I chose to address those topics that seemed most pressing when the teens in the study spoke about their worlds.

1

Interpreting Narratives

AS I RODE the subway each week to the school during the first year of the study, my mind was filled with questions about the validity, motivation, and limits of my project. What am I doing studying urban youth? Who am I to study them? What are they telling me? How will I represent their stories? Will I get it "right," and what is the truth? During the same time, I was a doctoral student in psychology, passionately immersed in the academic worlds of feminist, postmodernist, and hermeneutic theory. The perspectives advanced in these theories, loosely representing what Paul Rabinow and William Sullivan term "the interpretive turn in the social sciences,"[1] allowed me to eventually answer my gnawing questions. They offered me a window of clarity in the midst of my confusion. Feminist theory and postmodern thought, in particular, provided me with ways to make sense of my research project that resonated with my own perspectives on the world. They influenced not only how I conceived the project, but also how I analyzed the interview data, and ultimately, depicted the teens in this book. For this reason, it is critical for me to describe, over the next few pages, the beliefs held within this interpretive turn that shaped both the form and content of my study. Laying out the theoretical framework of my study is essential for understanding the teens' stories that follow.

Form

Objectivity?

Criticizing the objective ideal in the social sciences, Rabinow and Sullivan write:

> There is no outside, detached standpoint from which to gather and present brute data. When we try to understand the cultural world, we are dealing with interpretations, and interpretations of interpretations. Culture—the shared meanings, practices, and symbols that constitute the human world—does not present itself neutrally or with one voice, it is always multi-vocal . . . and both the observer and the observed are always enmeshed in it. . . . There is no privileged position, no absolute perspective, no final recounting.[2]

Like all other researchers, I came into my research on urban teens with a set of expectations and beliefs—a history, a gender, a race, a language, and a culture—that influenced how I understood and interpreted their stories. My stance as a researcher could not have been objective because I was not able to withdraw from my own perspective. In contrast to the beliefs characteristic of a more positivistic scientific tradition, the beliefs maintained within the interpretive turn assert that reality is not fixed and cannot be observed uninfluenced by the observer.[3]

Beginning with Schleiermacher in the early nineteenth century, various philosophers and psychologists have put forth theories making reference to a "hermeneutic circle." This "hermeneutic circle" centers on the idea that "understanding inevitably involves reference to that which is already known."[4] My study rests on the assumption, for better or worse, that we can never escape such a circle of interpretation. When we try to understand a new phenomenon, we are always coming into it with expectations and preconceptions. Furthermore, what we already know, or our pre-understanding, is itself not an unmediated knowledge of the empirical world but determined by the traditions and symbolic codes within which we live and which shape our lives and ways of making sense of it. Once this dialectical nature of understanding has been recognized, the illusion of a completely detached stance as a researcher is exposed as such. The belief in an absolutely blank mind—a mind without any biases, prejudices, or pre-understandings—is a powerful trope or figure for scientific research but an untenable research tool.

One outcome of this questioning of objectivity is that generalizations and universals that surpass the boundaries of culture, time, and region become suspect. As the feminist psychologists Carol Gilligan, Lyn Mikel Brown, and Annie Rogers have pointed out: "How can sex [or class, race, or culture] be a difference that makes no difference?"[5] Experience, perception, or ways of speaking cannot be decontextualized, taken out of culture, time, and place. To discuss how a person speaks about her or his world means to take into account and understand that these experiences are intimately connected to her or his specific location in the world.

One of the problems in the existing research literature on various populations of adolescents is that researchers frequently infer or explicitly state that what they have discovered from their data is the "objective truth" and that their findings can, therefore, be generalized to larger populations. The implicit and explicit denials by researchers of their lenses and biases often lead to distorted and misguided conclusions about the researched population. A striking example of such problematic conclusions is the "deficit model" of development used by many social scientists, which assumes deficiency or pathology when a particular population is different from what is typically a middle-class norm.[6] For example, ethnic-minority parents are often blamed for not instilling in their children the "right" (i.e., white, middle-class) educational values.[7] This deficit belief system, however, is rarely made explicit in the actual description of the research, and consequently the findings appear "objective." Employing this stance of objectivity, social science researchers have been able to maintain that urban populations *are* deficient or pathological because these populations *appear* deficient or pathological according to these unacknowledged biases. The alternative hypothesis has only recently begun to be explored—namely, that researchers have obtained certain results because they have worked within a deficit framework rather than within a culturally specific normative framework.

Biases and Expectations: What Do We Do with Them?

Recognizing that research always reflects the perspectives, ideals, and biases of the researchers need not lead to chaos or nihilistic indeterminacy. Biases allow researchers to maintain order and structure and gain access to meaning. In short, they allow us to *avoid* chaos. Prejudices are commonly perceived to inhibit truth-finding rather than to enhance it.[8] However, biases and prejudices are necessary for understanding. They allow us to take in and engage with the world.[9] Biases offer a perspective, and only through having a perspective can we see and possibly understand the vantage points of others.

But what are the implications of such beliefs? Since we always have biases, and, in fact, need biases to perceive different perspectives, what does this mean for researchers? I believe, along with many feminist researchers, that researchers should constantly evaluate and reevaluate their biases, assumptions, and expectations.[10] It is when prejudices are not reflected upon, and as far as possible, acknowledged in research that one is likely to end up with findings that do not accurately represent the research participants' views or perspectives.[11] Hans-Georg Gadamer, holding similar views, states: "Every textual interpretation must begin then with the interpreter's reflection on the preconceptions which result from the 'hermeneutical situation' in which he finds himself. He must legitimate them, that is, look, for their origin and adequacy."[12] Instead of trying to "forget" one's biases, prejudices, or expectations, one should engage with and challenge such biases and assumptions and determine their validity and limitations. In order to assess the "adequacy" of one's biases, it is critical to maintain an openness toward the views held by the participants. Such an openness involves raising questions such as: Are the views held by the interviewee consistent or inconsistent with my expectations? If they are inconsistent, what are the implications for my own preconceptions or understandings? Gadamer warns us:

> When we listen to someone or read a text, we discriminate from our own standpoint, among the different possible meanings—namely, what we consider possible—and we reject the remainder which seems to us unquestionably absurd. . . . We are naturally tempted to sacrifice, in the name of "impossibility," everything that we totally fail to integrate into our system of anticipations. . . . [However] the essence of questioning is to lay bare and keep alert for possibilities.[13]

For sound and meaningful interpretations, it is necessary for the "open" reader to remain receptive to interpretations that at first glance seem "impossible," "absurd," or unexpected.

In my own research, I attempted to remain alert to the unexpected. I took note when I was quick to dismiss an element of an interview as unimportant, uninformative, or "wrong," or when I was confused by an interviewee's statement. I sought to recognize, question, and challenge my own expectations and assumptions. The purpose of such a process is, once again, not to rid myself of such expectations or pretend that they can be left behind once they have been acknowledged, but to come to the edge of my own knowledge—to ask myself what did I know that, in fact, I did not know? What did I expect that did not appear in the interview? How far does the interview take me into territory that I have not yet charted?

Examples of my own biases include those that stem from my experiences of being a white, middle-class woman in the United States. These biases have led me to perceive the world as one in which power differentials exist between men and women, white people and people of color, and rich and poor people; in each case, the former has more power than the latter. Because of these power differentials, I believe that white women struggle more than white men on both a professional and personal level; that women of color struggle more than white women; and that poor or working-class people, especially those who are women of color, have a particularly difficult time surviving in the world relative to those who are more affluent. Nevertheless, as I listened to urban poor and working-class teenagers speak about their lives and the ways in which they do and do not struggle, I realized that my vision of the world did not include many of their views. Indeed, my understanding of surviving was challenged by various adolescents who had contrasting ideas of what it means to "survive." Some of the adolescents told me they do struggle but in ways in which I did not expect; others stated that they do not find themselves struggling either in or out of school. Some did not even know why I would expect them to be "struggling." My expectations that the adolescents in this study, particularly the ethnic-minority adolescents, would speak about struggling to survive, about having to make conscious and strenuous efforts to simply get through each day, were simplistic. Their lives were more varied than I predicted—my biases were not "adequate."

Throughout my analyses, I reflected upon my expectations and my interpretations. What was I *not* hearing? What was I not taking into consideration as I made an interpretation? I tried to maintain this reflective stance during my analyses to keep myself open to what I did not know or what my expectations prevented me from seeing. Having an awareness of and an openness to "the possibility that the situation may not fit any pattern of understanding in [my] repertoire"[14] led me to more perceptive research findings than would have resulted if I had limited my understanding to those theories and ideas that were familiar to me. This process of continual reflection, I believe, enhanced my ability to understand more fully those to whom I was listening.

Biases in Developmental Psychology

Although biases based on one's history, lived experiences, and present situation differ from researcher to researcher, there are certain biases or assumptions shared by many in the field of developmental psychology—the field in which I have been trained. In my study, I responded to three types of "professional" biases: (1) toward theory testing; (2) toward universal theories; and (3) toward specific theories of adolescence. My responses were, once again, influenced by the values maintained by the interpretive turn that I have been describing. Because these biases were both incorporated into my study and implicitly and explicitly challenged, I will elaborate briefly their content.

Theory Testing

The developmental theories of Sigmund Freud, Jean Piaget, Harry Stack Sullivan, John Bowlby, Mary Ainsworth, and Erik Erikson form the very meaning of "development" in the field of psychology. It is largely within these particular theoretical frameworks or several others depending on one's question or population of interest that researchers are expected to work when they conduct developmental research.[15] Developmental researchers are expected by others in the field to use a preestablished developmental theory—a theory that has been validated as representing a "real" phenomenon in development—to frame their research questions or to make sense of their data. To proceed without such a theoretical framework is frequently regarded as "unscientific," "atheoretical," or "not theoretically grounded."

While social scientists over the past thirty years have emphasized the importance of data-driven or grounded theory—theory that is built upon what is perceived in the data rather than theory that drives the interpretation of the data—developmental psychologists have typically continued to believe that the only valid knowledge is knowledge generated by testing theories. There has been a general neglect of "discovery research"—research that aims to discover rather than to test, prove, or explain. If one's intention is to test a specific theory, using a particular theory to frame one's research is clearly the appropriate path to take. However, if one's intention is to listen for developmental patterns, especially among a population that has rarely been studied by researchers, using a preestablished developmental theory to examine one's data does not make sense.[16]

Theory or hypothesis testing hinders researchers' abilities to perceive the unique experiences of those in their study and makes it harder for them to see the complexities and contradictions in lived experience. A researcher may, in fact, become all but blind to such complexities by looking only for data that fit a theory rather than a theory that fits the data. In a compelling and convincing critique of the social sciences, Albert Hirschman lashes out at the "the compulsive and mindless" theorizing. He emphasizes that connections must come from the material itself and not from a presupposed theory of explanation:

> [I recommend] a little more reverence for life, a little less strait jacketing of the future, a little more allowance for the unexpected—and a little less wishful thinking. . . . I am of course not unaware that without models, paradigms, ideal types and similar abstractions we cannot even start to think. But the kinds of paradigms we search for, the way we put them together, and the ambitions we nurture for their powers—all this can make a great deal of difference.[17]

While I sought, in my own study, to create theories from my data, I do not claim, following Hirschman, to begin my research from an atheoretical position. Given that my position as a researcher is bound up with the theories of my particular field, to claim such a starting point would clearly be naive. However, instead of deciding in advance which developmental theory would be most useful, I adopt a stance of theoretical openness. I am not looking for an assumption-free discovery, nor am I rejecting the usefulness of theory or hypothesis testing research; I am attempting to expand our theories to include context-sensitive and data-driven models of adolescent processes.

Martin Heidegger, whose work has greatly influenced and provoked much of the current interest in the interpretive turn, writes:

[The hermeneutic circle] is not to be reduced to the level of a vicious circle or even a circle which is merely tolerated. In the circle is hidden a positive possibility of the most primordial kind of knowing. To be sure, we genuinely take hold of this possibility when, in our interpretation, we have understood that our first, last, and constant task is never to allow our fore-having, fore-sight, and fore-conceptions to be presented to us by fancies and popular conceptions, but rather to make the scientific theme secure by working out these fore-structures in terms of the things themselves.[18]

I interpret Heidegger as warning against the adherence to a theory or "popular conception" that is out of relationship with what or whom one is studying. My "constant task" as a developmental researcher is to base my theories on the data themselves as opposed to basing my understanding of the data on what I have been told is knowledge or "valid" theory. This phenomenological process will lead, I believe, to a deeper understanding of the experiences to which I am listening—"a most primordial kind of knowing."

Universal Theories

A second bias found in developmental psychology that I tried to resist relates to what Jean-François Lyotard has called "metanarratives." Lyotard, who has written extensively about postmodernism in literature and philosophy, presents a critique of metanarratives which he defines as attempts to explain a particular process by making reference to a "grand narrative" or overarching theoretical framework (e.g., Marxism or psychoanalysis).[19] Lyotard claims that by relying on metanarratives, we tend to overlook the localized, shifting, and contextualized meaning that is present in everyday life. According to Lyotard, there are only local bases of understanding; there is no grand scheme or narrative that can explain it all. This rejection of metanarratives "refines our sensitivity to differences and reinforces our ability to tolerate the incommensurable."[20] Lyotard calls for the aim of science to be not for consensus but for "instabilities" or for "differences."[21]

In my view, many developmental theories are similar to Lyotard's metanarratives. Developmental metanarratives, as I will call those developmental theories that present a predominantly linear, universal, invariate, and progressive model of development, typically attempt to explain the whys, hows, and whens of human development across the lifespan or across a period within the lifespan. They create a story of development that tries to explain at the "meta" level the stages or sequences of development. These theories focus on describing underlying structures or themes in development that are purportedly universal. By definition, they attempt to describe a developmental process that is decontextualized, taken out of time and culture. Given the impact of context on both development and our understanding of it, the use of these metatheories to frame development for all people is problematic at best. The metanarratives of developmental psychology inevitably claim more than they actually provide.

My questions, as I come to understand these developmental metanarratives, are: What is left out of or missing in these theories? What types of experiences and complexities are neglected or obscured? What is not yet understood? Unlike Lyotard, I am not arguing for the rejection of these metanarratives, for they have clearly detected important developmental processes. Rather, I seek to expand our capacity to conceptualize valid theories and to determine good developmental research.

Sandra Harding, a feminist philosopher, tells us:

> What we took to be humanly inclusive problematics, concepts, theories, objective methodologies, and transcendental truths are in fact far less than that. Indeed these products of thought bear the mark of their collective and individual creators and the creators in turn have been distinctively marked as to gender, class, race and culture.[22]

The metanarratives in developmental psychology cannot be challenged on the grounds that they are "marked" by such factors as gender, race, and class; all theories are marked. Instead, they can be contested on the grounds that not only do they deny their marked status, but they also inherently discourage "sensitivity to difference" in development. Considering Gadamer's and Heidegger's suggestions that all interpretive efforts operate within a hermeneutic circle, and combining their ideas with Lyotard's and Harding's, it becomes clear that an openness to the unexpected and the unfamiliar cannot be maintained if one listens only for what is expected theoretically. How can one hear differences if one's ears are attuned only to that which is familiar or seemingly universal?

In my own work, I have been acutely aware of the professional demands to position my study within the rubric of a validated developmental metanarrative. Using such a universal framework to ground my research, however, was at odds with the purpose of my investigation. How could I put the stories of a sample of adolescents who have rarely been studied into a framework that had been developed in a different context and time? Why would I use a theory that either bears no relationship to these adolescents' realities, or specifically denies their realities in its search for universals? Although existing developmental theories are fundamental to our very definitions of development, and do successfully, at times, identify what seem to be common experiences within and across certain groups, I resisted listening with only one ear. I listened with both ears—the one familiar with existing "developmental metanarratives" and the other attentive to something new and unexpected. I listen with what Kierkegaard in the nineteenth century called a "passion for what is possible."

Theories of Adolescence

A third professional bias that influenced my study relates to particular theories of adolescence. Unlike the other two biases, however, I engaged rather than resisted this prejudice. While there exists an abundance of theoretical and empirical work on adolescent development, there has been a preference among social scientists, teachers, and other professionals for specific theories of adolescence. Certain theorists have dominated the adolescent scene for many decades (e.g., Erik Erikson, Peter Blos, Harry Stack Sullivan) or over the past decade (e.g., Carol Gilligan, Robert Selman), and their ideas have profoundly affected the ways we think about adolescent development. The core beliefs of these theories are critical to spell out because they reside in our psyche and in the culture at large; and they determine, to a great extent, what is considered sound and accurate data on adolescents.

One of the most pervasive beliefs about adolescents initially proposed by psychoanalysts and neo-psychoanalysts that has been fiercely adhered to since its introduction is the idea that adolescents are struggling to find an identity.[23] The aim of this struggle is to find a sense of self that is stable and continuous—adolescents want to answer the question, "Who am I?"[24] The identity struggle of adolescents, the topic of hundreds of articles, novels, and movies, forms the core of how we define adolescence. Closely related to this concept of identity are the concepts of autonomy and independence. Adolescents are striving for autonomy, freedom, and independence.[25] Indeed, adolescence has become synonymous with the arduous struggle for an independent selfhood or for an autonomous sense of self.

Adolescents are moving away from their parents emotionally and physically—"trying to free [themselves] from parents who made and partially determined [them],"[26]—and are relying more on their peers for guidance and support.[27] This vision of adolescence perceives this period in the life span as a time of searching, separating, and distinguishing oneself from others. It is also a model that is primarily based on studies of boys and has been criticized by numerous psychologists as being a "male model" of development.[28]

Responding to the absence of girls and women in developmental research, Carol Gilligan and her colleagues began to investigate the experiences of girls and women. Gilligan and her colleagues found that girls are struggling to stay connected to themselves and to others during adolescence. Adolescent girls typically find it difficult to be themselves—to be authentic—and to be in relationships with others. The research of Gilligan and her colleagues indicates that adolescent girls often feel the need to silence their real thoughts and feelings in order to be cared for by others.[29] Their work, along with similar research on girls and the research on adolescent boys, have reinforced the widely held belief that adolescent girls are more relationship oriented and adolescent boys are more interested in separation, independence, and autonomy.[30] For example, adolescent girls have intimate and self-disclosing friendships, whereas adolescent boys have competitive relationships with their male peers that focus on sports and playing games.[31] While these assertions have frequently been based on comparisons across studies using entirely different research methodologies,[32] they are firmly maintained and repeated frequently in the research and popular literature on adolescents.

These concepts and beliefs about adolescent boys and girls pervade our understanding of what it means to be an adolescent and have significantly affected my study. While I have attempted to generate theory from the data, I have never been theory neutral or absent. I have been responding to the theories I have been taught. I was struck by and drawn to stories in the teens' interviews that tell a different story from what we have heard. Yet, I was also pulled to stories that tell a similar story. And, as the reader will hear shortly, both types of stories are present in the interviews. While I sought to derive data-driven themes, these themes are always implicitly and explicitly a reaction to our popular theories of adolescence.

The Decentered Experience

Following feminist theory, I resisted framing my project within the unitary truths implied in many developmental theories, and refrained from creating my own unitary and totalizing truths as I listened to and analyzed the interviews. I tried to avoid creating theories that exclude or do not consider the fragmented, contradictory, ambiguous nature of human experience.

Recent feminist writers have emphasized the need to question and even break apart notions such as the unitary self. The "self," feminist theorists such as Linda Nicholson and Susan Suleiman have argued, is not a unified concept but has many conflicting sides—sides that are at times incommensurable and contradictory. Like the self, one's experience in the world also has many sides. Jane Flax encourages us to "tolerate and interpret [such] ambivalence and multiplicity. If we do our work well, reality will appear even more unstable, complex and disorderly than it does now."[33] I would add that developmental psychologists would also benefit from embracing a psychology, espoused by many psychoanalysts, that recognizes the multiple and contradictory ways in which the people we study experience their worlds, along with the numerous and conflicting ways we study and listen to people's experiences.

A problem evident in much of the research on urban adolescents from low-income families is that these adolescents are often portrayed as one-dimensional and static. They are frequently described by researchers as "hopeless," "present-oriented," or having low or high self-esteem without any acknowledgment that these adjectives or phrases may only be true for some of these adolescents part of the time. As suggested in my study, an adolescent may be "hopeless" when speaking about the state of the world, but optimistic when speaking about her or his own future; "present oriented" when speaking about an abstract future, but "future oriented" when discussing her or his own life; having low self-esteem when discussing relationships with friends in general, but having high self-esteem when speaking about a best friend.

In the present study, I listened for the shifts and conflicting aspects of the adolescents' perspectives or worldviews. The "sense of self" among these adolescents was not static but moving in many different directions at once. In my analyses, I aimed to capture some of this movement. I, as a reader, was also going in many different directions and, therefore, I noted in my analyses the various interpretations or experiences I had as I read the adolescents' interviews.

Although my findings are centered on various themes that I detected in the interviews, none of the themes I discuss are neat and compact. For example, one of the themes concerns the outspoken voices of the girls in the study. What the girls' interviews also suggest, however, is that these outspoken voices are only evident in certain contexts and relationships. Representing their voices as exclusively outspoken oversimplifies and thus distorts their stories. In my analyses, I note the nuances within each theme so that their stories do not get reduced to a simple set of patterns. Furthermore, there was, at times, a lack of clarity in the narratives (mine and theirs) and, therefore, my discussions often reflect these tensions: Was the theme really there? Was I only seeing it because I wanted to see it? When and why was it not there?

While I argue for heightened awareness of complexity, Susan Bordo warns us, and I concur, that there is always a limit to this "dance" of ambiguity.[34] At some point, there are patterns in the ways in which we experience or see our worlds, and these patterns may exist across or within specific class, race, gender, and regional categories. These patterns are not, however, evidence of a unitary self or story, rather they are evidence that experience is always traversed by consistency as well as inconsistency, ambiguity as well as clarity. The focus of my study is on capturing differences as well as commonalities in the ways in which the adolescents speak about their worlds over time.

My Purpose, Given My Form

What does it mean to adopt these "interpretive turn" beliefs in my research? What is the aim of such ambiguous, nuanced, and patterned interpretations? I do not seek to provide an "objective" or "subjective" account of the adolescents' narratives, but rather one that is engaged and concerned—an account that contextualizes their voices and mine within the culture that we share and that separates us. I aim to expand the repertoire of possible descriptions of adolescents rather than to find the single "right" description for all adolescents or for all urban poor and working-class adolescents. I want to offer my perspective on some of the ways urban adolescents speak about their worlds. To use Richard Rorty's words, my intention is to continue a "conversation rather than [to] discover Truth."[35] I want to add to the ongoing discussion about what adolescents think about as their bodies and minds undergo decisive changes and their lives progress: What is important to them? How do they speak about their lives as they grow older?

Practice

The practice or methodology of my research is embedded in the beliefs I have just outlined, and more specifically, in the work of researchers such as Michelle Fine, Joyce Ladner, and Carol Gilligan, who have put these insights associated with the interpretive turn into practice in their studies of human lives.[36] Although not all of these researchers have examined the experiences of urban adolescents in particular, all have been deeply influential in the formulation of my questions, my choice of methodology, and the general process of my research. They have provided insight into the ways or methods of exploring and understanding the richness and complexity of life.

Robert White, during the 1950s, was one of the first social science researchers to stress the importance of studying lives in progress. He believed that personality is a constantly evolving system: Both the person and the environment affect each other and undergo continuous change.[37] Tracking this change and evolution is critical, according to White, for understanding human development. Furthermore, he asserts that personality is inherently complex and that the method used for studying lives ought to reflect that complexity. He chose the case-study approach over survey methods because he believed that through case studies the intricacies of a person's personality can best be revealed.[38]

More recently, Carol Gilligan has underscored the importance of studying lives in progress, and has emphasized, in particular, the importance of *listening* to individuals speak about their lives. Gilligan and her colleagues at the Harvard Project on Women's Psychology and Girls' Development have been a primary source of inspiration and guidance for this study. By paying close attention to their empirical studies, I was able to formulate ways to address the gaps in our knowledge about urban adolescents. Gilligan and her colleagues have spent almost two decades conducting research on the lives of adolescent girls and women and, like the previously cited studies, their approach emphasizes the importance of lived experience. They also focus on coming into relationship with the girls they are studying rather than simply observing and recording the participants' behaviors or responses. Gilligan and her colleagues perceive the research process as inherently relational—the researcher is as much a part of the "findings" as the research participant. Consequently, discussions of the relationship between the researcher and the researched form a significant part of their analyses.

Through their methods of analysis, they underscore the complexity of development, the "nonlinear, nontransparent orchestration of feelings and thoughts."[39] And in order to reveal such complexity, they concentrate both on *what* was said (by the interviewee as well as the interviewer) and *how* the person expressed herself or himself. Their method, furthermore, is explicitly attentive to societal and cultural contexts. They believe the words of adolescents cannot be separated from the culture and the societal context in which they are spoken.

> Psychology has lost an awareness of voice and vision, and with it the recognition that a story can be told from more than one angle and a situation seen in different lights. In the absence of voice and vision, the ability to render differences fades into the stark alternatives of a universal standpoint—the presumption of a God's eye position—or the abandonment to riotous relativism—the claims to have no perspective or terms. We propose to solve our conundrum—to embed psyche and to speak about difference—by recovering voice and vision as concepts that link psyche with body, with relationship, and with culture.[40]

Psychological theory, and developmental theory in particular, has privileged only certain types of metaphors; namely, the metaphors of stages, steps, positions, and levels. These types of metaphors, found in many developmental metanarratives referred to earlier, have missed the polyphonic nature of human experience.[41] Gilligan and her colleagues call for a change in the language of psychology from one of stages, sequences, and linear development to one of musical metaphors such as "point/counterpoint" or "fugue." The metaphor of a fugue suggests a way to listen to many voices "as themes, and variations on themes" heard in the narratives of people speaking about their lives. These musical metaphors, they assert, better capture the varied nature of human interaction and experiences.

Gilligan and her colleagues have taken the beliefs that characterize the interpretive turn and created a method of listening called "The Listening Guide" (described in the next chapter). Their method of listening underscores the relational nature of research, the possibilities for both understanding and misunderstanding within this relationship, and the abilities of people to speak about their worlds in more than one way.

They warn their readers about the dangers of "striving for safety [or] clarity . . . at the expense of voice or vision and thus of oversimplifying or reducing the experience of conflict."[42] My own study was motivated by the wish to recognize and retain the potential for complex self-awareness that is usually sacrificed in accounts of urban adolescents for the sake of clarity. Gilligan and her colleagues' approach treats the research participants as authorities in their own experiences by revealing their voices in the text rather than replacing them with summaries of their stories or interpretations that cannot be questioned by the reader. They are also wary of psychological theories that attempt to explain development before they have "listened to" development. Through "The Listening Guide," Gilligan and her colleagues encourage the listener to hear the ambiguities, the subtleties, and—in order to avoid the "riotous relativism" of nihilistic indeterminacy—the patterns in each person's interview.

Questions about Power

This relational, voice-centered research approach compelled me to raise questions about what it means to be a white, middle-class female researcher studying poor and working-class adolescents who are primarily of color. Was I perpetuating a historical inequity that places the white researcher in charge of conveying the words of those with less power? Gilligan raises similar questions: "Who is observing whom and from what vantage point? Who is speaking about whom and in whose terms?"[43]

In relationship with the adolescents I interviewed, I find myself in a different position from researchers who come into their respective environments intending to stand outside of the research relationship in the name of objectivity, to study their "subjects," and to depart with "truths" to disseminate to their colleagues, the interested public, and eventually the policymakers who shape their subjects' lives. I understand the process of the interview to be a process of jointly constructed meaning. I listened to the adolescents knowing that I listen to how they respond to *my* questions and to *my* interests concerning their experiences of their worlds. I am not objective and the adolescents do not respond objectively or neutrally about their experiences. Each of my questions and each of their responses was filled with our own assumptions, expectations, and desires. Although I had the power to choose the questions and to interpret their responses, the adolescents in turn had the power of knowing their own experiences and deciding what to tell me and what not to tell me or the other interviewers. Even if we are socially constructed beings largely shaped by the cultures in which we exist, we are engaged in a relationship in which each of us has power over what we say and how we say it.[44]

I do, however, have power in these research relationships: power to decide what to include in my analysis and what to exclude; power to take the words of the adolescents and create meanings to which they cannot respond because I did not ask for their responses. But I assume this power with great care and trepidation, realizing throughout my analysis that I can misunderstand or misrepresent what they are saying. This knowledge makes me especially careful to "stick close" to the interview texts.[45] I quote from their interview transcripts, often at length, so that their voices can be heard throughout my interpretation. A common criticism of qualitative research has been that researchers paraphrase the narratives too much and, consequently, do not provide enough textual evidence for the themes being discussed. Broad strokes are made about human experience, and little detail is provided concerning the narrative(s) that provoked these assertions. I was mindful of such criticism as I analyzed and presented my findings. I paid particular attention to ensuring that my reader could see the narrative to which I was responding. I made interpretations only after I had reread each section of each interview repeatedly and believed that I could provide evidence in the interviews of a particular interpretation. I was wary of my own leaps of inference that take me away from the adolescents' actual stories and into the tunnel of my own expectations. As I interpreted their interviews, I was continuously engaged in self-reflection: How have I found this theme? Where does this theme come from?

The critical question of what it means to study a population different from my own racial/ethnic and social class background becomes less problematic when I acknowledge that my research is about relationships—relationships between me, as reader, interviewer, and a former counselor in the school, and the adolescents in the study. My power is limited by these relationships. This research project is about what the adolescents were willing to tell me and the team of interviewers (who will be introduced in the next chapter) in response to our questions. My analysis is not about what the adolescents said, but what they said *to us*.

But Were They Honest?

Since I am not able to stand outside of the research relationship, I cannot claim that what the adolescents told us is what they truly feel. However, three of the four interviewers (including myself) had worked as counselors in the school chosen for this study and were thus a familiar, and perhaps more trustworthy, presence to a number of adolescents. A consistent presence and extended relationship with many of the students in the school— although not with those who were interviewed—made it easier for my colleagues and me to engage with the adolescents we interviewed and most likely made it easier for them to relate to us. Our status as both outsiders and insiders, I believe, enhanced the students' candor and forthrightness. Had we been fully integrated members of this community, we might have been perceived as too risky since we could have spread their stories to others in their community. On the other hand, had we been complete strangers we might have been perceived as untrustworthy. Over several years of interviewing, I came to believe that the adolescents were sincere with us since most of them appeared to speak candidly about many sensitive issues, including their frustrations at home, with their romantic partners, with their teachers, and even with our questions at times. It is also significant, I believe, that we spoke with the adolescents over a period of three years and thus created continuing relationships within which it may have become safer to speak.

The tenets of the interpretive turn have significantly influenced the ways in which I conceive of and conduct this study. They have led me to raise questions about power; challenge, reflect upon, and engage with my own biases, expectations, and prejudices; and reframe the research endeavor as a relational process. These beliefs are firmly integrated into the specifics of my research project to which I will now turn.

2

A Study of Urban Youth

WHEN I FIRST decided to study urban adolescents' perceptions of their worlds, I had already been working for two years at the high school that would be my research site. I was a mental health counselor in training with ten assigned cases a semester—pretty plush circumstances given that the school's full-time guidance counselors each had more than three hundred cases. While there was a tremendous need for me to take on more cases, my school-based supervisor protected me from being overloaded because I was there to be trained. Since few of my peers in training wanted to work in this school (given the ratio of need to the resources provided and the fact that we were not paid), my supervisor feared I would leave if the work load became unmanageable. I stayed on after my practicum was over to counsel students for another few years; to help procure a federal grant to set up and codirect a five-year prevention/intervention project for at-risk youth in this school; and to follow, for my research study, a group of adolescents over three years.[1] None of the students whom I counseled, however, were involved in my study.

The Sample

Because my intention was to conduct an in-depth investigation of urban youth in their passage through adolescence rather than to generalize to larger populations, I chose to investigate a small sample of teenagers. Twelve girls and twelve boys from the urban school in which I worked were selected from a larger pool of students who had participated in a cross-sectional study in which I was also involved.[2] In order to recruit students, the research team from the cross-sectional study (including myself) announced the project to all the students in ten academically diverse classrooms. Eighty percent of those who were told about the cross-sectional project volunteered to participate, and 93 percent of those students who were eligible for my smaller, longitudinal project were willing to participate in my project. The adolescents in my study identified themselves as African American (12), Puerto Rican (3), Dominican (3), West Indian (2), Bolivian (1), El Salvadoran (1), Irish American (1), or half Irish American and half Puerto Rican (1).[3] Those who participated have spent most or all of their lives in the United States and speak English fluently. All came from poor or working-class families[4] and lived in the neighborhoods surrounding the school in which the interviews took place.

The Setting

The school in which I conducted my research had been a fairly prestigious boys' school with a predominantly white student body in the 1960s but has gradually transformed into a coeducational, almost exclusively ethnic minority school with a poor reputation. The mostly white teachers typically blame the students for the school's decline; and the students, for the most part, also blame themselves, as will be seen in a later chapter. At the time of the study, the school had an approximately 33 percent dropout rate, among the highest in this northeastern city. About 25 percent of the students (girls and boys) became parents by the time they graduated from or left high school. The city's primary newspaper has called this school "violent and dangerous": the principal has been held hostage by a student at gunpoint, both teachers and students have been attacked in the hallways, and students have been shot at the subway stop next to the school. Black as well as white security guards roam the hallways, stand at the doors, and interrogate any "suspicious-looking" persons. I rarely got stopped by the guards while I searched for kids to interview, while my partner, Stacy, an African American middle-class man, was stopped repeatedly. During the last year of the study, metal detectors were installed at the front doors, but this novelty was quickly criticized for slowing down the morning surge to classes, and for its lack of success in preventing weapons from coming into the building. The suspension rate was high during the first two years of the study. However, when the principal was reprimanded by the school superintendent for such a high suspension rate, efforts were quickly implemented to cut it down.

The school's physical building is in fairly good condition. There are only a few seriously damaged sections, and paint peels in only a few of the rooms. The greatest problem is lack of space. The building is much too small for the twelve hundred students who attend. Between classes, students push and shove as they try to make it to the next class in the allotted three minutes. Fights often erupt between classes because a student has pushed another one into the wall and one or both of them are angry. Like so many other public school buildings, this building was originally designed for a much smaller student body. Designed to be a junior high school, it was transformed into a high school when the high school was moved from its former location in an affluent neighborhood in another part of the city. The building looks like a factory, with no "real" windows, only large panes of scratched plastic "safety" windows dully covering the gaps in the walls. On sunny days the rooms feel dark and dirty, with the smudged windows preventing the light and air from coming in. Students, many of them suffering from asthma, complain that it is difficult to breathe in this building. I felt similarly whenever I spent any time there. The circulation in the building is poor and musty smells of sweat and stale science projects float through the air. This lack of circulation may be, in part, a reason why students are seen sleeping in virtually every classroom.

The school is considered an "okay" school academically but since a more academically demanding "school within a school" left the building (it used to be located on the top floor and recruited some of the best students in the city), many have complained that all the good students have left. The school is now divided into two programs or houses—"the bilingual program" and "the traditional program." Each program has its own floor. The bilingual program consists primarily of Puerto Rican and Dominican students. A good part of the school's resources goes into the bilingual program and the more inspired teachers are likely to be found teaching here rather than in the traditional program. Students and teachers in both programs are acutely aware of this discrepancy, creating an obvious tension between programs. The traditional program is made up primarily of African American students and houses many of the teachers who have been teaching at the school for over twenty years. The students who participated in my study came predominantly from the traditional program.

During the time of the study, eighty percent of the students in the school were on the city's reduced or free lunch plan, which means their families' incomes were close to or below the national poverty line. Dotted with empty lots and boarded-up buildings, the neighborhoods surrounding the school are considered the city's most dilapidated and desolate and testify to a general reluctance both by city officials and the business community to invest here. A subway stop is located a block away from the school, a working-class Irish pub/restaurant sits across the street, and a small luncheonette is down the street. While many students buy lunch at the luncheonette, no students are ever seen in the pub/restaurant that is closer to the school and has food as cheap as the luncheonette. Tensions between white ethnic groups and people of color abound in this neighborhood and are practically palpable when students skirt past this Irish working-class establishment before and after school.

When I arrived at the school from the subway stop down the street, as I did every week for five years, I was often greeted by small groups of students hanging out in the parking lot or on the steps of the school, cutting classes or being denied access to their classes because they were late to school. On a daily basis the front doors are locked and students are not allowed into the building after the second-period bell rings. However, there are many secret routes into the school, and students seem to go in and out of the building throughout the day. School security is not as thorough as the administrators claim it to be. The school is a place where some kids want to be because, they told us, it is better than being at home or out on the streets. For many others, however, it is a place of frustration, boredom, and, at times, humiliation. Nevertheless, this school is the place in which the teens in this study spent most of their days, and it is the place where the students told us their stories.

Strategies

My colleagues and I conducted semistructured interviews as our method of inquiry. The adolescents were first interviewed when they were in the ninth or tenth grade and then twice more in the two succeeding years. My colleague Helena Stauber and I interviewed all of the girls and some of the boys, while Mike Nakkula, Stacy Scott, and Jamie Aronson interviewed most of the boys.[5] We tried to match interviewee and interviewer by gender in the belief that this would enhance the possibility of eliciting open and honest responses from the adolescents. Our experience eventually suggested, however, that this was not necessarily the case. Some of the boys specifically stated that they would feel more comfortable being interviewed by a woman and, subsequently, we accommodated their preference. Given my belief that continuity over time would enhance the quality of the interviews, I also tried to have each adolescent interviewed by the same interviewer each year. Due to scheduling difficulties, only ten of the adolescents were interviewed by the same interviewer during all three of their interviews. The remaining interviewees typically had the same interviewer in at least two of their three interviews.

The interviews were open-ended and lasted from one to two hours; during the third-year interviews, they typically lasted between two and three hours. The interviews took place in the school—any available space we could find—during lunch periods, class periods, after school, and, in a few cases, during the weekends. The weekend interviews took place in a community-based health clinic down the street from the school. The interview protocol included questions concerning self-perspectives; the future; drug and alcohol use; relationships with parents, siblings, best friends, romantic partners, and role models; and perspectives about school as well as the larger surrounding community (see Appendix A for interview protocol). Although each interview included a standard set of initial questions, follow-up questions were open-ended in order to capture the adolescents' own ways of describing their lives. I wanted to find out how, why, and when these adolescents think, feel, or act with respect to the topics we were exploring.

To provide incentive for the students to participate, we paid them ten dollars for each interview. However, we realized after the first year of interviews that a greater incentive for some of the students was the opportunity to miss classes. While we tried to avoid having them miss core classes, inevitably they ended up missing all types—from gym to science. Teachers occasionally balked at our intrusiveness and were understandably unhappy about their students' absences. To thank teachers for their cooperation and to give something back to them, we devoted time each week to helping them with difficult students. We ended up having good relationships with a small group of teachers who helped us find students and spaces for us to conduct the interviews. An ongoing difficulty with conducting school-based research studies is finding time to conduct interviews with students when the students are willing to do them and when the teachers will allow them to be done. In the end, however, we were able to interview all but one of the adolescents over three years (one student was only interviewed over two years). All interviews were tape-recorded and transcribed by a professional transcriber. Once the interviews were transcribed, the analytic process began.

In order to begin to make sense of what amounted eventually, after three years, to seventy-one interviews—each approximately forty to fifty pages in length—I sought immediate help from other qualitative researchers. While there is some consistency in the ways in which qualitative researchers collect interview data, there is little consistency in the ways in which they analyze it. After spending considerable time in the vast amount of literature on analyzing qualitative data, I decided to apply three data-analytic methods. These methods seemed the most effective in helping me sort, categorize, thematize, and understand the piles of data lying on my office floor. The methods, which I will describe below, were "The Listening Guide";[6] narrative summaries;[7] and a content analysis using conceptually clustered matrices.[8] As most qualitative researchers do, I revised slightly each method to fit this particular project. The integration of three revised methods, each emphasizing different aspects of the text, allowed me a detailed examination of the interview data.

"The Listening Guide"

"The Listening Guide," a method created by Lyn Mikel Brown, Carol Gilligan, and their colleagues, highlights the multilayered nature of people's experiences of self and their relationships as conveyed through interviews.[9] This method underscores and draws out the complexity of voice and of relationships by paying close attention to the language used by the interviewees. It attunes the reader's ear to what is being said and also, perhaps, to what is not being said. Moreover, it stresses the relational nature of interviewing, analyzing, and interpreting narratives.

"The Listening Guide" involves a sequence of four readings, each focusing on a different theme or voice. In the first part of my analysis, I undertook the first two readings, and in the latter part, after I created the narrative summaries and the conceptually clustered matrices, I conducted a revised version of the latter readings. The first reading in "The Listening Guide" focuses on how the narrator tells her or his story. As the reader, I sought to understand the story being told by the interviewee by listening for the "who, what, when, where and why of the story."[10] In this first reading, I also listened for and recorded contradictions or inconsistencies as well as repeated words or images. I looked for places in which there appeared to be absences or revisions. I also recorded the ways in which I responded to the narrator and the story being told, and I thought about the ways these responses affected my interpretations and understanding of the person being interviewed.

In the second reading, I listened to, examined, and recorded the ways in which the narrators spoke about themselves. I became attuned to "the voice of the 'I' speaking in the story"[11] by locating the references to self throughout the adolescents' stories (e.g., "I am outspoken" or "I am always worrying about my mother"). Without using preexisting categories to determine self-perspective, the second reading invites the reader to listen to the narrators on their own terms: What are they saying when they refer to themselves? How are they describing themselves? Together, these first two readings enabled me to listen and respond to the adolescents' stories of self and relationship.

Narrative Summaries

After these first two readings, I created narrative summaries of each topic within the interviews. Barbara Miller, in her study of adolescent friendships, created this method as a way to preserve the natural storyline and the context of the adolescents' relationships.[12] According to Miller, the two most important features of the method are that it accentuates "the elements by which we understand something as a story," and it reduces the data to a more manageable quantity.[13] Narrative summaries involve three steps: (1) the determination of a narrative; (2) a summary of that narrative;

and (3) the exploration of all the gathered narrative summaries to find evidence of similar themes.

Miller defines a narrative as a story based on an adolescent's personal experience, such as a relationship or a particular event. The story may have a beginning, a middle, and an end, or it may be a history of a relationship without a clearly definable beginning, middle, or end. The summary of the narrative is meant to be a condensation of the story. Miller suggests using direct quotes in the summary in order to maintain the "flavor of the story." There may be many narrative summaries created from a single interview or only a few, depending on the number of stories the adolescent tells the interviewer. When exploring common themes across the narrative summaries, one can look within an interview, across interviews (if longitudinal), and across individuals.

For my analyses, I created narrative summaries for each topic discussed during the interviews (e.g., self-perspective, relationships with best friend, mothers, fathers, etc.). For example, when Eva spoke about her relationship with her mother, she told me that she and her mother do not get along, and she provided various explanations for these difficulties. I summarized the entire discussion of her relationship with her mother, quoting her as much as possible in my narrative summary of this topic (see Appendixes for an example of a narrative summary).

Conceptually Clustered Matrices

After narrative summaries were created for each topic in the seventy-one interviews, I created conceptually clustered matrices in order to detect themes across and within narrative summaries. Miles and Huberman suggest this matrix technique as a way to consolidate and present the data.[14] The conceptually clustered matrix has a simple respondent by topic (or variable) format. All the topics in a matrix are conceptually related to each other. For example, I created a matrix for the general conceptual category "relationships with peers"; within this matrix the topics were relationship with best or close friend(s), and with boyfriend or girlfriend. Beneath each topic, I placed the three narrative summaries for that particular topic (representing each year of the interview) to the right of each adolescent's pseudonym. For example, next to Marie's name and under the topic "relationship with best friend," one would find three entries summarizing her relationship with her best friend for each year she was interviewed (see

Appendix B for an example). I created separate matrices for each of the five general conceptual categories: (1) self-perspectives; (2) relationships with family members; (3) relationships with peers; (4) perspectives on school; and (5) views on the larger society.

From these matrices, I detected themes across narrative summaries. Themes were repeated phrases, terms, or concepts that I heard within and across narrative summaries. For instance, when the adolescents spoke each year about their fears of betrayal by close friends, I considered betrayal a theme *within* the topic "relationships with close or best friends." When the girls spoke about being outspoken in their relationships in and out of school, I considered this a theme *across* the topics of relationships with friends, family members, and school. In addition, I also went back to my notes taken during the initial two readings of each interview (the first two readings in the analysis based on "The Listening Guide"). I used these notes along with the conceptually clustered matrices to determine the central themes in the data. Those themes that were evident in half or more of the interviews in any one year were considered common themes. I then searched for evidence of each common theme in the original interview transcript of each participant.

"The Listening Guide" Revisited

Reading for specific themes is an approach based loosely on "The Listening Guide"'s third and fourth readings. In the original version of the Guide, the third and fourth readings consist of reading for voices of justice and care. However, my analysis was data rather than theory driven and, therefore, I did not read for such voices. Instead, I read for the common themes detected in the conceptually clustered matrices and the first two readings of the interview texts. I read the interviews searching for the location of where and how frequently each common theme emerged in the adolescents' interviews. The conceptually clustered matrices offer only a rough outline of this information. Unlike the two previous methods, "The Listening Guide" focuses on both the narratives' content or *what* was said, and on the form or *how* it was said. Reading becomes a process whereby the reader listens not only for evidence of a theme, but also for points where the theme is revised, drops away, or is conspicuously absent. The reader highlights each theme with a colored pen, creating a trail of evidence indicating where and how frequently a particular theme emerges in the text. I, as the reader, look for the nuances in the theme and the places where the theme is not as clear as it is in the other parts of the text. As I discussed in the previous chapter, I attempted to remain aware of the interplay between who I am, what my expectations are, and what I see and hear in the adolescents' interviews. In each reading of an interview, I sought to "hold and represent the sense of tension that people often convey . . . in order to capture the situational, the personal, and the cultural dimensions of psychic life."[15] I attempted to track the common themes that weave throughout each person's narratives. The themes I followed were clear at some moments and difficult to detect at others. I aimed to incorporate these tensions into my analysis of the interviews.

My three methods of data analysis—the revised version of "The Listening Guide," narrative summaries, and the conceptually clustered matrices—helped me to hear the veritable pitch of a given theme as it rises and falls throughout the narratives I follow. They encouraged me to be sensitive to difference, variation, and contradiction while at the same time enabling me to perceive patterns and continuities. Most important, they allowed me to begin to understand and make sense of the masses of data we collected over three years.

These methods, furthermore, helped me meet a central goal of my research; namely, to describe and interpret what the adolescents said and how they said it. Given the lack of knowledge and the stubbornly maintained prejudices about this particular group of adolescents, I wanted to simply listen closely to their stories. I wanted to resist the immediate temptation to explain why they told such stories (although I do provide explanations at times). Explanation, though necessary, involves distancing oneself from the actual words of the participants, and I wanted to stick close to their words. In future studies, I can begin to explain more thoroughly, and these explanations will, by that time, be firmly grounded in the teens' perceptions.

INDIVIDUAL LIVES

Part I

In this book, I present two case studies of adolescents who were interviewed over the three years of the project. Malcolm and Eva inspired and provoked me. As I listened to their stories, I was compelled to focus on them for my case studies. Malcolm, first interviewed by Mike in the spring of his freshman year, is presented in the first part of the book, and Eva, first interviewed by Helena in the spring of her sophomore year, is presented in the latter part of the book.

In these case studies, I describe what Malcolm and Eva said about themselves, their futures, their relationships to their mothers, fathers, sisters, brothers, friends, lovers, and role models, their school, and the larger society. In some respects, Malcolm and Eva are similar: both are black and live in the same neighborhood; both go to the same school; both live with their mothers; and both struggled academically at the beginning of high school only to finish on the honor roll. However, they are also different: Malcolm is African American and Eva, though raised in the United States, was born in the West Indies; Malcolm is relatively isolated from his peers while Eva is extremely popular; Malcolm is not involved in any extracurricular activities while Eva takes part in many. Their perspectives on their worlds, furthermore, differ as dramatically as the quality of their relationships.

In presenting these two case studies, I want to remind the reader of the complexity of each individual life. While the focus of this book is on the patterns detected across adolescent lives, it is important to remember that each adolescent had a different story to tell, and a different way of telling his or her story. I also want the reader to hear how the specific patterns I focus on in chapters 4 through 9 are a part of larger stories—the two case studies provide a context for the patterns. And finally, I want the reader to hear the wide-ranging and deeply moving stories that two adolescents told us when we asked them about their lives. Michelle Fine and Lois Weis emphasize the importance of representing the "mundane" or the "rituals of daily living." They note that as socially responsible researchers we should "recognize how carefully we need not to construct life narratives spiked only with the hot spots . . . like surfing our data for sex and violence."[1] I present the details of two individual lives, in part, to avoid representing only the patterns, or the "hot spots," in the data. In these case studies, I want to present the regularity and texture of everyday living.

Throughout the case studies, I frequently provide a verbatim account of Malcolm's or Eva's responses to our particular questions. Although I offer interpretations of their responses, my primary aim here is to have the reader hear the details of the lives of these two adolescents. Chapters 4 through 9 are structured around the patterns that I detected among the adolescents and the interpretations I have of these patterns. Consequently, these chapters leave little room for listening freely to their stories. I have chosen, therefore, to present the case studies in a format that is more conducive to open listening—listening that is less constrained by a specific interpretation, that lets itself be guided by the rhythms of the stories. I begin and end this book with a story of a life in progress.

3

■ ■　■　■　■　■　　■　　■　　■

Malcolm's Story

MALCOLM, a tall, lanky, light-skinned African American student walks into the room that has been set aside for interviews. This closet-sized, hot and sleepy alcove is the only room in the school where one is guaranteed not to be interrupted by students or teachers wanting to use the space. Formerly a piano practice room, it has the added benefit of being one of the few soundproof rooms in the school—the interview can proceed undisturbed and confidentially. Sporting a flat-top haircut, baggy pants hung low around his hips, a colorful shirt, and untied sneakers, Malcolm looks like a typical urban teenager. Although he has volunteered to be interviewed, he seems shy and self-conscious with Mike, his freshman-year interviewer. He shifts in his seat as his eyes explore the small room. On the room's lone poster hanging next to him, which offers the only visual distraction from the white cork walls, a Hispanic young man proclaims that becoming a teenage father "isn't cool." Malcolm briefly glances at the poster, and without reacting (his gaze indicates that he has seen the poster many times before), turns to Mike. He is ready to begin the interview.[1]

Malcolm's Freshman Year

Malcolm lives with his mother, a secretary at a beauty salon, and his younger sister in a part of the city plagued by "a lot of violence" in the streets. He doesn't belong to a gang but the scars on his face and back (he shows them to Mike) provide evidence of his involvement in street fights where he "backed up" friends who were being attacked. He claims, however, that he has been involved in only two fights and that he generally avoids them altogether. Malcolm has a knife at home for protection, but says that he does not typically carry it on him unless he should "do something stupid like go outside, you know, way late at night in some area I don't know. You know?" He keeps the knife because he is worried someone will break into his house. He seems more threatened by an intruder at home than in the streets.

Malcolm has no memory of his father, who left the family when he was two years old. His mother's ex-boyfriend lived with them for a few years when Malcolm was younger but moved out several years ago. Malcolm says his family has moved a lot—they have lived in Florida, California, and in the Northeast—and by moving they have frequently left extended family behind. Unlike many of the other boys in the study, Malcolm claims that his extended family members have played only a minor role in his life.

Mike begins the interview by asking Malcolm about his family relationships:

Tell me about your relationship with your mother.
We get along pretty cool most of the time when we do see each other. She gets home about eight most of the time. And then I'm still probably not in the house. So then when I get in the house, I'm like, "Hi, how you doing? Good night." And just make sure I've done my [house] work. If I ain't done my work, then I might get fussed at. That's it.

Malcolm's relationship with his mother appears to be relatively uncomplicated and not particularly intimate. At home, Malcolm says, he is responsible for taking care of his cat, dog, and bird, cleaning his room, and, generally, keeping the house in order. His mother will ask him about his schoolwork, but she doesn't check it: "She only waits for the report card." Malcolm says he does not tell his mother much about his personal life. He prefers to talk to a friend, or "figure things out" by himself. There have been no men in his life whom he has considered a father figure. Malcolm explains that since his mother has provided him and his sister with "everything we have needed," his mother has served as both father and mother in his family:

Was there ever a male that you looked to as a father figure?
Myself mostly. I never really—I just looked at my mother as strong, you know, 'cause she kept me and my sister and she raised us both. It wasn't really my mother's boyfriend paying a lot of attention to us. He did help out money-wise. But she was there when we needed her, so she's mostly if anything the father figure.

While describing why he sees his mother as a father figure, Malcolm repeats a theme that is heard among many of the teens in the study who did not have fathers in their lives. Mothers were typically considered "strong" people who were "there" for their children and were often deemed both mother and father figures because they provided emotional *and* financial support. Although the teens did express anger, at times, at their fathers' neglect, they rarely spoke explicitly of yearning for a male father figure and seemed generally content with their mothers' abilities to fulfill both roles.

Malcolm believes that his mother listens to him and that they talk to each other "as equals."

She'll respect what I—what I ask or something.
How do you think you've grown into that position where you've earned that kind of respect from her?
Just by being able to listen and not really getting into trouble. Stay in school. Do my work. You know, I also have a few jobs. Like when she was in the hospital, I was working. And that was when I was paying the rent.

Malcolm suggests that his mother not only takes care of him but that he takes care of her and his sister as well. During the period in which his mother was in the hospital to have a benign tumor removed, Malcolm worked at a convenience store during the week and at a gas station on the weekends. I was immediately struck, while listening to this interview of a freshman, by Malcolm's sense of commitment to his family. While his appearance fits the stereotype of an adolescent, his actions clearly do not.

Malcolm is sensitive to the needs of others and willing to assume adult responsibilities.

Malcolm identifies his relationship with his mother as most important for him at this point in his life: "'Cause like with her, all these years we'd be at each other's back. Just like that, so that's the most important one." As will become evident, Malcolm's relationship with his mother is not only mutually supportive and most important for Malcolm, it is also the only relationship about which he feels good. Malcolm and his sister get along "okay" but they argue often because she takes his tapes and clothes from his room without asking him. This, Malcolm says, is the main problem in their relationship. Over the three years Malcolm is interviewed, his sister will play an increasingly important role in his life.

When asked about close or best friends, Malcolm mentions close friends from his childhood who no longer live in his city. Currently, he has no close friends who live nearby:

> *So you really don't have a closest friend here at school?*
> Oh no, nobody. Not even around my way. It's like everybody else is just associating, you know. No. . . .
> *Why do you think you don't have closer friends?*
> Nah, it's just like things like friendships take time. Just like a relationship. You can't really, you know, rush into that. You have to just take it slow and be able to know for true who's your friend, who's not.

Malcolm begins to suggest what will emerge as a common theme in each of his interviews. He is wary of close relationships with his peers and worries about "rushing" into relationships before he knows he can trust the person. By referring to his peers as "associates," Malcolm is distinguishing between casual friends and those "people that [you] really get into deep depth conversation."[2] Malcolm says he "hangs out" with his "associates" but does not share personal thoughts and feelings with them. In each of his interviews, Malcolm claims to have only "associates" but no close or best friends. It is not until his junior year, however, that he begins to clearly articulate why he does not have close or best friends.

In this freshman-year interview, Malcolm mentions that he has had a few girlfriends "here and there" but has never been involved in a long-term relationship. At this point in his life, Malcolm says, he has no interest in staying with "only one girl." "I just wanna expand mostly, you know? When I see something I like, I try for it, you know." During this section of the interview, Malcolm and Mike bond as they laugh together about Malcolm's reluctance to make a commitment to one girl.

> *What's your thinking behind that? That you would prefer not to get involved in a relationship but be available to get involved with whatever [sic] comes along?*
> It's mostly just testing, testing to see how good you are, really. 'Cause like you know sometimes you might not really like the girl. You might not even want to talk to her. But sometimes something about her that you want to talk to her for. . . . You know, that's where me and my boy Paul differ like. 'Cause he got one girl and he's been with her for a while now— well a few months. But like, see I be thinking to myself—I even told him sometime, "That's crazy. I can't do that, man." I mean just for one girl. I get tired of her.

While describing the subtleties of affection and desire, Malcolm speaks about his unwillingness to enter into a steady relationship with a girl. Although "his boy Paul"[3] maintains such a relationship, Malcolm has no interest. Malcolm's response, unlike his earlier responses, sounds stereotypically adolescent and male.

When asked if he thinks his opinions about girls will change in the future, Malcolm says:

> So I don't know if I'm gonna be able to quit or if I'm, you know, just going to keep going the way I am [seeing many girls at one time].
> *Do you mind if it just continues to stay this way?*
> Well, I do mind in a way because I'd rather have a girl that's trustful, that's faithful, and trustful and I want to be the same way to her. And have a kid so he can look up to me like that. But then when I be thinking about having a little son. I want him to be able to do the same [as me], but I don't want him seeing me do that to his mother, though, you know?

Malcolm describes a complex relational dilemma. He understands that he has separate desires, and in order for one set of desires to be fulfilled he may have to sacrifice the other. Although there is a "youthful" quality to Malcolm's perspective, there is also a certain sophistication: the answer to

Mike's question is not simply "yes" or "no." Malcolm engages with Mike's question, tosses it around, weighs the pros and cons of following different paths of action and ends on an unresolved note. Malcolm seems reflective, forthcoming, and honest during this freshman-year interview.

When asked about his feelings about sex, Malcolm moves into what sounds like a "cool" voice:

What is sex for you?

Well, I don't really know how to put it but like . . . it makes you feel more re-laxed so after a while you can't really—I can't really say that I put all my feelings into it. But like when I do it, it's like it's mostly like an accom-plishment. Where like, I, in my mind, I be like, "Yeah, I got that." You know I won't go around telling. But sometimes like, if a dude asks you, you know, I be like, "Yeah, I been with her," and stuff like that. You know certain girls—I mean certain dudes'll look up to you like if you got a real fine girl. And you know for yourself that'd be an accomplishment because you want it. But see they'll look up to you, be like, "Yeah, he must be good because he got her."

Similar to his relationships with his "associates," Malcolm says he doesn't "put all [his] feelings" into his sexual relations. Even when he admits to getting emotionally involved in sex, his focus immediately shifts to speak-ing about sex as an achievement. He perceives "getting certain girls" as a route toward gaining both self-respect and respect from his peers, al-though the respect from his peers does not seem to enhance or lead to close male friendships. He wants his peers' approval even though he keeps his distance from them.

Malcolm claims that he uses condoms most of the time because he is afraid of getting AIDS but does not use condoms with girls who he "knows are faithful." With those particular girls, however, he worries about getting them pregnant. Yet, if that happened, he says he would let the girl choose whether to have an abortion:

It sounds like pregnancy's not that much of an issue because you wouldn't mind really being a father.

Yeah, it's not like I'm trying to get one 'cause, you know, if that happens, you know. I'm there.

So it wouldn't be the worst thing in the world for you?
So, I wouldn't really—so, what I'm saying, I wouldn't mess around with
somebody, you know, and try and mess up and make that mistake with
somebody I don't even really care about, or don't really like.

Malcolm's ambivalence about having a child is palpable as he states in one
moment that while he is not trying to have a child, he would "be there" if
he were to become a father; and in another moment, that although it
would be a "mistake" to have a child, he would not want to make such a
"mistake" with someone for whom he did not care. Given such uncertainty, Malcolm seems more likely to become a father at a younger age than
his male peers in the study who, like the Hispanic boy in the poster, were
unambivalent about not wanting to have children. Malcolm will, in fact,
become a father by his junior year.

When asked about high-risk behavior such as drug and alcohol use,
Malcolm says that he currently smokes marijuana and occasionally drinks
alcohol because, like sex, it relaxes him. He would never try drugs such as
cocaine or crack because he has seen the "statistics" and knows how dangerous those drugs can be. He has, nonetheless, sold drugs a few times in
the past and admits to having stolen coats, pants, hats, and gloves and then
selling them to make money. He has recently stopped these illegal dealings
because he grew too worried about getting caught and because he found
a job. What seems particularly noteworthy about Malcolm's confessions is
that despite his past and current involvement in risky behavior, he is also
an adolescent boy who takes care of his family and works two jobs when
necessary.

Among his current role models, Malcolm mentions rap artists such as
Public Enemy because they "get positive messages across." Unlike many
of the role models of the teens interviewed, Malcolm's role models are not
his immediate or extended family members, but rather people whom he
admires because they put "knowledge into words that flow." He thinks
that rap is an important way to get messages across that "tell the truth
about how things really are": "Even though some people use profanity,
they're still telling the truth. Some adults, black, white, whatever it may be,
they don't even understand that. They just think they're kicking out profanity. That's all they pick up." Malcolm strongly believes that rap music

can offer people much more than most adults are willing or able to grasp. He hopes to be able to become a rap artist in the future to convey his own messages in a powerful medium. He wants to speak out about the realities of his world. Malcolm's passion and intent to express himself in the world and to make a difference through his music is manifest throughout his freshman-year interview.

In school, Malcolm feels "somewhat" satisfied with his grades, which are mostly B's and C's. He emphasizes to Mike that he firmly believes that his grades are important and admits that he hopes to get better grades next year:

> I used to think to myself, like, "This quarter, I can mess up." But now I'm thinking, you know, mostly it's just better to do good all quarters and try to like, you know, it's really a thing trying to impress. You know what I'm saying? So they know who you are. They recognize you better.
>
> *Who's they?*
>
> Like upper people that be looking down at the schools or children. Like, "Yeah, have him work for me." When you go out and try to get a summer job, you be able to show them that you can back up your word.

Malcolm's wish for recognition by the "upper people" is evident in each of his interviews and, in fact, is met in his junior year when his teachers place him on the honor roll. His belief in the importance of good grades and his search for recognition eventually appear to pay off.

When Mike asks Malcolm about his plans after high school, he says: "Well, I'm trying to get this rap thing started. But I'm just gonna go to school as long as I can. Just keep thinking positive—try to get as much info as I can—expand my vocabulary." Malcolm repeatedly discusses his desire to "think positively" and to learn new words to effectively convey positive messages. "I feel as long as I expand my vocabulary, I'm able to get a positive message across." Developing his ability to express himself is a critical component of how Malcolm sees himself gaining power or making a difference in the world.

When asked what he fears most about the future, Malcolm says his mother's death as well as the consequences of his own death for his mother:

Do you fear your own death?
Not really. . . . I just be thinking how, I want to leave them. And then I be thinking, you know, if—if I ever die before my mother, you know, that hurt her a lot. That's why I try to just not really think about that.

In keeping with his positive outlook, Malcolm avoids thinking about that which he most fears. Fearing death and the death of one's parents or family members, and maintaining a positive attitude, was a theme in all of the adolescents' interviews and is the focus of chapter 7.

Asked about whether "life is worth living," Malcolm states:

I like to live because I feel like I want to be able to experience a lot of things, you know. And be able to give back what I've received.
So getting a lot out of life and then giving something back?
Yeah, like from where I've grown up. 'Cause times are hard for some people. And I'd rather be a—I ain't gonna try to be no, um, whatcha call him—Martin Luther King—nothing like that. But I'm gonna try, myself, to do anything I can.
What would you like to give back?
Well, you know, I just like if I make it big—if I have dough—I'd rather be able to start some kind of scholarship or something like that. I would like to just help in the community. Start up, you know, new gangs, help with clubs or something like that, you know, parks and stuff.

Malcolm's determination to spread his "positive messages" is, once again, evident. Although he is quick to point out that he does not have grandiose dreams for himself, he does have dreams, and they include "giving back" to his community.

I am drawn to Malcolm's reflectiveness, sensitivity, and intelligence as I listen to his freshman-year interview. His perspectives sound "young" at times, but also sophisticated. He thinks about his life ending but worries about the effects of his death on his mother. He does not have close peer relationships but seems aware of the complexities of close relationships. He uses marijuana and has a history of delinquent behavior but remains mindful of gradations of risk and is responsible at home and at school. Malcolm represents himself as resisting simplistic classifications and in need of respect:

Okay, anything else about you that I didn't ask that would be important to know in knowing who you are?
Just, you know, as long as you can respect me and I respect you and, after that, everything comes. We be cool.
So respect is a big thing for you?
Yeah.

Malcolm's Sophomore Year

In Malcolm's sophomore year, he is again interviewed by Mike in the "piano" room. Malcolm still has the same appearance as in the previous year, only his hair is now cut in a "fade" in keeping with current fashion. Malcolm seems more confident this year as he virtually struts into the room and sits down in a chair he has nearly outgrown. He begins the interview by telling Mike that he still lives with his mother and younger sister and "nothing particularly" has changed over the past year except that his mother now works as a receptionist at a local hospital.

When Mike asks Malcolm about his relationship with his mother this year, Malcolm says:

> We, like, respect each other. We don't communicate too much on certain things. Some things you know we—I talk with my friends or whoever. But we talk about certain things, you know, like she communicates. She's sick of something, she tells me. And she tells my sister too 'cause she doesn't want nothing to be a surprise. She goes to work. That's really influenced me 'cause she proves to me that she's strong. She doesn't have the best of health, but she feels that she's strong. She goes to work, gets up, like that.

Malcolm's response conveys a closeness to his mother although he still maintains certain boundaries within this relationship. He admires and respects her strength, worries about her health, and seems to appreciate her frankness. It is unclear, however, whether Malcolm reciprocates this directness. Malcolm once again says his relationship with his mother is the most important of all of his relationships: "It's just my mother 'cause she's the one really supporting me and stuff, you know. None of [my friends or girlfriend] are."

Malcolm's mother, however, doesn't *always* support him:

> Last night I cooked for everybody—my mother and I ate and my—my mother's friend came over 'cause he was watching my little nephew. So then he ate, you know. Then my sister comes in with McDonald's almost every night and stuff. Eating that nasty stuff too much.
> *So she doesn't really eat at home that much?*
> No, like she keeps getting stuff to drink, bringing it up to her room, leaving it there. And she don't clean up and then when my mother argues about no one cleaning, that's not true and that's what gets me mad. That's really the only thing. Because you know I clean because I see my mother working and sometimes she like works three to eleven and then sometimes she works a double shift so she don't get off until seven in the morning. So then, you know, I be trying to clean up, but I can't be all cleaning, plus doing my schoolwork. Then I have the responsibility of the dog . . . I walk her myself and stuff like that.

Malcolm's frustration with his sister's behavior and his mother's accusations, as well as his desire to take care of his mother, and perhaps his sister, are immediately apparent. The variability of Malcolm's relationship with his mother is evident in his stories—he admires, respects, and cares for his mother and is also angry and frustrated with her. Perhaps he also feels a bit guilty that he does not help her as much as she needs. Unlike many of his male peers in the study (see chapter 6), Malcolm is consistently willing to speak about the range of his feelings for his mother. He seems comfortable with Mike's questions and willing to reflect on the details of his relationships.

Speaking about his sister, Malcolm does not suggest a similar range of feelings. He is angry at her irresponsibility and outraged that, though younger than Malcolm, she expects to enjoy the same privileges. Because she is not doing as well in school as Malcolm, however, his sister is not allowed to stay out late, go to movies, or attend concerts, and Malcolm says this causes a lot of tension in their relationship:

> *Okay, does that come into play between the two of you [that his sister is not doing as well in school as he is]?*

Well, not really. My mother doesn't bring that up 'cause she doesn't try to
compare us. I just try to prove—show my mother that I'm capable of
doing good. You know, being responsible and stuff. 'Cause I slept late this
morning and she woke me up and it was 7:00. Supposed to be here [at
school] at 7:30. I got here on time.
You were here even though you slept in late?
Yeah. Washed up, ironed my clothes, everything.

Moving swiftly from a discussion of his sister to a discussion of the extent
to which he is responsible, Malcolm demonstrates the intensity of his desire to "prove" to his mother, and perhaps to Mike, that he can take care
of himself. He clearly wants to continue having the privileges his mother
gives him and to be respected by her. He is also, perhaps, competing with
his sister for his mother's praise and attention.

Malcolm says that although he had no interest in seeing his natural father, his father recently visited him at home:

To me he's just a stranger, really. When he came over, I didn't know who he
was. I had like the door open, screen door locked. He knocked on the
door, he was all talking about—He didn't even say "Hi," that's how much
communication we got. He didn't even say, "Hi."
Did he know you?
Yeah, he knows me 'cause he said he walked in, he was all—he was like,
"Can I use the bathroom?" Like who are you? He was like, "I'm your fa-
ther."
Wow, what was it like seeing him after so many years?
Didn't do nothing to me. It just made me mad the way he came to the door
and stuff. You know, all talking about, "Can I use your bathroom?"
It must have felt kind of weird or strange in some way.
It didn't really faze me. I just saw him as a stranger.

The "I" statements in Malcolm's story ("I didn't know who he was. . . .
Didn't do nothing to me. It just made me mad. . . . It didn't really faze
me") suggest that he is denying his anger while feeling angry. He does not
want to be "fazed" by the presence of his father, but his shaky tone indicates otherwise (this was the first time that he can remember meeting his

father). While his sister will occasionally have contact with their father, Malcolm prefers not to have any.

> *As you're getting older, do you ever think that you want to talk to your father about anything? I don't mean about problems that you have, but about any feelings you have toward him not being around when you were growing up?*
> No, 'cause I feel I turned out pretty good, so you know. It probably would've been more better. I would've had an easier view. I'm not saying that I had it hard, 'cause I had plenty of time to play and all, but I'm just saying, you know, I don't feel nothing.

In his shifts from saying he "turned out pretty good" to "it probably would've been more better" to "I don't feel nothing," Malcolm suggests, once again, that he is trying to ward off feelings of hurt and anger. "I just try to, like, grow up, take things as they come. I don't try to be like '[I] depend on nobody' or 'you're not here, now we're having all this trouble.' You know, I feel we can do for ourselves." The absence of his father, Malcolm maintains, has made him neither wary nor desirous of dependency. He seems resolute not to be affected by his father's absence.

When Mike repeats the previous year's questions about having any adult males who he looks up to, Malcolm says:

> Not really, 'cause there wasn't really nobody around besides my mother's boyfriend. He was, you know, cool and all. He liked to tell us things. He used to play with me and my sister. But besides that there was nobody else because [my mother] was always trying to do for us. She'd like come home, clean, and all that stuff. And then after a while, I just like—somehow she— I just took over that role really. I started cleaning and stuff. Trying to keep things in shape, whatever. Keep my room neat so everything would be decent.

Malcolm's repeated stories to Mike of his duties at home suggest pride but also, perhaps, a sense of feeling overwhelmed (his frequent reference to needing "to relax" also suggest a sense of burden). The roles at home have changed since last year so that now Malcolm appears to feel more like the mother and/or father figure in the household. It is not clear from his discussions whether, for Malcolm, this apparent shift in roles ("I just took over that role") is frustrating, enjoyable, overwhelming, or, perhaps, a mixture of all these emotions. However, he has taken on the caretaker role and he wants Mike to know this.

In response to a question about whether or not he has a best or close friend this year, Malcolm says:

> Just my girlfriend really. I be chilling with her, but besides that I'm getting tired of being crowded really. I like hanging out but it just gets boring when you, like, do the same things so much. So when, like, people say, you know, "Why don't you come out anymore," I don't feel like just going out, sitting on the corner or nothing.
>
> *What exactly do you mean by being crowded?*
>
> Well, it could just be one person. But sometimes, that one person just get aggravating. Not what he says and stuff, it's just that he's being—that he's there. 'Cause it's just most of the time I like to be alone, you know, just me and my dark side. I like music a lot. So I just buy a lot of albums and stuff, but I don't like people always around me and stuff.

While Mike asks Malcolm about "friends," Malcolm responds by referring either to his girlfriend or to "people" (last year it was "associates"). Like last year, Malcolm is seemingly frustrated with his male peers and does not believe he has a close male friend.

Malcolm mentions, at a later point in his interview, that spending time with his male peers may not only be "aggravating" but also dangerous:

> So like I'd rather just go [out] by myself if anything's going to happen it's gonna happen with me alone. Therefore, I won't have to bring nobody else into it. You know, 'cause when you're hanging with a gang, there might be a dude that's hanging with you that got a beef with these people over here. And then all of a sudden you getting stabbed up or you in a fight or something or arrested over that.

Remarkably, Malcolm's peers do not provide him with a sense of security but rather with a grave sense of peril. Keeping to himself, however, has not protected Malcolm from all threats of violence. He was recently shot at by a gang of boys while walking his dog. Since these situations frighten him, he tries to stay "out of trouble" and not make any "enemies." For Malcolm, there are dangers to being alone as well as being with his peers. He is caught in an environment that has no clear route toward safety.

Malcolm prefers to spend time with his girlfriend rather than with his male friends:

> We could talk, you know, we go out, we go to the movies. But we could do certain things that you can't—you don't—well you can do it [with male friends], but it is just not the same feeling like when you're walking with a girl because with a girl you can express certain feelings and stuff. Like, say if you don't really want to spend no money, you just go for a walk on the river, whatever. You know, you can do that with a girl. And you can talk about certain things, you know, be laughing, have fun. That's the kind of stuff I do with her and stuff. You know, me and her, we went to the park and stuff, chill, walk, took pictures. . . . [With boys] it's just harder to like—'cause some of the things you may [want to do] make you seem as if you're gay or something. You know, . . . it's more relaxing when you're with a girl so you can just chill. Seems like you have more to talk about.

In dramatic contrast to his dismissive attitude about girls in his freshman year, Malcolm tells Mike that he finds girls more relaxing and easier to talk with than boys. Interestingly, Malcolm discusses "certain feelings" with Mike while, at the same time, claiming that he can only express such feelings with girls. Malcolm may feel that his male peers are less trustworthy than an adult male—even an adult male who is a stranger to him. However, as suggested by some of his peers, Malcolm may feel comfortable with Mike precisely because he is a stranger: there is no risk that Mike will spread his stories to others and tarnish his reputation.[4]

About his feelings for his girlfriend, Malcolm says:

> I don't feel myself falling in love or nothing like that because you know—I feel if she left me, it would leave a little emptiness but after a while I could fill that with a different girl . . . so I feel like if she left me, I feel empty because I ain't got a girl there. But see, once I do have a girl there, then all thought of her is gone. [My girlfriend] claims she's in love with me, but you know, I just, you know, don't let myself—I don't even think like that. Therefore, I won't fall in love, I guess, because it ain't the right time in my life. I gotta be handling things for myself right now.

Describing how he would know if he were in love ("I feel if she left me . . ."), Malcolm makes it clear to Mike that, although he enjoys spending time with his girlfriend of two months and considers her a close friend, he is not in love with her. Like last year, Malcolm seems cautious of being intimate with others. He also explains that while his girlfriend is a close friend, she is not a best friend because "if you have a best friend, you know, you express yourself more and . . . you, like, feel lost without them." Articulating the subtleties of relationships, Malcolm vividly conveys a personal understanding of love and friendships.

Malcolm explains to Mike that he likes his girlfriend because she has encouraged him to do things that he has never done before:

> That's helping me really to expand like when you learn a new word in your vocabulary. You open up more vocabulary words. She's just like expanding in a different variety of things you can do instead of just going to the park, playing ball, hanging on the corner you know. . . . But she was like, "Let's go take some pictures," And while you're actually taking pictures, when you're done with that, you go get some ice cream, then go chill in the park, you know, go ride the [boats] or whatever, you know, and just chill. And that's really things that girls like.
>
> *Do you like doing those things?*
>
> Well, yeah, they're cool.

Despite his previous concerns about sounding "gay," Malcolm describes the pleasure he takes in doing things that are not stereotypically male activities. In fact, he perceives such "girl" activities as mind expanding and as "cool." Malcolm's comfort in communicating these potentially risky thoughts and feelings attests not only to Mike's skill as an interviewer (Malcolm seems to trust Mike), but also, perhaps, to Malcolm's growing self-confidence and pride in his ability to transcend his peers' expectations.

Malcolm says that both he and his girlfriend consistently use birth control, but if she got pregnant he would support her in whatever decision she would make: "I want her to do what's right for her. Whatever she feels she could do." Once again, Malcolm seems uncertain about whether or not he wants a child. He claims, however, that he is more cautious than he was last year:

> [Everything is] more of a struggle. So you gotta make—I gotta make sure my life's right first before anything surprising happens.
>
> *When you say it seems more like a struggle, what do you mean?*

You know, it's like—'cause it's now the time when I'm in the tenth grade and stuff and this year's ending so I'll be in the eleventh grade. So therefore, I'm growing up, you know, I'm about to get out of school. I gotta figure out everything. If I'm going to college right away or whatever.
So you try to be especially safe so nothing gets in the way.
So I won't have this responsibility that holds me off from that, you know.

Malcolm seems particularly focused on "figuring things out" for himself this year. His sense of "growing up" has heightened his concerns about his future and has made him more careful.

When Mike inquires about Malcolm's role models, Malcolm says, as in the previous year, that he likes certain rap stars such as Public Enemy because they "talk knowledge":

They speak of the history and stuff. Certain stuff that could help you so you can fill that confidence inside you. 'Cause if you just know what's going on now, sometimes you might hear the wrong things and you feel like you can't do nothing, you can't get out. But that's not always true because when you see other people done it, there are just certain ways you gotta go about things. You can't always go about things with your fist. You gotta go about it with your mind.

"Filling" his confidence, dispelling feelings of hopelessness and despair, and providing him with positive messages on "how to get out," rap music plays an important role in Malcolm's life. While he never explains and is never asked what he means by "getting out," Malcolm suggests in other parts of his interview that he wants to "get out" of living a life in which both being at home and in the streets of his community is fraught with danger.

Malcolm wants to be a rapper who speaks

clear and stuff, not all hard. But you know [I want] everything to sound nice. You know, I want it to be like a memory song—a song that people play after a while.
What are some of the messages you want to get across?
Like I said be confident, you know, try your hardest, don't look back too much. Just 'cause you done wrong then, just look forward to what you can do now. Stuff like that.

A strong but not mindless sense of optimism, trying hard, and "looking forward" are themes that are evident in each of Malcolm's interviews and summarize well his strategy for living.

Asked to describe himself, Malcolm says:

> Somewhat mature. I'm sort of caring. I could say I'm caring. You know, understanding at some level. I'm responsible, I feel. That's really it. I won't try to get all conceited or nothing 'cause I don't really try to judge myself. I just try to be who I am and go for what I want.
>
> *Anything you don't like about yourself?*
>
> No, I feel that I'm fine. You know, I'm not gonna try to say I wish I was like this or like that because I just have to accept myself for who I am now. I can't say I'm all good. I can't say I'm all bad. I just try to do my best. If you try to be all good, sometimes you just—what you think is good might not always be right.

Malcolm again reveals a capacity to understand the variation of his personality and of his relationships. Malcolm's self-description seems honest ("I'm *sort of* caring") and astute.

> *Does anything stand out for you [over the past year] as having been especially good or bad?*
>
> Just [my] grades. It shows people feel that I'm good, but then I take it as like, you know, I can go out and be in a gang or whatever, come to school and do my best. You know, so, therefore, those grades don't mean I'm good. But then it's just when I'm in the gang they think I'm bad. So it's really odd.

Malcolm's critique of one-sided perceptions is unique among the adolescents we interviewed. He is cognizant—perhaps due to his own experiences (although he currently does not belong to a gang)—that one can be both "good" and "bad" at the same moment and is baffled by the fact that most people refuse to allow for such complexity. Offering evidence of his different sides, Malcolm tells Mike of his arrest last month for being in a stolen car (he received a short probation), and of his recent academic achievements that include making the honorable mention list.

Malcolm is quite proud of being on the honorable mention list. He tells Mike that he received a "little medal" for that honor, but immediately explains that he is not on the more prestigious honors list because he is getting a C in one of his classes. He is pleased with himself for improving his grades from last year, but believes he is capable of doing even better. He has done well in school because for "the first time" he "really tries to listen" when he is in class. Relying exclusively on homework to help him understand the class material does not work for Malcolm because "I do get lazy when it comes to like reading the whole section like I said, I do [homework] while I'm at school. I'll say I'll do it at home, then when I get home, I just get lazy." Malcolm speaks about his own "laziness" in the midst of telling Mike of his academic achievements. While he listens in class and is doing better in school, he admits to not completing his homework. When I listen to Malcolm speak about his school performance, my professional training leads me to want to categorize his school performance as "good," "average," or, perhaps, "lazy." Malcolm's perception of himself in school, however, resists these flat categories. He is a student who is doing well and who is struggling to do better.

Reflecting on his high school, Malcolm considers the only problem to be the absence of a Black History course "because it could help [black] students realize that they can be somebody." Learning for Malcolm is an experience directly linked to his life. Through education, and particularly education about the past and present lives of his ancestors, he believes that he and his black peers would realize their potential. In a school where almost half of the student body is black, Malcolm is, I think, justifiably distressed at the lack of such a course.

Aside from this gap in the curriculum, Malcolm, to my surprise, likes his high school. Because his junior high school did not enforce the rules or encourage learning, he says he did not do as well in school as he does now in high school (he says he was also spending time with the "wrong people" in junior high). He appreciates that the administrators and teachers at his high school are strict because their actions, he believes, create an environment that is conducive to learning.

When asked about his plans for college, Malcolm responds affirmatively but sounds unsure whether he will really go. After high school, Malcolm says he would like to be an entertainer or an engineer.

When you think of the future, what do you think of?
I just think of me growing up. I just wanna be well-set even if I gotta work.
'Cause I rather be an entertainer, therefore, I can, you know, have fun at
what I'm doing, at what I like to do. But like if I gotta work, I just wanna
have a well-set job where I'm getting paid a good amount of money where
I could save stuff. Being—doing good for me. I'm standing on my own
feet, not asking people. Even if I do gotta ask, I wanna make sure, I'm able
to—I got the right things in my head, so I could pay it back, give it back.
How likely does it seem to you that that will happen?
Well, I feel like there's a great possibility 'cause it's just that I gotta get out of
this lazy mood. 'Cause like getting in shape, that seems so hard. So far I
been doing that. So I think that's like my first step to doing anything
'cause once I got everything in order, then I feel I could do it even though
I might need a break once in a while.

Malcolm's standards for himself are clear: he wants independence yet allows himself to ask for help when needed as long as he returns the favor.
He "can do it" even though he may need a "break once in a while." By repeatedly stating, throughout his interview, that he needs to "get everything in shape," and make "things neat" or "decent" before he can "do
anything," Malcolm implies that he does not feel that his life is in order or
"neat." He is, however, intent on finding such order.

When Mike asks Malcolm, "When is the future?" Malcolm answers:

Everyday. I just, you know, take it as a new day because I don't ever know
what might pop up, you know. Therefore, I don't try thinking too far ahead
'cause the way things are today. I don't try to think too negative, but you
gotta think in the right perspective where you're at, you know, where you're
living. You know a lot of people getting killed, especially innocent people,
for no reason. You gotta think like, "Well, I could be one of those people so
why should I sit here and just wait for this to happen." Make a name for
yourself while you're here. So, therefore, people can remember you for not
being lazy, drinking beer all the time. They could think that you were trying
to do for yourself, trying to make a name, trying to get out.

One reason for Malcolm's concern with his own laziness becomes clear in
this passage. He wants to be remembered as self-reliant and as someone

who "got out." Strikingly, his awareness of death pushes him to want to "be somebody." He tries not to think "negatively," but believes that he has to think realistically, and this "right perspective" seems to enhance his perseverance.

> *When you think about the future, is there anything that you're afraid of?*
> Death, really. I'm not really afraid to die. I'm really afraid of the outcome after I die. If I died before my mother or my sister, I just think about how hard it would hit them. . . . I'm not saying they couldn't go on, but I know it'd be very hard. Even when like me and my mother argue, all of a sudden she be like, "I don't wanna argue like that." She always wants to settle things and stuff.

Malcolm speaks each year about his worries concerning the effects his own death would have on his mother and sister. He knows that given "the way things are today . . . where you're living," his life is constantly in danger and this knowledge seems to haunt both him and his mother.

When Malcolm is asked what makes his life worth living, he tells Mike:

> Just the fact that I feel I know I can make it. That I have the strength and the whatever it takes to succeed. Really, that's really what makes me feel like "yeah, my life is worth living." 'Cause if I was doing bad in school and I felt there was nothing I could do about it, I feel that there would be nothing else really going for me. You know, I would probably be drinking more, whatever.

A sense of optimism pervades Malcolm's interviews. Knowing that he has the strength and ability to do what he wants and the control to change his life makes him want to live his life.

His optimism is evident as well in his response to a question about potential discrimination:[5]

> *How do you see being black having an effect on what you would do in the future?*
> Well, it depends on how the person sees me—if they see me as black and therefore won't speak to me at all, I feel that it's just gonna make things even more difficult. But if they see me as black but don't like me too much . . . but if they speak to me, I feel like I can influence them in some way to make them understand I got the quality, I could do the job, I give it my

best. You know, I'm gonna be here on time. If you wanna put it all hard on me, you know . . . I'll prove myself, that's what I'm saying.

Keenly aware of the racist stereotypes that will follow him into the work world, Malcolm is intent on proving them wrong. Yet he understands he will only be able to challenge such beliefs if his future bosses are willing to give him a chance. His determination to defy his bosses' negative expectations reminds me of his conviction to "prove" to his mother that he can be responsible. While it is impossible to know what is not being said here, since Malcolm may feel that he is, in fact, speaking to one of those "bosses" ("If *you* wanna put it all hard on me you know . . ."), Malcolm appears to believe he can prove his potential to others. This confidence, hopefulness, and persistence are typical of Malcolm's outlook on his world.

Malcolm speaks about fearing an early death and about having hope for the future; he speaks about being responsible and about being arrested for being in a stolen car; he speaks about being lazy and about being on the honorable mention list at school; he says he does not want a committed relationship with a girl and claims that the closest relationship he has right now is with his girlfriend. Malcolm seems caring and reflective and, at other times, tentative and disengaged.

His presentation of himself and his life in his freshman and sophomore years is typical of the adolescents we interviewed. While there were a few students who presented themselves as one-dimensional (e.g., those who were seemingly the most depressed), the stories of the majority of students were three-dimensional, alive, and filled with ambiguities, contradictions, and continuities.

Malcolm's Junior Year

Because of scheduling difficulties, I am Malcolm's interviewer in his junior year. Malcolm does not seem bothered by the switch. He is much as I expect him to be from Mike's descriptions—a tall, lanky, handsome African American young man. He wears the latest "hip hop" fashions, a brightly colored sweatshirt and baggy pants riding low enough on his hips to reveal the waist band of his boxer shorts. I interview him in the "piano" room where he was interviewed in the previous years. The small, claustrophobic, soundproof closet seems to get smaller with each passing year. When I go to Malcolm's classroom to ask him if he is willing to be interviewed again this year, he and a friend (who is also a participant in the study) enthusiastically agree. They tell me that they like getting out of their class for one period, and I suspect, judging from their enthusiasm, that they also enjoy speaking to someone who wants to listen to their stories.

Malcolm and I begin the interview by going over the past year and discussing the changes that occurred in his life. His fifteen-year-old sister has been diagnosed with malignant cancer and has been given six months to live. Also, he has recently become a father to a child born three months premature (a few weeks before the interview). Malcolm has had an eventful and difficult year.

Malcolm tells me that he and his mother do not have time to be close with each other this year because most of their time is spent trying to care for his sister. His mother stays home because they cannot afford a home nurse, and his sister is too ill to be by herself. He or his mother is constantly with his sister "because it's really scary like, you know, how she [his sister] can go to sleep and not wake up or something." Because his mother's attention is directed toward his sister, he says he has been mostly by himself this year: "I don't feel that my mother's neglecting me because I understand the situation. But it's just that it's not like she's around all the time or anything" (she goes to the hospital frequently with his sister). Malcolm sounds and looks depressed and scared. He tells me that his sister is undergoing chemotherapy and spends most of the time in the hospital. When she is home, she hardly eats: "It's real hard 'cause, you get her a plate like—a regular meal from McDonald's or something, she won't even finish a whole Happy Meal. Sometimes she'll just throw it up." Malcolm is clearly struggling with his sister's illness.

When I ask him directly how he is doing, Malcolm replies: "I really take it from what my sister tells me. If she's having a real bad day, then that's when I start feeling bad. If she's feeling good, then I feel good. I don't feel bad when she's feeling good to make her feel bad, you know. You know, I just go with how she reacts." As Malcolm explains how he carefully monitors his own feelings to make sure they are consonant with his sister's, his concern for her is unmistakable. Briefly looking away from me, Malcolm says that he and his mother are "just barely keeping things together," and that he and his mother try not to show their feelings too much "so that way it won't affect us in our ability to do what we have to get done."

Growing increasingly concerned about Malcolm's well-being, I ask him:

> *Are you able to really talk with somebody about your fears with your sister?*
> I don't really talk about it with anybody. . . . People thought I needed to have somebody to talk to and they tried to like—well, when I did speak to them, they said that I'm handling it pretty well on my own 'cause like I'm on the honor roll in school and I'm still working and all.

While "people" have told Malcolm that he is doing well (based on his behavior), it is not clear from his response whether he himself thinks he is okay. When I ask him again if there is anybody with whom he could share his feelings, he says "there ain't nobody there" and he is "tired" of people telling him that he should talk to somebody. Malcolm sounds defensive, predicting, perhaps, that I too will recommend speaking with somebody. His willingness to be interviewed, however, suggests that while he is not interested in counseling per se, he is interested in telling his story to someone.

Malcolm does not really have time, he states, to think about what is happening at the moment because he is so busy with schoolwork, going to the hospital, or going to work: "There's so much going on, it's really hard to let myself get down. You know, I know it's good at times to, like, feel sympathy, which I do. It's just that I don't want it to affect me real bad, then it affects my schoolwork and I have to work at my job." His school and work responsibilities may be important for Malcolm because they provide him with some sense of control over the events in his life. Although in the previous year he also spoke about "maintaining order" and "keeping things decent" and "neat," this year these themes return with a new kind of urgency.

> *How are you able to be so strong? It's not like you're surrounded by people that are supportive.*
> Well it's not people supporting me, but people showing the same strength.
> *And so they inspired you?*

Yeah. Not in school, but people that I've seen as I grew up. You know, like
my mother, she has some real hard times. But she is always doing her best.
She always tried, you know. She never gave up. To keep myself from the
same struggle that she went through and to keep my girlfriend and my
child now, I'm doing what I can. I wanna make something of myself. I
don't think it's just that I got this way like it just happened to be. It's just
that from what I've seen . . . my own sight, you know, what I hear and
stuff. How people act.

Notably, Malcolm refuses to believe that his resilience is an inborn trait ("I
don't think it's just that I got this way") or the outcome of overt support.
He perceives it as a product of watching and being in relationship with
others, especially with his mother. Observing and listening to his mother
has given him clues of how to persist and thrive in the midst of ongoing
adversity.

This year, Malcolm is not only dealing with a sister who has been given
a limited time to live, but he has also recently become a father to a child
born three months early. He says he is very happy to be a father, but he is
unsure what it is going to be like since his child is still in the hospital. When
I ask him if it was scary to have his child born prematurely, he says with a
pained expression on his face, that while it was difficult, he was happy that
his sister got to see his child before she died. His daughter, he says, is giving him the courage to carry on during this difficult period.

Over the past year Malcolm and his girlfriend have grown closer and, in
a shift from the previous year, he "thinks" he loves her. He still wants to
take things slowly with her, however, because he does not want anything
to go wrong in their relationship, especially now that they have a child together. Although his girlfriend's jealousy and possessiveness irritate him,
he seems committed to her in his discussion of "loving her" and hopes
their relationship will last a long time. Yet, he does not feel ready to marry
her: "I wanna make sure that's what we want because we're going through
so many stages now. Before we like move into the same house and stuff, I
wanna make sure that we can happen." Malcolm's hesitation about marriage may be connected to his feeling that he was not cautious enough
when he and his girlfriend had a child.

Although Malcolm's thoughts and feelings about his girlfriend have
changed from the previous year, they have not changed regarding his male

peers. When I encourage him to tell me why he doesn't discuss his troubles with his male peers, Malcolm says:

> Like 'cause I feel that what I got to say, everybody can't handle it or really wouldn't understand it, you know. They'll sit there—they'll take it as if I'm talking about the sports game or something. Like, if I were to talk about my sister, and they'll just change it up. Like, "Yeah, how are the Bulls doing?" You know?

Malcolm's thoughts about communicating with his peers this year are more complicated than he had indicated to me earlier in his interview. He wants to talk to others about what is happening in his life, but only to those people who will listen and understand him. While he seems to believe that I, as his interviewer, can "handle it," he doesn't hold such faith in his male peers.

Malcolm states, as he did in previous interviews, that he doesn't have a best or close friend this year:

> I had a couple [of friends] like once when I was real young, around ten, and then when I lived out—and then me and this dude got real close, we was cool. But right now, nobody really 'cause it seems that as I've grown, you know, everybody just talk behind your back and stuff, you know. So I just let it go because it seems like no people that can hold—well, not no people, but the people that I've been meeting can hold up to their actions. Like you know . . . something might've happened like between me and a person where other people felt that we shouldn't even be friends no more. So they sit there and talk about me to that person while I'm not around or something. And then that person will just talk about me too, you know, whatever, 'cause you know all throughout my neighborhood, I always hear, "He talks about you, he says this or he says that." . . . So I just don't really bother with it, you know, trying to make best friends.

Although he had a close friend when he was young, Malcolm currently believes, like most of the other boys in the study, that his male peers will betray his trust. He, consequently, does not have a close or best friend and has given up on trying to find one (chapter 5 is focused on this theme in the boys' interviews).

Malcolm explicitly tells me that he does not tell his male peers when he is angry:

Why don't you confront your friends when you are angry with them?
I don't know. . . . I guess it's sometimes like it could be just their family or
something like they're nice or something. You know, I don't really wanna
cause no conflict. I just leave it at that and just avoid them.

Malcolm's reservations about "causing" conflict seem to lead him to neglect his desire for close friends. He does not get angry with his peers because he believes that maintaining friendships entails avoiding conflict; yet,
when he is angry he removes himself from his peer relationships ("[I] just
avoid them"). His strategies with his peers fail to maintain the relationship.

Do you feel like you have any friends?
I feel, well, sometimes I be thinking they're jealous or somewhat. Because I
hang with them and all, but they're getting C's and D's. . . . I'm getting
A's and B's. Like in the program I'm in [an advanced placement program],
I've been the student of the month.
Oh wow!
And like when something's going on, yesterday, they [the teachers] wanted to
use me, my image like to represent the program. Like if there's an interview of how—what the program's about or something, they ask me to do
the interview. And I hang with them [his friends]. But I'm getting all this
attention. Sometimes I do the same things as them, like I might skip a class
or go to the store or just cut school one day. But it's like, see, I do all that,
knowing that what I gotta get done is gonna get done . . . and I notice
that when they do it, they're not caring about like getting it done. They
just saying forget school, you know. So then when that report card comes
in, I got A's and B's and they got C's and D's and they wonder how you
do this and why I got this because even though I did that—skipped that
day, I still went back and got my schoolwork done.

Malcolm's ability to be both responsible and irresponsible is causing envy
and resentment among his friends. Furthermore, the attention he receives
for his ability to be responsible (being chosen as the student of the month)
may also cause his peers' jealousy. In a school where very few students receive individual attention, to be favorably singled out may not only encourage a student, such as Malcolm, to complete his schoolwork—even

when he skips classes—but may also prompt those who do not receive such notice to put little effort into their own schoolwork.

In Malcolm's junior year, he is on the honor roll all year: "I feel that I'm pretty well focused at my age and stuff so that's really gonna help me." He claims to feel fairly sure of his intellectual abilities, and this confidence seems to stem primarily from his performance in school. His school achievements, he tells me, make his life "worth living." Malcolm's grades may not only prove to him that he has potential, but may also provide him with an adult support network beyond that of his mother. At times, however, he feels insecure in school:

> Most of the time I try to open myself up to learning. Because like if I go into something new I always like get that attitude where [I think], "Oh, man, I don't think so." Instead of saying, "Well, maybe I can do it, let me try, you know." I found myself doing that.
> *So you sort of slip into this insecurity.*
> Yeah. Even though I still try most of the time.

While Malcolm is proud of his school performance, he also finds himself doubting his capabilities. Yet he typically does not allow himself to give up because, as he explains in a later part of the interview, he needs to do well in school in order to be "somebody." Education, learning, and "expanding [his] vocabulary" are critically tied to opportunity and success for Malcolm. He does not want his self-doubts to prevent him from reaching his goals.

When asked to describe himself, he says:

> Intelligent, responsible, independent to a point where you know I've done things on my own. . . . I could be forgetful at times. Irresponsibleness, but that—everybody you know has some faults, so I can't be perfect [giggle]. You know, I can't just be mature, responsible, and all this. I feel that I do have matureness but I'm also immature.

In matter-of-fact tone, Malcolm describes himself precisely as I had perceived him in his earlier interviews. As suggested in all his interviews, he clearly appreciates who he is and both understands and seeks to maintain his three-dimensionality:

When you say you're independent to a point, what's the point?
I feel that I still find myself not all the way saying, no, I don't need nobody else, I don't need my mother 'cause I always find myself doing so much on my own, but I still have to come back and ask her to help me.
Do you think you'll probably stay that way, or do you think you'll change?
Hopefully [I'll stay the same] 'cause that's something I wanna teach my child.
What do you want to teach her?
To be independent, you know—don't be afraid to ask for help but you know, try your hardest, you know.

Malcolm sees himself as both dependent on and independent from others, and he expects to stay this way throughout his life. His understanding of independence as not excluding the need to depend on others is not unique among his peers, for whom independence and dependence were typically seen as equally important and necessary. Malcolm asserts that people who deny that they are dependent on others have a problematic "type of attitude" and he simply "does not believe" them. Following this conversation, however, he warns me that it is hard to be dependent on someone for a long time because "nobody lives forever." With his mother having had a benign tumor (mentioned in his freshman-year interview) and his sister currently afflicted with a malignant tumor, Malcolm has every reason to be wary.

When I asked him to explain why he considers himself irresponsible, Malcolm refers to his and his girlfriend's decision to have a child at such an early age. He states that although he loves his child, they were "not thinking clearly" when they made this decision. Despite this momentary lapse, Malcolm makes clear to me that he is also responsible:

You know, I act a little crazy sometimes. I may do things that you're not supposed to do, but I'm still doing the things that gotta be done. So, no matter how much I do on the side, everything else is still getting done that needs to be done to keep me where I need to be going. . . . I always think that having so much responsibility at such a young age has made me more self-disciplined where I could be acting real stupid.

In each of Malcolm's interviews, self-discipline is a central theme. He wants to be and considers himself focused on what he has to do. In fact, Malcolm states that, instead of leading to feelings of being overwhelmed, as I had interpreted his statements earlier, the responsibilities of his young life have enhanced his ability to be self-disciplined. While he readily admits that he has been and can be irresponsible or "crazy," he also believes that he has and will accomplish his goals.

Malcolm tells me, not surprisingly, that what he most likes about himself is his determination, and what he most dislikes is his tendency to become violent when upset. He has been told by his mother that his father used to get violent when angry. Although he does not want to replicate his father's behavior, he finds himself doing so at times. He has taught people, however, how to respond to his "fits": "Even though real inside I'm raging like but somehow [when people say certain things to me] it works, you know [I calm down]." I am surprised by Malcolm's confession about his potential for violence, and I find myself questioning what other aspects of Malcolm's way of being I have failed to understand or ask about. Although Malcolm has clearly discussed many layers of his world, his unexpected admission of violence and of "raging" reminds me that I am being exposed to only a small part of his world.

When Malcolm thinks of the future, he says he thinks of going to college and being a rap artist. However, since he has to make sure his child is "comfortable," he may choose college over becoming a rapper to ensure her well-being. Having a child has led Malcolm to reassess his future goals and become more intent on following a traditional path. For the first time, Malcolm discusses going to college as a real alternative rather than an abstract concept.

Malcolm, however, is still interested in rap music and expects to continue to write rap music even if he goes to college. When I ask Malcolm again what kinds of messages he wants to convey in his music, he responds by telling me:

> [In my rap music] I try to tell people they gotta—you know, if you want something done, do it yourself. You know, 'cause like the killing and the deaths within the area are not caused by the white person or the other color, whatever they want to call it. Like yeah, the Colombians, they bring drugs in, but we gotta take it upon ourselves not to use them. You know, gotta get—push them back out. And certain people got to take it upon themselves not to sell them. You see all that money, but you got to take it upon yourself to think differently. It's a poison, it's really not helping no-

body. You know, so if they could take it upon themselves to realize that what they're doing is killing, then that could help get rid of it. We can always get rid of it no matter how much they bring in, they would have nowhere to put it. You see?

So there needs to be a buyer.

Yeah, and there's always somebody there forcing it [on others]. So the people just need to get smart. There's rehabilitations if they really work and then maybe those people that were once on the drugs will realize and just help. . . . It's an individual effort . . . but it also takes the whole to make it all work.

In a passionate and angry voice, Malcolm tells me about the importance of individual obligation and effort in creating societal change. Although he briefly mentions the importance of collective effort, he is primarily focused on the individual. As with most of the adolescents in the study, Malcolm firmly maintains individualistic values while being deeply engaged with others.

When I ask him what makes his life worth living, Malcolm says:

Because I'm doing well in school. . . . There's so much positive coming out of what I been doing. That makes me feel good. To be alive and stuff, to be around.

So that makes you feel good, that you're doing so well?

Yeah, to show the others. Yeah, even my friends you know . . . they be like, "Yo, you're real smart you know, that'd be stupid, if you dropped outta school," or something and I like be hearing them say that. I just be like, "Yeah, no, I ain't planning on dropping out, anything like that." So that makes me feel good.

His academic achievements seem to anchor Malcolm's confidence, which, in turn, is the key to his positive attitude. Even though Malcolm has gone through a particularly difficult year, he has found a way to maintain his hope and perseverance.

Throughout his junior-year interview, Malcolm has direct eye contact with me and speaks with ease about his thoughts and feelings and his strengths and weaknesses. Malcolm seems more reflective and vulnerable this year than in previous years, most likely the result of his difficult experiences over the past year. The depths of his introspection may also be the result of speaking with a woman, given his ease in speaking with girls about "certain things."

As in each of his previous interviews, Malcolm's interview is filled with surprising as well as expected responses. He speaks about his responsibility and his irresponsibility; his confidence and lack of confidence; his future and present orientation; and his independence from and dependence on his mother. He also tells me about the sensitive ways he interacts with those about whom he cares and his violent attacks when he is "raging." Malcolm is in control, out of control, passionate, and provocative.

At the end of Malcolm's senior year, I hear from one of his peers that he will begin taking classes at a local college in the fall and is excited to begin his new life. Malcolm's sister died a few months after our final interview. I am profoundly saddened by his loss. He nonetheless graduated with honors and continues to be a proud and caring father of his baby girl. I hope to contact him again to hear more about his life—the life of an ordinary and extraordinary young man.

PATTERNS

I started the book with the story of an individual. I now turn to the patterns or themes that I detected after reading, sorting, categorizing, and rereading the interview data of twenty-four adolescents over three years. While in qualitative research it often seems as if the researcher simply read the interviews and immediately detected themes, this is typically not the case. The themes presented in this book are the outcome of two years of sifting through and analyzing over three thousand pages of interview transcripts and listening repeatedly to over 120 hours of audiotapes. My goal in this long process was, once again, not to determine themes within *each* topic addressed in the interview protocol (e.g., self- and future perspectives, drug and alcohol use, relationships with each family member), but to detect themes when the adolescents spoke about their worlds (which includes all of these topics). I listened to their interviews in a holistic way, trying to capture the most prevalent themes. Therefore, some of the topics addressed in the interview protocol are discussed (e.g., relationships with friends and mothers), and some are not (e.g., drug and alcohol use). When a topic is discussed, it is because I detected a pattern regarding this particular topic.

Listening to seventy-one interviews (twenty-three adolescents over three years and one adolescent over two years), I detected six common themes—and numerous subthemes—in the data. Some of the themes overlap across chapters while others stand alone. The location of each of the themes varied from being topic-specific to being evident across topics in the interviews. For example, those discussed in chapter 4—speaking out or being silenced in relationships—were evident when the adolescents spoke about their friends, parents, role models, school, and society (i.e., across topics). On the other hand, the themes discussed in chapter 5—themes of betrayal and distrust in peer relations—were evident only when the adolescents were asked about friendships (i.e., within one topic). The theme discussed in chapter 6—the importance of mothers—was evident throughout each interview, not only when the adolescents were asked about their mothers. The themes discussed in chapters 7, 8, and 9 were either evident across or within individual topics. A consequence of such a theme-centered discussion is that not all of the adolescents will be discussed in each chapter. The chapters focus only on those teens who suggested the particular theme being discussed. In addition, in some chapters where gender differences are discussed, the boys' and girls' stories are presented separately while in other chapters they are presented together.

4

■ ■　　■　　　■　　　■　　　■　　　　■　　　　　■　　　　　■

Voice and Silence

I have a voice. I mean I like to be heard.

Are you heard?

In most of my classes, yeah. They look to me for answers. 'Cause, you
know, I'm always trying to make a point or a statement. . . . I express myself no matter what, I mean I've always made a strong statement. . . . I'm sensitive to people's feelings, but if you're not sensitive to my feelings, I'll come straight out and say it.

> —Eva, a West Indian student
> in her senior year

SPEAKING ONE'S MIND, expressing one's opinions, daring to disagree, and speaking the truth in relationships were values emphasized by
the majority of girls in the study. This outspoken group, consisting of
African American, Dominican, Puerto Rican, West Indian, and Irish American adolescent girls, either specifically stated that they were "outspoken"
or underscored their ability to be candid about their anger and affection in
their relationships. Their voices exemplified what Annie Rogers calls "ordinary courage" or the ability "to speak one's mind by telling all one's
heart."[1] The girls discussed open conflict and honest speaking not only as

an ideal but as a necessity; they needed to tell people what they thought or felt because if they didn't, they would "explode." The boys, on the other hand, reported being silent in or silenced by their relationships, especially with their male peers. Speaking out, for the boys, was associated with being angry and frustrated and they feared that such candid expressions would threaten their relationships or would simply be "rude." While outspoken voices were occasionally evident among the boys, they never spoke with such passion as the girls about their abilities to express themselves.

Girls' Voices

Speaking Out over Time

The girls were most willing to speak out when they were juniors or seniors.[2] As they went through high school, they grew increasingly able to speak their minds and "tell their hearts." They typically referred to a period when they kept quiet followed by a time in which they began to speak openly.

Mary, an Irish American girl, suggests such a pattern when she is asked to describe herself over the three years she is interviewed.[3] As a sophomore, Mary says to Helena: "[Laughs.] I'm not good at describing myself. I don't know, oh, I don't know, I just can't—I never can . . . I'm patient [laughs]." In her junior year, Mary says to Helena:

I don't know. Well, I don't like that question 'cause I can't describe myself. I don't know how I am. My boyfriend says I'm too, like, overprotective of people. Not overprotective of people, but that I'm very caring about, you know—there's certain things that I care about with other people.

In her third-year interview (she has dropped out of school by this time), Mary describes herself by saying: "I will listen to people's ideas but I'm still gonna say what I have to say and tell them the way I feel about it." When I ask her what she likes about herself this year, Mary mentions her openness and "the fact that I don't let people walk all over me." In other parts of the interview, she tells me:

I used to be, like, anything [would happen] and I would just let it keep on passing and passing, and just get over it. But I only made myself aggravated and I became a royal pain in the witch and I was taking it out on everybody

close to me and not the person that's really being the source of my aggrava-
tion. So, you know, I can't do that to people that haven't done nothing to
me, so I have to tell people that do it. . . . Now 'cause I speak up about everything that bothers me I'm just gonna say it. I'm not gonna hold anything in
no more. Now I always say what I believe, especially if I think what they are
saying is wrong. . . . Finally now I can open my mouth and say what I feel.

In previous years, Mary had neither mentioned her desire nor her ability
to "open [her] mouth." In her third-year interview, this is clearly a central
theme. Although she continues in this interview to tell me that she is caring and protective of *others*, Mary's self-description is not dominated by
this characterization. Instead, her focus is on her ability to give voice to her
opinions, thoughts, and feelings, and to take care of *herself* by not being
"somebody's bridge."

Mary discusses her willingness to speak out with her sisters, brothers, father (her mother died when she was younger), peers, teachers, and with
her boyfriend. Unlike many of her female counterparts in the study, Mary's
self-described outspoken ability seems to exist across her relationships:

My father's older son, he's the one that always wants to like walk over my
father and see, I haven't seen him in a while. So, I haven't said anything,
but I know next time I see him like I'm gonna say something 'cause finally
now I can open my mouth and say what I feel. And, you know, he hasn't
been there in a while and . . . my father seen him the other day—and thank
God I wasn't there, 'cause I would've had a mouthful for him, but when
he does come, his time will come and I'll just tell him. . . . Because before
I couldn't—I couldn't just like speak out [with] anybody—I wouldn't. I
just let people walk and I wouldn't say nothing. Now I can't see people
doing that.

Mary feels the need to use her voice not only to protect herself from being
"walked on" but also to protect her father. Her tendency to care for others exhibits itself in her newly acquired candor. In this discussion of her
"father's older son," however, there are hints that she may find it more difficult to articulate her anger than she is willing to admit to me. When Mary
says: "My father seen him the other day—and thank God I wasn't there,"
she may be suggesting that she was truly relieved not to have felt called
upon to express her anger at her "father's son." While speaking honestly is
possible for Mary this year, it may still be difficult for her.

When I ask Mary, who recently passed the GED exam (and thus received her high school equivalency diploma), why she was able to change so dramatically over the past year, she says:

> Well, when I went to my GED program, I met a lot of new people and I got along, you know. I don't know. I found myself feeling more freely to talk and, you know, it was like we were all coming from the same boat. You know, none of us could stand the high schools and it just—I ended up—like I matured a lot in the few months getting my GED. It's like since then, there's been the change in things.

Mary learned to voice her own thoughts and feelings in a space in which she found a common community and in which she felt a sense of freedom. Strikingly, it was only after Mary *left* school that she was able to find such a "home."[4]

Aside from her sheer exuberance and energy, there are other indications that Mary feels more self-confident in her third-year interview than she has in the past. During her first- and second-year interviews, Mary rarely looked at Helena and giggled nervously throughout. During her entire third-year interview, however, she maintains direct eye contact with me and tells me with obvious pride that she is pleased to have "finally" lost forty pounds as a result of working with a nutritionist (she had been overweight in previous years). There is a calmness and conviction in her voice that I had not heard previously.

Shakira, an African American student on the honorable mention list at school, also emphasizes her outspokenness during her third-year interview. In the first two years, Shakira suggests a willingness to speak her mind, but it is not until her senior year that this becomes a core theme. In her sophomore year, she tells me about her relationships with her teachers:

> You know, I snap—I get—I yell at the teachers sometimes. When they get on my nerves, I'll yell back. But most of the time I just listen. But sometimes I get so nauseated, I just say, "Leave me alone." When they call me out of all people in the class just makes me just want to say, "Okay, everybody else talking and you gonna call me?" I always say that when they call me out of everybody, but that's not most of the time.

Despite her occasional challenges, Shakira seems ambivalent or uncertain about her willingness to express her feelings to her teacher ("most of the time I just listen," "[it] just makes me *want* to say . . . ," "I always say that when they call me out . . . but that's *not* most of the time"). It is not clear just what she is telling me. She may *want* to say something to the teacher when she believes her teacher is acting unfairly but typically chooses not to. Her assertion that most of the time she just listens may have been made for my approval (as the adult listener) or because it truly reflects her behavior with her teachers—sometimes she is able to articulate her anger but most of the time she is not. Whether or not "yelling" at the teacher is an effective or even appropriate means of expression, her desire to respond verbally to her teachers' accusations are clear here. This is the only time in her sophomore year, however, that she mentions her desire to speak out.

In her junior year, Shakira suggests that she speaks openly in some of her relationships, but it is neither a part of her self-description nor a focus of her interviews. She describes herself as "a modern teen—an average student. I'm a modern teenager. I like to get out sometimes. I like to stay in the house. I like what the average teen likes."

When I ask Shakira to describe herself in her senior year, she says:

> [I am] outgoing, outspoken, and out everything. Yeah, out everything. If I had something to say I'm just gonna say it. Some case it'd be rude and I know it'd be rude, but, you know, when you're not listening to me, sorry, I'm rude. I'm rude. So I never let anyone intimidate me. . . . I learned that, you know, just moving [here]. I had an accent out of this world, everyone was bothering me. I used to cry. Then I was like forget this, you know, I can't be crying for something that's mine. I can't help it if I got it, you know. So after that I guess everything turned.

There was a time when Shakira, like Mary, felt she could not speak openly. However, she eventually overcomes her silence, and, quite literally, recognizes that she has to be proud of her *voice*—its "out of this world" accent, its absolute uniqueness. In contrast to her previous interviews, this year's interview is filled with stories about directly expressing her anger and frustration in and out of school. She says she is a "very bold" person and will "always" speak her mind. As an example, Shakira tells a story about a school-sponsored "Latino Expression Night." She was enraged because the organizers chose to exclude people from the "Black Islands" and Shakira felt that this discriminated against her "black West Indian friends." She circulated a petition in the school and spoke with teachers until the teachers and administrators agreed to include black West Indian students. Shakira tells me: "People know me. They know I'm outspoken." According to developmental researchers, being able to disagree openly in one's relationships is a sign of strength.[5] By their third-year interviews, Shakira and Mary are both speaking their minds with peers and with adults.

Shakira's outspokenness is not only focused on expressions of anger and frustration, but also on love and loyalty. After she performed a song in a talent show, Shakira ran to the front of the stage, saw that her best friend was sitting in the packed audience, and yelled: "I love you, Nina!" Having attended that talent show, I remember being impressed and moved by her expression of such strong feelings of affection for a female friend in front of virtually the entire student body. When she is asked to describe her relationships with her two best friends, Shakira begins by saying: "Well, I love them." Unlike in her sophomore and junior years, Shakira in her senior year is not only open and honest in her relationships but also quite passionate.

The Variations of Voice

The outspoken voices of the girls in the study did not simply fit the stereotype of typically loud, bold, and brassy inner-city girls.[6] The voices heard among these ethnically diverse adolescents were more complicated. Their motivation to speak out depended upon the immediate situation, the surrounding circumstances, and the type of relationships to which they referred. Speaking out was seen as serving various purposes at different times and in different situations.

Expressing Anger and Frustration

Chantel, an African American adolescent, claims that she is very outspoken—even with her teachers. In her junior year, Helena asks her:

So you think you are the type of student who will say something in class and speak up?
Yep. Plenty of times, 'cause . . . I know in one discussion that my teacher, my English teacher, he's like strictly against abortion and he was like, "That's wrong and I think they should make it illegal." I said, "Well, I'm not say-

ing that I'm for abortion or anything, but, you know, you're only one person and it's like I feel though you all shouldn't take the right from other people—to tell people they can't have abortions." I was like, "Who are you? You don't have to deal with that kid when that kid comes here." We had a big old discussion in class and he was like, "Okay, Chantel, we both made our point." I was like, "Yeah, but . . ." He was like, "I still think it's wrong." I was like, "Well, that's your opinion, but I don't feel as though you should put your opinion on everybody else's life." He was mad at me, so I was mad with him.

Chantel is insistent on speaking out on issues about which she feels particularly ardent. She refuses to be silenced. She expresses her contrary opinion, risking her teacher's displeasure. Moreover, she resists his effort to "put [his] opinions on everybody else's life." In this instance, Chantel represents herself not merely disagreeing with this teacher, but speaking out for the common right to self-expression.

Marie, a Dominican American student in her sophomore year, tells me about her classroom behavior: "I always speak my mind. Like, some students can't really go up to the teacher and talk about, like if they have problems. I'm usually the one in the class that's always like we believe that we should get this and that and we should be treated that way and not this way." When I ask her to describe herself in her sophomore year, Marie once again discusses her need to respond verbally to unfair treatment:

I can't stay shush on anything. Like my father, he'd always be like, "You did this and you did that." My brother'll be just standing there like, and he don't answer, he don't say nothing. I can't be like that, I can't keep it in myself. I gotta talk back, you know, speak my mind, tell him my side of the story even though you're gonna lose. My brother's like, "You're gonna lose anyway. They ain't gonna listen to you so why talk back." Like I just can't, I try but I can't.

Even when she is told by her brother that "speaking [her] mind" is not going to make a difference, and when others "don't say nothing," Marie speaks up.

When asked about her relationships with her parents in her junior year, Christine, an African American student, suggests a similar pattern with her father:

[My father and I] have discussions every once in a while. But then I don't agree with his view so when he says something, you know, I try to challenge it. You know, find out why he thinks that way. And he'll get mad, 'cause he doesn't like when people try to challenge him. I'm really the only person that will stand up to him. Talk to him word for word. . . . I get it from him. He doesn't back down either. He likes to be his own boss. And I'm the same way 'cause he always taught me never to let people take advantage of you or take control of you. You should always speak up, talk for yourself. And that's what I do. It just so happens I do it with him.

Christine feels comfortable challenging her father. She sees herself as uniquely direct and attributes this ability to her father. She won't "bug down" to him because he has taught her to be self-assertive, and she is, to her fathers' dismay, using these skills with him. Strikingly, the girls in the study, like Christine, were more apt to indicate that their expressive abilities came from watching their fathers than their mothers. Fathers were the ones who were either directly or indirectly teaching their daughters to speak their minds, and their daughters were following suit.

Christine also speaks about her directness with her mother in her junior year: "My mother would try to put me in my place. But I wouldn't buckle down, so I guess now she realizes I'm not trying to be grown or anything but I have my own opinions." While the girls commonly provided stories of being outspoken with their fathers and mothers, their discussions about being expressive with their mothers were never as frequent, lengthy, or as intense as their discussions of their fathers. It is unclear what the reasons are for this difference. When daughters have more daily contact with their mothers than their fathers, as is the case with most of these girls, being candid with their mothers about their thoughts and feelings may seem more commonplace, and less worthy of discussion, than their outspoken experiences with their fathers. Girls may also feel more pride in their abilities to be outspoken with their fathers—the parent who may hold more power in their families and who does hold more power in the larger society—than with their mothers. And, of course, girls may also feel less angry with and, perhaps, have more respect for their mothers than for their fathers (as suggested in chapter 6). Consequently, they may be less willing to challenge their mothers. As Milagro suggests below, they may also feel more protective of their mothers.

Milagro, a Dominican American student, tells me in her junior year about her need to speak up when she believes her father mistreats her mother:

> Sometimes my dad makes my mother cry and I don't like that and every time he does that I go up to his face and tell him that I, you know, that I really love my mother and he shouldn't be doing that to her. . . . And I always get on his case real bad 'cause I remember he's going to be getting on everybody's case but I told him not on mine, you know, 'cause I've taken a lot of stuff, you know. I'm up to my head already with all of this stuff.

Sometimes, as Marie indicates, the motivation to speak up comes from wanting to shield oneself, and other times, as Mary and Milagro indicate, the motivation comes from wanting to protect others. These girls, however, seem to stand alone within their families in their courage to be outspoken.

Gabriela, a half Irish American and half Puerto Rican student, also indicates in all three years of interviews that she is the only one in her family who is willing to stand up to her father:

> He expects me just to keep my mouth shut but I don't. I'm not gonna keep my mouth shut. . . . He'll yell at me for nothing and he expects me to keep quiet and take it. I ain't taking it from him. . . . I've been quiet for too long. My brothers and sisters just tell me, "Just be quiet with him." My sister went through the same thing, you know. But I'm the only one that's spoke out to him. Like he gets mad when I'm like this, but he gave me [my outspoken voice].

Like Shakira and Mary, Gabriela discusses her previous silence ("I've been quiet for too long") and her newfound voice in her relationship with her father. Unlike the other girls in the study, however, Gabriela expresses only her anger and frustration in her relationships and not her pain and vulnerability. Gabriela does not tell any stories of affection, loyalty, or love. She was one of only two girls in the sample who begins saying in her junior-year interview that there is *nobody* she can really be close with while telling me about her direct expressions of anger with her father, mother, friends, and teachers. In all three of her interviews, but particularly in her third interview, Gabriela seems lonely and depressed. Gabriela says "a lot of people say [to me], 'Oh, you got courage,' it's not courage, it's just that I don't care." Gabriela expresses her anger because she does not *care* about the consequences. In contrast to those adolescent girls who discussed being outspoken precisely because they cared about themselves and others, Gabriela asserts that she does not care about either: "'Cause the thing about me is like life to me means nothing. You know what I'm saying? . . . Like I don't know . . . when they're saying, like, I'm very negative about things now. Like I don't care about nothing no more." Gabriela may be claiming not to care to protect herself from deeply caring or caring too much. If she cared, I suspect, she might truly feel the depths of her loneliness. Worried about her psychological well being, I referred Gabriela to counseling at the end of her third-year interview.

Marie, Milagro, and Gabriela were remarkable in their willingness to voice their thoughts and feelings in situations in which they readily acknowledged that they were not being heard. They persisted in speaking out even when others told them to keep quiet. They insisted on breaking silence with the hope, perhaps, that they would eventually be heard. In contrast to Gabriela's personal assessment, the determination revealed by Marie, Milagro, and Gabriela suggests tremendous courage.

Unlike the other girls in the study, however, Marie begins unexpectedly to silence herself with her father by her junior year: "I don't respond [to my father] . . . because when I do, it's like it gets worse because he always says, 'Oh, you always talking back at me.' So, I just ignore him. I just be quiet, I don't say nothing. I'm tired of it. I've heard it, so what's the use. I don't get nowhere by saying anything." Marie has apparently lost her hope that she will make a difference with her father by speaking her mind. By her junior year, she has chosen to remain silent with him although she continues to be outspoken in other relationships. While she has given in, perhaps, to the strictures of her father, she has also seemingly devised a way to protect herself from further frustration and, possibly, further harassment. Being outspoken may be an effective strategy for responding to injustice, rudeness, or differences of opinion. However, it may not always be the best way of protecting oneself from psychological or physical harm.[7]

For the Sake of Connection

The girls spoke out about anger and frustration not just for its own sake, but also for the sake of maintaining connection. They did not typically speak of fearing isolation or alienation from others if they spoke honestly, but rather of having closer relationships. Eva tells Helena in her junior year: "You know you always argue with your family and friends but that don't mean you don't care about them. So it's always, you gotta have disagreements in a relationship and then happiness comes along with it. In order to have happiness you also have to have quarrels." In her junior- and senior-year interviews, Eva repeatedly tells stories in which she "had to" speak her mind in her relationships with her friends because she believes honesty is necessary in, and for, a good or "happy" relationship: "My friends and I always argue but that's okay because that's what friends do."

When I ask Chantel, in her junior year, about what has changed in her relationship with her best friend, she says that her best friend used to take advantage of her "niceness" by talking "for hours" about her problems. This year, however, Chantel told this friend that she wanted her to stop. Her best friend did indeed change her behavior and, consequently, Chantel says, their relationship improved. Chantel suggests that expressing her frustration preserved the relationship. She could not have continued the friendship without openly articulating her feelings.

Chantel's self-description in her junior year also emphasizes the importance of honesty in her relationships:

How would you describe yourself?

I don't know, I try and be honest with people. . . . If I feel like somebody's doing something, and they ask me, they want my honest opinion, even if I think it's gonna hurt them some, I just have to tell them 'cause it'll bother me if I say, "Oh you look fine," and then I'll leave. So I just answer them, "No, you look awful. Please go do something with yourself." I feel as though I have to say it regardless [even] if I'm gonna hurt somebody's feelings or not, I'll say it. But I think before I speak. I be like, "Oh, this person might get their feelings hurt," so I'll put it nicely. I will tell people what I'm thinking, but I'll say it nicely.

Voicing one's thoughts and feelings in relationships, for both Chantel and Eva and most of their female peers, involves both taking care of one's own needs and the needs of others—it is deeply embedded in relationship.

With "Attitude"

Occasionally the girls framed their outspoken voices as having "an attitude." When Florence, an African American adolescent, tells me in her junior year that her "attitude" has become worse over the years, I ask her why she believes this is true: "It lets people know that I'm serious, that I'm not playing and it's a good way for, you know, for people to listen, to know that I'm trying to get a point across." Christine says in her senior-year interview: "I get an attitude. My mother says I have an attitude. Sometimes I don't wanna be bothered and I let her know. She says I have an attitude. I don't think it's an attitude. I just don't wanna be bothered, you know, so she doesn't bother me anymore." Gabriela says in her junior-year interview: "I have an attitude with people sometimes. You have to have an attitude nowadays, you know what I'm saying? Like somebody says something [bad], I snap back at them." Shakira also tells me in her senior-year interview about her attitude: "You could do just a little thing like step on my feet, and I just be like, 'You stepped on my feet.' Especially if I don't like you, you really gonna get it. I be like unbelievable. If it's somebody I don't like, I'm like, 'You stupid, don't be stepping on my feet.'"

"Having an attitude," for these girls, is a way of forcefully expressing themselves. While it may be considered inappropriate, ineffective, or rude at times, such confident articulations force people to listen and take their thoughts and feelings seriously. Christine wants people *to know* when she does not want to be bothered. Felicia says her "attitude" encourages people to acknowledge and listen to her. Shakira wants those she does not like to know it. These girls implied or directly stated that they had an "attitude" when they wanted to convey criticism, their need for privacy, or their negative or hostile feelings. While many of these girls initially stated that they needed to "change their attitude," when their interviewers asked whether they liked having an "attitude," most of the girls stated that there was "something positive" about such a stance. They fully recognized that adults and many of their peers thought "having an attitude" was problematic (e.g., Christine's reference to her mother), but, at the same time, they found this posture "sometimes necessary."

The Complexities of Voice

Variations across Relationships

When Christine is asked to describe herself in her senior year, she says:

> There goes that question. I don't know. I'm sensitive, but outspoken, you
> know.
> *How are you outspoken?*
> I don't tolerate anybody disrespecting me. Or putting me down or saying
> something derogatory. I don't, you know, I have to speak up.

However, she also states:

> I have a low self-esteem. I'm not—I'm not low self-esteemed. I'm self-con-
> scious. I don't know. 'Cause see when I was growing up people called me
> ugly and naturally I believed them . . . and then like some of the boys will
> try to talk to me, you know, I wonder why. What do they see? I don't like
> speaking up to people I don't know. Well, not speak, I'll say, "Hi," but you
> know, you see somebody on the street you go, "Hi, how you doin'?" I can't
> do that, I don't know why, unless it's someone I know really well.

While Christine describes herself as outspoken with people when they are
impertinent, she struggles to speak with people whom she does not know
well, but who are, in fact, not "disrespecting" her. Christine's stories suggest that being able to speak up when someone "puts you down" may not
indicate complete or unconditional self-confidence or an ability or willingness to express oneself in all situations. Christine's stories also suggest that
experiences that lead to "low self-esteem" may not only inhibit one from
speaking out ("people called me ugly. . . . I don't like speaking up to people"), but may also motivate one to speak up. When I ask Christine why
she thinks her father is able to be so outspoken (she mentions this early in
her senior-year interview), she tells me of his struggles as a child: "Everybody thought he was dumb and even his own cousin picked him last in this
kickball game." Because of his earlier experiences, her father "wouldn't let
anybody tell him what to do or try to take control of him or try to take advantage of him [as he grew older] . . . he would always speak up." Christine, who herself was called "ugly" when she was younger, may identify
with her father and consequently be intent on responding when others insult her. Her "low self-esteem" seems to overwhelm her when casual con-

versation is called for, but when someone is "putting [her] down" she has learned from her father that she must speak her mind.

Chantel, who spoke so fervently about her desire and ability to speak honestly with her friends, discusses her frustration that she is occasionally "too nice" to people. She expresses anger at herself for letting people take advantage of her by lending them money although she knows they will not pay her back. She does not know why she resists "saying something" to them. Chantel and Christine suggest that being able to speak one's thoughts and feelings can vary within and across relationships. The type and meaning of the relationship, the specific act or request (e.g., to borrow money), as well as the girls' own self-image and past history determines when, where, and with whom they will bring forth their voices.

Silencing in the Midst of Voice

Although most of the adolescent girls explicitly discussed their willingness to speak out with their friends, teachers, and family members, these outspoken voices faltered when they discussed their relationships with boys. Most of the girls[8] spoke of not trusting boys and of feeling wary of becoming involved with boys because they were not certain they could protect their own feelings or listen to themselves in these relationships.

Milagro, who so boldly articulated her willingness to speak her mind with her father, says in her junior year:

> What I don't like about myself is that I'm so light on guys. After they do something really bad, like they call me, I talk to them and I'm kind of like, you know, a couple of days later I just forgive them.
> *Why do you forgive so easily?*
> Because I fear that the guys might hate me.

Milagro's fear of losing her relationships with boys inhibits her from communicating her anger even when they do "something really bad." For girls such as Milagro, honestly expressing themselves with male peers may feel more risky ("because . . . the guys might hate me") than speaking out with their fathers. While boys may "hate" or abandon these girls as a result of their outspokenness, fathers, at least theoretically, will not.

Gayle, an African American student, finds speaking with boys and men in general too "dangerous," and has consequently cut herself off from most boys and men in her sophomore and junior years. She believes that they will inevitably betray or manipulate her and concludes that "you should just stay quiet" with them: "I don't talk to males about any problems I have, rather keep it to myself." In her senior year, Gayle says that she has a boyfriend whom she thinks she loves. She is not going to tell him, however, because she believes he may take advantage of her if he knew how she felt. She says she may tell him in "a year or so" when she feels more certain about the relationship. Although Gayle says that she is not afraid to talk to her boyfriend about certain things (aside from love), she still does not trust older men and avoids speaking to them: "They start looking at you strangely and I just don't like people looking at me strangely. I feel like, 'Dag, what did I do?' . . . I watch TV, and I see the shows about how older men molest little kids and I try to avoid anything that could be hazardous."

Shakira, who claims to be "outspoken and out everything," is unwilling to speak openly with boys because "I don't feel like dealing with their problems and things." Shakira tells me about her anger at boys who *hit* her and who pressure her to have sex with them. Such experiences are examples, she says, of why she finds boys unworthy of her trust and, therefore, undeserving of hearing her "real" thoughts and feelings. When I ask her in her senior year to describe how she sees herself in relation to boys in the future, Shakira says: "I don't know. Maybe more open, I don't know. I don't share or anything with them what, you know, what I want them to hear, want them to know. Oh I don't know, maybe I'll meet somebody I could open up to." Shakira speaks her mind with people, such as friends and family, whom she does not consider dangerous, and silences herself with those whom she deems unsafe.

While most of the girls seemed silenced by the actions and reactions of boys, there were variations in the kinds of silences these girls described. Gayle and Shakira actively choose not to speak honestly to boys because they believe that this is their safest strategy. Milagro, on the other hand, doesn't seem to make an active choice ("what I don't like about myself . . ."); she seems more silenced *by* boys than silent *with* boys. In addition, unlike Gayle and Shakira, she does not remove herself from her relationships with boys in response to how they have treated her. Because her silence seems more passive than active, Milagro may be more "at risk" psychologically than Gayle or Shakira. Silencing oneself may be an effective

way of protecting oneself in certain circumstances. However, the consequences will likely be determined by the amount of agency experienced in
one's silence.

Silencing with No Voice

Two of the girls in the sample seemed to silence themselves in most, if not
all, of their relationships. They rarely told stories of speaking their minds
or saying what they felt or thought. I heard no distinctions, typically, in
how they spoke, or rather did not speak, to their friends, family members,
or boys. To avoid replicating the girls' silences by silencing them in this
chapter, I will describe one of these two girls as she speaks to me about herself and her relationships over three years.

Tyiesha, an African American girl, seems confident in her freshman year.
There is a clarity and honesty to her stories as she speaks to me about caring for her friends and family. When asked to describe herself, Tyiesha says:

> I describe myself sometimes nice and sometimes mean, most of the times I'm
> nice but sometimes when I don't get what I want I get mad . . . I'm not hon-
> est all the time. . . . I'm sort of mean sometimes because when I was younger,
> I used to have to walk—walk in the streets because me and my mother and
> my sister didn't have nowhere to stay so I guess that's why I'm so mean now
> and because when I was younger, my father used to try to hit my mother and
> I guess that's what also makes me mean now, too.

Tyiesha is reflective and direct with me as she describes herself and her difficult life. This honesty, however, diminishes over the course of the next
two years, and by her junior year she seems profoundly troubled. In her
sophomore year, the frequency with which Tyiesha says "I don't know"
sharply increases from her first interview; she appears not to know what is
happening to her or why she finds it difficult to express herself with her
friends and family members. By her junior year, Tyiesha has almost completely shut herself off from others who care for her. When I interview her
this year, she has just returned home from an adolescent shelter to which
she was sent after she ran away from home for five days. She says she ran
away because she wanted to spend time with friends, although she admits
they were not "really friends." Her decision to run away, she explains, did
not have anything to do with her mother or sister (the two people with
whom she lives), and, furthermore, she "did not mind" staying in the shel-

ter. The only reason she came home, she says, is because her mother asked her to return. Tyiesha sounds acutely disconnected from her own feelings and confused in this interview (she did not remember being interviewed in the previous two years).[9]

When asked whether she will voice disagreement with the people in her family, Tyiesha says in her junior year:

> I'll keep quiet.
> *Why?*
> I don't know. I don't—it's none of my business. Like if my stepfather [who does not live with them] touched me or something, I'll say something. Well, I don't know. I don't know if I would say something. I don't know. Probably scared that it would hurt my mother 'cause she really loves him.

Tyiesha wants to believe that she would say something to her mother, and thereby protect herself, if her stepfather molested her, but she also feels the need to protect her mother. If she found out, however, that her stepfather was having an affair with another woman, she says she would definitely tell her mother "cause that's my mother he's hurting." While she is willing to protect her mother, Tyiesha is uncertain about her ability to protect herself. Her recent running away suggests, however, that there are even limits to her willingness to take care of her mother.

Tyiesha's apparent silence becomes more obvious when she speaks of a male friend with whom she would like to become romantically involved. Tyiesha says she has had sex with this boy for many months in the hopes that it will turn into a steady, monogamous relationship. Yet she has not told him directly of her desires because she fears he will leave her and she does not want to risk such a consequence. In the meantime, Tyiesha says with an angry voice that this boy is also having sex with other girls. Even though she is upset, she will not express this to him for the same reasons she will not speak to him about her desires.

When I ask her to describe herself later in this interview, Tyiesha says:

> Vulnerable . . . 'cause I know that this girl's having sex with [him] and I'm not gonna say nothing about it . . . I don't know.
> *How else are you vulnerable?*

Like when my friend asked me to go somewhere and I can't go and they keep
asking me and asking me, "Come on." I just say, "Yeah." And people ask
me for stuff and I let them use it and they mess it up and I don't say nothing.
How come?
I don't know.

When asked to define the term "vulnerable," Tyiesha says: "[W]hen people walk over you. Telling you what to do. When people use you, when
sometimes I let my friends tell me what to do and stuff. I don't listen to
myself." Seemingly afraid of the consequences of "listening to [her]self,"
Tyiesha chooses not to and ends up feeling like, in the words of Mary,
"somebody's bridge." Tyiesha's silence and depression are readily apparent this year. As with Gabriela, I refer her to counseling at the end of her
junior-year interview.

While Tyiesha and one of her female peers in the study appeared to be
silenced by and silent in most if not all of their relationships, most of the
other girls were not. They related numerous stories, especially in their junior and senior years, of directly expressing their feelings of anger, frustration, love, and affection. These tales of outspokenness, however, were frequently interspersed with stories of being silent in, being silenced by, or
entirely avoiding relationships with boys. The girls indicated that being
able to voice one's thoughts and feelings in some relationships neither
generalizes to all relationships, nor suggests an earlier ability to do so, and,
finally, does not necessarily imply self-confidence or feelings of being
heard.

Boys' Voices

In contrast to the girls, few boys identified with being "outspoken" or
being able to "speak one's mind." Furthermore, none of the boys discussed "having an attitude." The boys spoke, instead, of retreating or remaining silent when they were angry or upset.[10] They were fearful, they
said, that if they directly expressed their angry feelings, particularly with
their male peers, these relationships would "most definitely" end. Speaking one's mind was typically framed by the boys as "disrespectful," dis-
ruptive, and dangerous.

Silencing in Relationships

Marvin, an African American student, speaks in a soft voice and has a hard time looking directly at his interviewer in each of his three interviews. When Mike asks him in his sophomore year to describe himself, he contrasts himself to an outspoken older sister: "Like my older sister, she gets in there. Like she don't be lying, she be telling the truth. Like whoever's right, she be on their side . . . I try to not even get in it." Concerned about openly expressing himself with his mother, he says: "I see my older sister talk back and it just makes my mother upset." While Marvin recognizes the risks of outspokenness and may want to spare his mother frustration or anger, he nevertheless seems to admire his sister for her "truth telling" abilities.

Marvin expresses his frustrations to his mother on occasion, but is hesitant to do so: "Like sometimes like she'll aggravate me and I be telling her how I feel sometimes, like I don't be meaning to be rude or anything." Surprisingly, Marvin's perspective and cautious attitude was typical of the boys in the study. They indicated that speaking directly in relationships was admirable but potentially rude and risky and, therefore, undesirable unless one wanted to be disrespectful.

In his senior year, Marvin tells me:

> When I'm mad I usually keep it to myself, 'cause I'm not outspoken. I'm kind of shy. Like some of my friends they could just come out and say it with no problem. Me, I'm like I never say it. Mostly just with girls, I don't know, like I do it with boys too—they ask my opinion, like if something looks ugly, like they really like it so I probably be like, "It looks okay," but I really think it looks terrible. But I don't know. I think different, I guess. . . . Like they probably won't like you no more because you said something that made them mad.

Marvin views speaking out as an act of courage that would endanger rather than enhance relationships. When asked about his closest friendship, Marvin says he is able to get mad at this person sometimes but "not all-out mad." When I ask him why, he says: "I don't know. I guess because we know each other and like grew up together." Since friends may not "like you anymore" if opinions are expressed, Marvin may feel particularly wary of speaking up in, and therefore losing, a long-term relationship.

Albert, a Puerto Rican teenager, also seems to silence himself in his relationships. Like Marvin, Albert reveals these difficulties in a discussion in
which he contrasts his own behavior to the fearless, and, perhaps, dangerous actions of his younger sister:

> [When my father used to hit my mother when I was younger] I would hide
> under the bed, but my little sister used to get in the way of my father. She
> used to get in the middle of my mother and father, just push, push, she
> would scream. . . . She would never be scared. . . . She is real strong. She
> gets mad very fast, you know. She has an attitude, you know, like you can't
> bother her too much, she'll get mad . . . I am not like that.
> *Do you have any of her willingness to fight back?*
> Not as much, but sometimes I will, but she's more, you know—she has more
> guts. Even though she's eleven and a half, she *still* has more guts, I think
> than me.

Albert's tone of voice suggests a desire to have his sister's courage. He
seems impressed with her fearless ways of protecting her mother despite
the fact that his sister may be putting herself at great risk.

In his senior-year interview, Albert says to me that what he dislikes
about himself is that he is "too nice" sometimes:

> Some people do take advantage of me. Some of my friends, you know, like I
> would leave them alone in my room, they would take things. But I would
> let 'em and I would be like, "Oh lemme see if they do bring it back." They
> would never bring it back, so whenever I used to go over to their house, I
> used to take it back.
> *Why didn't you say anything when you noticed tapes were missing?*
> I would try to convince myself that the tape was just lost but then I would see
> it in their house. I also thought if I say anything they would tell me they
> didn't take it . . . I don't trust friends no more, when they go to my room
> I'll be there, you know.

Instead of directly confronting his friends, Albert has chosen a strategy of
silence and disconnection. Although some of the adolescent girls also
spoke about being "too nice," their discussions were interspersed with ex-

amples of speaking unabashedly about their feelings. Albert and Marvin, in contrast, speak only of people taking advantage of them, of being "too nice," or of not being able to express their anger or frustration with their parents and friends. When I ask Albert in his senior year how he typically responds when he is upset with his friends, he says:

> I would keep it to myself sometimes, you know, sometimes I would tell 'em, "Don't do that, 'cause I'm getting mad already," but sometimes I won't, you know, I'll just laugh with them but it's hard because I'm getting mad. *Why will you choose not to say anything?* So I won't create no problems, so they won't get mad at me and then break up.

Although he occasionally expresses his irritation directly, Albert, like Marvin, generally avoids communicating such feelings for fear of a "breakup." The irony of Albert's situation is that he avoids conflict with his friends in order to protect the relationship, but, in the process, he also concludes that he can't "trust friends no more."

Malcolm suggests a similar dilemma. In his junior year, when I ask Malcolm why he does not confront his friends when he knows they have betrayed him, he responds:

> I don't know how to put it besides we're friends like, you know, if he wants to talk go ahead but he don't say nothing to my face. I guess I think of it as that's how they have to let their steam off or whatever, you know. They have to just say something bad about somebody, so, I don't talk to him about it because I don't want to occupy my mind with little stuff. I guess it's sometimes like it could be just their family or something like their family is nice or something. You know, I don't really wanna cause no conflict.

Malcolm continues by saying that as a result of his experiences of betrayal, he does not have close friends. He remains silent because his anger may lead to conflict and, at the same time, he distances himself from his friends because of his anger. Albert and Malcolm use the same strategy and experience the same outcome: they avoid conflict with their peers when they are angry in order to protect these relationships, but since their anger remains unexpressed and their problems unresolved, they trust fewer friends and distance themselves from their male peers. They diminish the intimacy of their relationships in order to preserve them.[11]

Albert's avoidance of conflict and disagreement with his friends is also evident in his relationships with his teachers. In his senior year, Albert speaks about his hesitation to say something when he disagrees in class because he has "too much respect" for his teacher. Like Marvin, he connects speaking openly and honestly with being rude: "I wanna tell 'em [the teachers] it's not true. I just respect other people. I'm like that, inside of me, just respect other people. I won't argue with other people. They might keep on arguing and it'd never stop." Although Albert avoids disagreeing with his teachers for fear of being rude, he also implies that the possibility of an ongoing conflict is so uncomfortable for him that he avoids disagreements altogether. While the issue of respect may be one reason for not speaking out with his teacher, his aversion to or fear of conflict emerges as another.

Albert also retreats in his relationships with girlfriends when he is angry. In his senior year, he tells Mike why he broke up with his girlfriend: "Like every time she used to go out someplace, she used to go and she never told me nuthin'. . . . She never told me like she would make up something and I knew something was going on, so I said I would like to end this relationship." Instead of confronting his girlfriend with his suspicions and allowing her to respond, Albert terminates the relationship as his sign of protest.

Like Albert and Marvin, Victor, an African American teen, also struggles to speak openly in his relationships. When I ask Victor, a senior, what he would like to teach his two-and-a-half-year-old son, he says: "Number one, to be a very outspoken person 'cause that's a key element that I never had. . . . I would want him to express his opinions, you know, whether good or bad, at least express them. I was never able to do that." During all three years of his interviews, Victor speaks about his desire to be more outspoken:

> When I look at other people and like they're so upfront and forward and stuff like that, right, I'm not that type of person.
> *Why aren't you more upfront?*
> I feel I'm gonna say something wrong, I'm gonna say something out of context that I shouldn't have said. . . . I really don't like talking that much. . . .

It's not really to do with trusting other people, I just don't really—I don't really have no confidence to even, you know, come to a person and share. It's hard. It's hard for me 'cause I never really had any confidence. . . . I think that's gonna hurt me down the road the slower it comes.

In contrast to Christine, who indicated that even though she lacked confidence she remained outspoken, Victor equates being open and honest with having confidence. Without such confidence, Victor feels he is unable to "share." Victor's openness with me, and his willingness to reveal what he perceives as a problem, is striking in the context of his struggles to speak with others. He may perceive less risk of being "wrong" or "out of context" within the structure of an interview than with his friends and family members. In addition, I may have created a safe space within which Victor feels free to express himself.

In all three of his interviews, Victor struggles to voice his anger as well as his opinions. In his senior year, Victor tells me a story about his friends throwing food at him in the cafeteria and not letting him play basketball with them once he started becoming liked by, or "getting in" with, the teachers. He says: "I didn't really hate them for it. . . . I feel more like a man because I will still help them if they need it even though they hurt me." He seems to equate being "like a man" with maintaining his equanimity and caring for his "friends" even when they do not care for him. When asked why he did not really "hate them for it," he says: "I have no room in my heart to be angry 'cause life's too short . . . 'cause I feel a whole lot better being happy." While Victor may wish to believe this, his agitated voice suggests otherwise. He may be trying not to hate his friends while he harbors strong feelings of resentment toward them. Victor may not want to admit to himself the intensity of his anger or may not be willing to speak openly with me about these seemingly humiliating experiences.

The boys in the study commonly indicated that they were unwilling to speak out with their peers, teachers, and family members. They spoke about being silenced by and silencing themselves in their relationships and, unlike the girls, about wanting to avoid conflicts or retreating from their relationships when there were disagreements or conflicts. Some of the boys were fearful that their experience, if openly expressed, would endanger their relationships. Other boys were not willing to disagree or argue with others because they would be perceived as rude or disrespectful. The boys' avoidance of conflict did not suggest a lack of interest in openness and honesty with others, but rather a fear of the potential interpretation and consequences of such behavior.

The Variations of Voice

There were a few boys, however, who discussed being outspoken in their relationships, particularly as they got older. For these boys, as for the silent ones, speaking out was typically framed as stemming from anger or frustration and was rarely described as an act of care or love. Tyrone, an African American student, tells Helena in his freshman year about a time in which he had to speak up with his mother:

> [I told her] I'm old enough that I can be talked to instead of someone trying to beat on me. I said, "Well, listen you're not going to beat me, for one. I still have my respect for you but you're not going to beat me, I'm older than that. I'm above all that. It's time for you to open your eyes and notice that."

After saying this to his mother, Tyrone left his mother's house to live with his father. While Tyrone's verbal directness resembles the outspokenness of the girls', his subsequent action is similar to many of the boys: he retreats or leaves when conflicts arise.

Tyrone tells Helena in his freshman year that he and his mother have many arguments because he was the first among his siblings to challenge her "strict" religious beliefs. He could not abide by his mother's dogmatic religious rules which would have prevented him from playing sports. His rejection of his mother's religion has caused severe difficulties in their relationship. Tyrone says he expresses his anger directly to both his parents for not being responsible parents. With his voice shaking with anger, he tells Helena that he recently discovered that his father was buying crack from one of his friends. As a way of "getting back" at his parents, Tyrone has decided not to do well in school so his parents will "suffer." Tyrone seems, at this point, to disconnect from his own needs and develop a self-destructive strategy, which he readily admits is not going to "really" make him feel better. While Tyrone openly communicates with his parents, his needs, feelings, and desires are not being heard by them and are, even more seriously, barely audible to himself.

In his second-year interview (he is still a freshman), Tyrone, once again, speaks to Helena of being direct with his father and mother about his anger. Speaking of the shame and anger his father caused him, he says:

> You know he wasn't giving up nothing. Like we didn't know right from left. I was like, you know, "I'm above all that, and you're treating me as if I was just like a bum off the street and was just uneducated." And I was like, "You didn't raise me to be that way. You always told me to fight for what I believe in and this is what I believe in." [These days] I tell him straight out how I feel and you know all the time I couldn't do that, but it's like [now] I say it in front of him. I don't fear him or nothing like that. . . . When I found out [about my father buying crack], I lost respect for him, you know, I say what I want to say when I want to say it and I have no remorse in what I say.

As this angry and disturbing passage suggests, speaking out for Tyrone was not about maintaining connections. Rather, it was a tactic and last resort in a relationship with little or no respect. Tyrone speaks out with both his parents because, he implies, he has little regard for either of them. Perceiving the act of speaking out to be a way of disconnecting rather than a way of connecting may begin to explain why the boys appeared more hesitant and resistant than the girls to being outspoken.

Speaking out for the boys, however, was not consistently about disrespect, just as speaking out for the girls was not consistently about maintaining connections. For girls and boys in the study, speaking out was also a response to injustice. In his third-year interview, Tyrone describes an argument he had with school administrators who accused him of stabbing a peer in the bathroom. Claiming innocence, Tyrone explains:

> I'm like I ain't gonna take this lying down. I'm getting transferred here, I haven't done nothing. So I'm gonna fight it as much as I can. Because I know I'm innocent. If I was guilty, I'd have no cause to fight it . . . but if you're in the right, you know you'll fight it to any degree, to any extent. . . . You won't care what others say because you know now you're right.

Like many of his male and female peers, Tyrone believes that when one is "right," one should express oneself. Self-expression is necessary for self-protection.

When Helena asks Tyrone to describe himself in his third-year interview, he responds:

Determined and outspoken. . . . Outspoken for the fact that if I see something I dislike, I know I only live once, I'm not gonna sit down and just say
nothing about it, I'll speak upon it. . . . I'm quick to point out something
that's wrong or something I don't understand. And, you know, people'll be
like, "Well, you got a good head on your shoulders, you can go somewhere,"
and stuff like that.

Here Tyrone, as in the previous passage, conveys a sense of urgency in his
outspoken ways that is similar to that expressed by many of the girls. This
is the first time that Tyrone describes himself as outspoken and he was the
only boy who described himself in this way. His experience of being
wrongly accused of a crime may have enhanced his determination to speak
up.

Notably, Tyrone also tells Helena that people are telling him that he has
"a good head on his shoulders" and that he could "go somewhere" because he is outspoken about his beliefs. Jamal, a peer of Tyrone's, indicates
in his interviews that he, too, is frequently told by teachers that because he
speaks his mind he could be a "leader" in the future. This type of encouragement was remarkably absent from the girls' interviews. There were no
stories of girls being told they could be leaders because they were outspoken. In fact, girls' outspokenness was more likely to be perceived by others and by themselves as having "an attitude." The boys and girls in this
study appear to receive quite different messages from their teachers, parents, and, perhaps, from their peers about being outspoken.

"Speaking Out" through Violence

Three of the boys in the study implied that they expressed their thoughts
and feelings primarily through physical aggression. While physical and verbal expressions and responses are clearly different, the desired effects are
similar. Those who are outspoken either through their voices or through
physical aggression want to be heard, noticed, and taken seriously, and
they are willing to let people know of their desires. Guillermo spoke at
length in all of his interviews about his violent impulses when angry. In his
senior year, Guillermo said to me:

Like this person who really hurt my mother when I was in Miami. She took
my mother to court and made a lot of problems for her. So I really got mad
when I found out that. . . . Most of the time I am a calm person, okay? Kind,

I don't bother anyone. But when somebody really gets on my nerves, I just lost my head. . . . If I had a chance to get up to grab a gun I'd just use it, that's one thing about me. My temper, it's too strong and when I get mad that gives me a headache too. Like when I get mad about something in school I just go home and sleep. But when somebody special like bothers me a lot, just gets on my nerves, talks a lot of things about me, I just don't know how to control myself.

When Guillermo is angry, he either strikes out violently or retreats into sleep. Using his voice as a way to express himself is not an option. When he gets angry or mad at his mother or sister, he will "just be quiet. I don't say nothing. Just go to my room or get out of the house." He has, however, hit his sister because his sister "was being really disrespectful of [his] mother." Guillermo claims not to like his short temper but when people are "rude" to him or his family members, he feels he cannot control his violent impulses. He suggests that "being rude"—as many of the boys described the act of speaking out—can be physically dangerous. Boys like Guillermo can become dangerous as a result of their peers' outspoken ways.

In contrast to the girls, the boys typically had difficulty communicating their angry thoughts and feelings. They interpreted such acts as disrespectful, if sometimes necessary. Speaking out, for the boys, was commonly perceived to be an aggressive act, a perception bolstered by their physically aggressive peers. They rarely discussed being openly expressive with others about love, care, and affection. Speaking out involved making oneself vulnerable, and these boys, for the most part, were not willing to allow themselves to experience such vulnerability.

Reflections

Over the past ten years, several important research projects have indicated that adolescent girls and women "silence themselves or are silenced in relationships rather than risk open conflict and disagreement."[12] From pop psychology[13] to more scholarly books based on empirical research,[14] we have learned that as young girls reach adolescence, they begin to struggle to speak out in their relationships about their anger, frustration, and pain. Luise Eichenbaum and Susan Orbach found that for many women, "the mere idea of mentioning a hurt, expressing a grievance, showing a friend that she has made one angry . . . can make a woman very nervous."[15] Furthermore, they claim that "women rarely develop the facility of talking directly to one another about difficulties between them."[16] According to these popular and more academic reports, which have almost exclusively focused on white middle- and upper-class females, many adolescent girls and women struggle to express their real thoughts and feelings directly in their relationships.[17]

In the present study, however, the willingness "to speak one's mind by telling all one's heart"[18]—to speak out about anger and pain as well as love and loyalty—was expressed by the majority of the adolescent girls in their junior- and senior-year interviews. This theme was heard among the girls who were struggling as well as the girls who excelled in school;[19] it was heard among girls from different ethnic communities; and it was heard most frequently when the adolescents spoke about their relationships with female friends, parents, and teachers. In contrast to studies of primarily white, middle-class, adolescent girls and women, these urban poor and working-class, ethnically diverse adolescent girls were willing to speak their minds in many of their relationships.[20]

These girls, however, also suggested that they were silent in or silenced by their relationships with boys. They spoke about fearing and not wanting to cope with boys' reactions as the reasons for their silences. Some of the girls appeared to be silenced by their relationships with boys but maintain them, while others chose to silence themselves and, consequently, avoid relationships with boys altogether.

The boys, in contrast, commonly spoke of struggling to speak openly and honestly in many of their relationships. While some of the boys spoke of being direct and open, many feared that if they spoke candidly, particularly with their male peers, these relationships would end. The boys' reluctance to directly express their thoughts and feelings with their peers and family members stood in stark contrast to the girls' open and honest expressions in similar relationships.

Questions raised as a result of these findings include: (1) Why do the girls in this study have the courage and strength to speak out in relationships when many white, adolescent girls and women from middle- or upper-income families appear to have great difficulties doing this? (2) Why are the girls more likely to openly express themselves in their relationships (although not with boys) than the boys? (3) Why do both boys and girls have difficulty speaking out with boys? and (4) Why does the capacity for speaking out increase for many of the girls and a few of the boys by their junior and senior years?

There are various reasons that may explain the first question. Adolescent girls growing up in urban America may not be raised to be as passive and quiet as girls growing up in suburban, white middle- or upper-class environments. Gloria Wade-Gayles suggests that black mothers (and, according to the current data, black fathers as well)

> do not socialize their daughters to be passive. . . . Quite the contrary, they socialize their daughters to be independent, strong, and self-confident. Black mothers are suffocatingly protective and domineering precisely because they are determined to mold their daughters into whole and self-actualizing persons in a society that devalues black women.[21]

Joyce Ladner similarly writes that "black females are socialized by adult figures in early life to become strong, independent women, who because of precarious circumstances growing out of poverty and racism, might have to eventually become heads of their own households."[22] In keeping with these findings, Lourdes Torres asserts that Puerto Rican girls and women are less passive and more outspoken than they are commonly portrayed in the social science literature.[23] While these researchers are not specifically addressing urban poor or working-class girls and women, it is possible to draw hypotheses concerning such populations from their observations given the prevalence of black and Puerto Rican girls and women in poor, urban environments. Low-income black and Puerto Rican parents and parents from other ethnic minority communities living in urban areas may want to socialize their daughters to be outspoken and strong. They may realize that if their daughters are passive and quiet, they may simply disappear in a society in which they and their daughters are already pushed to the margins.[24]

Urban poor and working-class adolescent girls may, furthermore, realize that to survive in a world that routinely marginalizes them, they must speak up. Jennifer Pastor and her colleagues note that "urban girls of color must learn how to assert themselves within white, often male-dominated institutions, because they know that these institutions are often not designed to protect them or promote their interests."[25] White middle- or upper-class adolescent girls and women may understand that even if they remain silent (or, perhaps, especially if they remain silent), they will still be granted certain, albeit limited, opportunities. Their race and class almost ensure these opportunities despite the prevailing sexism in our society. Adolescent girls, especially girls of color from low-income families, may realize that they will be offered little, if anything, if they do not ask for or demand it. Even then, their opportunities will be slight, although greater than had they remained silent. Some of the outspoken girls in this study may also be learning such skills by watching their female peers. If, for example, black mothers and fathers are socializing their daughters to be outspoken, perhaps Latina and white girls are learning from their black female peers. This may be especially true in a school such as the one in this study where the majority of the student body is black.

Finally, since many of the girls in the study seemed more willing to speak openly in their junior and senior years than in their freshman and sophomore years, it is possible that girls from different socioeconomic, racial, and ethnic backgrounds find it particularly difficult to speak out in early adolescence. Hormonal changes, school transitions, and other shifts in their lives, including their growing cognitive capacity to understand cultural expectations, may silence most girls during this period.[26] The capacity for open expression may increase as girls' lives stabilize when they reach late adolescence. Previous studies focusing on the silences among primarily white middle- and upper-class adolescent girls have focused on those who are in early to midadolescence. Had we interviewed the girls only in their first two years of high school, outspokenness would have been a barely detectable trend rather than a pervasive theme. Researchers have, however, detected such silences among adult white middle-class women[27] as well, which suggests that there may be differences across social class, race, and ethnicity in the willingness and ability to speak one's mind.

Answers to the second question regarding the gender differences in outspokenness lie with the culture and society in which these adolescents are raised.[28] In a society in which girls, particularly those who are poor or working class, are neither heard nor taken seriously, girls may learn quickly that they will have to speak up for themselves if their needs are going to be addressed. Boys, even poor and working-class ethnic-minority boys, may believe that their wants and needs will, to some extent, be addressed even if they do not speak up; or, perhaps, they believe that they may lose what little privilege they have if they speak out. Those with the least power in society—poor girls and women of color—may experience more internal pressure to speak out in their relationships than those with even slightly more power. Speaking out may be more fundamental for survival for those lowest on the proverbial totem pole. If they do not speak for themselves, they will surely be "somebody's bridge." "By necessity, not choice, black women have had to be resourceful, assertive, and self-reliant in order to survive."[29]

Furthermore, the girls in this study live in a society that encourages them to express themselves in their relationships. Boys, on the other hand, are commonly discouraged from doing so on the grounds that it is "unmanly" or effeminate to expose one's vulnerabilities (this belief was expressed directly by some of the boys in the study). These mainstream messages, however, are conditional: girls are encouraged to express only their feelings, particularly their sentimental feelings, and boys are encouraged to express their thoughts or opinions—particularly their intellectual ideas. Yet most boys in the present study had difficulties expressing their sentiments as well as their thoughts and opinions, and the girls were willing to communicate both emotions and opinions. While socialization pressures regarding the appropriate gender-specific behavior may partially explain the present findings, these pressures clearly do not fully explain them.

The gender differences in the adolescents' narratives may also spring from the idea that boys do not think of being outspoken as a distinct quality and, therefore, particularly noteworthy. While this was clearly not true for the boys who explicitly discussed their silence in relationships, this may have been true for the remaining boys in the sample. Jamal rarely discusses his outspokenness, but speaks frequently about his potential for leadership. Perhaps for Jamal, outspokenness is something that is assumed and hence not necessary to articulate. In a world where men's voices are heard everywhere and women are still struggling to be heard, boys may not think that "having a voice" is a unique quality, whereas girls may perceive being outspoken as an accomplishment and as something definitely worth talking about.

The culture in which these adolescents live may also explain the third question regarding the silences among the girls and boys in their relationships with boys. The girls, like Milagro, may be responding to cultural pressures to maintain relationships with boys and men. In order to maintain even tenuous relationships with boys, girls may believe that the best strategy is to remain silent, especially when they know, as many indicated, that some boys perceive outspokenness as grounds for terminating relationships. The girls are cognizant of the risks of speaking out with their male peers. Elizabeth Debold suggests that girls may adhere to mainstream expectations regarding male/female relationships with the hopes of experiencing the security and safety offered to those who most closely resemble the cultural ideal.[30] A few of the girls, however, appear to resist such expectations by removing themselves entirely from their relationships with boys. These girls appear to believe that it is simply too dangerous. They want safety and security but they are not willing to have such safety at the expense of their voices and, in fact, do not believe that safety and security are offered within male/female relationships.

The boys may also be responding to cultural pressures when they silence themselves with their male peers. While having male friendships for boys and men is highly regarded in our culture (maintaining the "old boys' network"), having such relationships, especially if they are intimate and self-disclosing, is also considered odd and unnatural in our homophobic society.[31] The tension of these opposing cultural demands is evident in the boys' stories of maintaining connection with other boys despite anger, and of disconnecting from or terminating these relationships despite a desire for companionship. The boys, like the girls, may be sharply aware of the risks of speaking out with other boys *and* have ambivalent feelings about the extent to which they want to maintain close friendships with their male peers. The consequence of such awareness and ambivalence may be that they silence themselves in and remove themselves from these relationships.

The fourth question concerning the increase in outspoken voices over time can be addressed by examining developmental changes. As adolescents prepare to enter the world of college or work and some prepare to leave their families' homes, they may become increasingly aware of the need to communicate their needs, wants, opinions, and expectations. Researchers have also noted that the self-esteem of adolescent girls appears to increase following a sharp decrease in early adolescence.[32] This increase in self-esteem may enhance the girls' abilities to be outspoken. Although, as Christine suggested, low self-esteem is not necessarily associated with being unable to speak out in relationships, it may make it more difficult. It is likely that adolescents who feel good about themselves will be more outspoken than adolescents who do not. In addition, Mary, the Irish American young woman who only "found [her] voice" after she dropped out of school, suggests that becoming outspoken is possible only within the context of a safe environment. Michelle Fine and Lois Weis describe these safe spaces as places that "offer recuperation, resistance, and the makings of a home."[33] For Mary, her GED class provided her with such a space. In this setting, she was able to speak freely and challenge widely. Finding such a space or a "home" may be more possible when adolescents are older and have more autonomy to make their own choices and find their own spaces.

Eva reminds us, however, that while many of the adolescents were outspoken in their relationships, they did not necessarily feel heard. In *Talking Back*, bell hooks describes this phenomenon:

> This emphasis on woman's silence may be an accurate remembering of what has taken place in the households of women from WASP backgrounds in the United States, but in black communities (and diverse ethnic communities), women have not been silent. Their voices can be heard. Certainly for black women, our struggle has not been to emerge from silence into speech but to change the nature and direction of our speech, to make a speech that compels listeners, one that is heard.[34]

When Eva, the student who said "I express myself no matter what," is asked what she fears most in the future, she says:

> I fear becoming someone that is not heard.
> *Why?*
> 'Cause I believe too many people, black people mainly, are not being heard. You know, they're turning the "well nobody's listening to me" into "I must be a nobody." You know, turning to crack, drugs or whatever. I don't want to be like that.

Eva, aware that she lives in a society that listens only rarely to black people (and even less often to poor or working-class black girls and women), knows that speaking out will not guarantee her a listening audience. Few of the girls or boys in the study seemed confident that they were being heard by those to whom they were expressing themselves.

The present findings suggest that urban teenagers—boys and girls—need help in developing or maintaining their ability to listen to themselves and to speak their minds. They also may need help learning how to speak in voices that can and will be heard. This task, however, will be realized only when adults begin to listen to them. Their voices can be strengthened only if adults take these adolescents seriously. Such a response is a first step toward increasing the number of poor and working-class adolescents who grow up to be resistant, healthy, and confident adults.

5

■ ■   ■   ■   ■   ■   ■   ■   ■

Desire and Betrayal
in Friendships

GUILLERMO, a Bolivian American adolescent with jet-black hair pushed behind his ears, watches me closely as I prepare to interview him for the first time during his junior year. Once we begin, he immediately reveals what will be a key theme for him over the two years he is interviewed.[1]

Do you have a close or best friend this year?
Not really. I think myself. The friend I had, I lost it. . . . That was the only person that I could trust and we talked about everything. When I was down, he used to help me feel better. The same I did to him. So, I feel pretty lonely and sometimes depressed . . . because I don't have no one to go out with, no one to speak on the phone, no one to tell my secrets, no one for me to solve my problems.

Why don't you think you have someone?
Because I think that it will never be the same, you know. I think that when you have a real friend and you lose it, I don't think you find another one like him. That's the point of view that I have . . . I tried to look for a person, you know, but it's not that easy.

A "real friend" for Guillermo is someone with whom he could "go out," talk about everything, and to whom he could entrust his "secrets." Unable to find another such friend, Guillermo speaks about his loneliness and depression. Intimate and emotionally supportive male friendships—"chumships" according to Sullivan[2]—are what Guillermo appears to have "lost." What will become increasingly clear as the adolescents' stories unfold in this chapter is that Guillermo's discussions of having no close or best friends and his yearning for the type of friendship he had at a younger age are not isolated sentiments expressed by an exceptionally sensitive boy. Instead, they are emblematic of many of the adolescents, particularly the boys. These boys and girls told us that while they *wanted* to have close or best friends, they *no longer* did.

The following year, I ask Guillermo once again about his close friendships. He says that he has a friend this year but he sounds uncertain, if not ambivalent:

Do you have a close or best friend?
If you could call it that. Because I don't tell him my secrets, right, you know.
I told you that I have a very good friend in Miami and with him it was very different. I used to tell him a lot of things. But this guy, I don't trust him that much. Even though I hang around with him all day, all that, and we talk about things. Maybe he considers me his best friend and tells me things. I tell some things, but not all of them.

Lacking trust in his current friend, Guillermo limits the extent to which he will reveal his intimate life to him. While he used to have a friend with whom he saw no need for such limits, his current friendship is "different." Guillermo, however, seems to have an easier time trusting girls. In his senior year, he has fallen in love with a girl whom he trusts and who has made him feel good about himself: "Well, I remember that I told you that I was never going to find a good friend, right, and the only good friend that I have found is my girl. Besides my girlfriend, you know, is, um, besides being my girlfriend she is my good friend." While he has not found a close *male* friend, Guillermo *has* found a close friend.[3]

Along with Guillermo, almost all the adolescent boys and girls in the study[4] discussed their difficulties trusting their same-sex peers.[5] Like the theme of outspokenness among the girls, these feelings of distrust were particularly evident in the teens' junior- and senior-year interviews. Many of the boys also told us, by their junior or senior years, that this lack of trust prevented them from having close or best friends. In contrast, the girls indicated that although they too did not trust their same-sex peers, they still had close or best girlfriends. Not having close or best friends because of distrust or having close friends despite distrust, yearning for intimate same-sex friendships, and articulating a relational language filled with vulnerability and passion were the common threads that wove together the adolescents' narratives of friendships.

Listening to Boys

Maintaining Distrust

Malcolm

Malcolm, whose case study I presented earlier, tells a story that resembles Guillermo's. Sensitive and introspective, Malcolm does not trust his male peers, is not close to other boys, and, by his junior year, trusts his girlfriend the most. When Mike asks Malcolm whether he has a best friend during his freshman year, Malcolm says he used to have a best friend when he was in middle school but he no longer has such a friend (the following quotation and some of the quotations from Malcolm over the next few pages were also heard in the case study):

> *So you really don't have a closest friend here at school?*
> Oh no, nobody. Not even around my way. It's like everybody else is just associating, you know. No . . . it's just like things like friendships take time. Just like a relationship. You can't really, you know, rush into that. You have to just take it slow and be able to know for true who's your friend, who's not.

Malcolm is cautious about whom he calls a friend, calling those he knows "associates" until he is more certain. Although he does not directly state that he is wary of trusting his peers, he implies this in his phrase "you have to take it slow." When asked to explain what he means by "associates," Malcolm says:

> Yeah, like they're not the people that you really get into deep-depth conversation, you just be like you talk about such and such things. You know, you

go places, yeah, but they're not the ones that you really be like: "I want to go do something, you know, I'll call up," you know?

With his "associates" Malcolm keeps the relationship superficial both in conversation and in his day-to-day contact. The boys commonly referred to having "associates," and these "associates" were commonly given such titles because they were not considered trustworthy enough to be called "friends."

In his sophomore year, Malcolm says in response to Mike's questions concerning whether or not he has a close or best friend:

> No, right now, I don't know, I don't like to be crowded too much. No . . . just my girlfriend really. I be chilling with her, but besides that I'm getting tired of being crowded really. . . .
> *What exactly do you mean be being crowded?*
> Well, it could just be one person. But sometimes that one person just get aggravating. Not what he says and stuff, it's just that he's being—that he's there. 'Cause it's just most of the time I like to be alone, you know, just me and my dark side . . . but I don't like people always around me and stuff.

With not much affect in his voice, Malcolm expresses little interest in having a close or best male friend and, in fact, claims to feel uncomfortable with his male peers. When he discusses his girlfriend, however, his desires concerning male friendships become more complicated than this dismissive attitude initially suggests:

> With my girlfriend, I could relax . . . we could do certain things that you can't—you don't—well you can do it [with male friends] but it's just not the same feeling like when you're walking with a girl because with a girl you can express certain feelings, and stuff . . . you can talk about certain things. . . . [With boys] it's just harder to like . . . 'cause some of the things you may [want to do] make you seem as if you're gay or something. . . . It's more relaxing when you're with a girl so you can just chill. Seems like you have more to talk about.

Although Malcolm may desire intimate male friendships ("where you can express certain things"), he seems to find them too risky ("makes you seem as if you're gay"). Instead, he chooses to spend intimate time with his girlfriend with whom he does not have to fear breaking social norms. He feels safer and, perhaps, more accepted with her than with his male peers.

Malcolm points out, with a vulnerability apparent in his hushed tones, that while he expresses himself freely to his girlfriend, he does not think of her as his best friend: "'Cause if you have a best friend you know, you express yourself more and you're like—you, like, feel lost without them. So, you know, with her it's really just we have a close relationship where we can express things." Distinguishing between close friendships and those that one feels "lost without," Malcolm describes the complexity of friendships. According to Malcolm, being close with another person "where [you] can express things" does not necessarily indicate that one feels deeply attached to that person.

Such careful distinctions between close and best friends occur repeatedly in the adolescents' interviews. They were consistently attuned to the layers of friendships, and their understandings revolved around the concept of trust, betrayal, and loss. Boys and girls carefully described why certain friends were only "associates" and not close friends, and why other friends were only close friends and not best friends. Best friends were those whom one could trust, and "associates" were those with whom one spends time but does not "really" trust.

During his junior-year interview with me, Malcolm articulates specifically why he finds it difficult to have close or best male friends:

> I might talk with people but it won't get real deep . . . there is nobody there to talk to.
>
> *Do you think you have a close or best friend in your life right now?*
>
> Right now, no. I had a couple [of friends] like once when I was real young, around ten. . . . But right now, nobody really 'cause it seems that as I've grown, you know, everybody just talk behind your back and stuff, you know. So I just let it go because it seems like no people . . . that I've been meeting can hold up to their actions . . . something might've happened like between me and a person where other people felt that we shouldn't even be friends no more. So they sit there and talk about me to that person while I'm not around or something, and then that person will just talk about me too . . . all throughout my neighborhood, I always hear, "He talks about you, he says this or he says that." . . . So I just don't really bother with it, you know, trying to make best friends. Say whatever you

want behind my back, I don't care . . . whatever you do behind my back, I don't care.

Although there are suggestions in Malcolm's earlier interviews that he is struggling to trust his peers, it is not until his junior-year interview that he makes these difficulties explicit. By then, Malcolm has given up hope of having the kind of close friend he had when he was younger because people do not "hold up to their actions"—they betray you "behind your back." Following this seemingly direct, angry statement, however, Malcolm seems to distance himself by claiming not to "care" about his friends betraying him. Malcolm may not *want* to care, but he seems to have isolated himself from his friends in response to caring precisely about how his friends are treating him.

When Malcolm is asked why he thinks he has not found a friend whom he trusts, he says:

> I don't know . . . it's like certain areas affect the, you know, the whole. Like the environment like around [my neighborhood], mostly there's gangs and everybody talks about everybody. I don't know if there's still those in there that can like hold their own and not think about talking about other people. A baby's born innocent but it grows up in there and you know it does the same thing . . . 'cause around my area there's few people that move in, you know, from other places.
> *So what do you think it is—what is it about the environment you live in that makes—that causes this?*
> It's just the violence. . . . The—the arrogance. The arrogance. Most of the people, you know, it's like people wanna be number one and stuff. It's like if somebody's downing me behind my back and somebody I know is with him, I might know both of them, but to make them both feel good, I guess they both gotta go along with it.

Malcolm tells me that the problem of "talking behind people's back" is not inherent in one's way of being, but is rather learned as a result of living in a particular community. He locates the source of the problem in his community specifically with people wanting to "feel good" about themselves. In order to raise their standing among their peers, Malcolm's peers choose to denigrate each other. Malcolm also implies a connection between violence and arrogance when he slips from saying "violence" to "arrogance" in response to my question. Victor, another adolescent involved in the study, says that the reason for so much death in his community is "people wanting to be important." Wanting to be important (or "number one") may lead to betrayal which, in turn, may lead to distrust, and, finally, to violence (wanting to be important may also lead to violence directly). Violence may not only be a cause of distrust but also a consequence of it among these adolescent boys.

The apparent consequence of distrust for Malcolm is that he chooses not to have close or best male friends. When I ask him if he wishes that he had a close or best friend, he says:

> Somewhat because then they [his "associates"] wonder why like I don't call them and stuff or you know. Because I really don't wanna be with them. . . . It's not somebody I could trust. Because like there's even times that I found stuff missing. Like I try to like hang out in my room and I find that things are gone, you know they're gone. Certain things like my tapes are missing and stuff.[6]

Malcolm wonders aloud why his friends betray him and steal from him and speculates that they may be jealous of his academic achievement and the attention he receives from his teachers. In the struggle "to be important," students who are deemed important by others, including figures of authority, may be particularly resented by their peers.

In his junior year, Malcolm has given up his search for a best friend ("So I just don't really bother with it, trying to make, you know, best friends"). In Malcolm's world, male peers betray him and steal from him and he is, therefore, unwilling to consider any of them close or best friends. There is apparently no male friend in Malcolm's life without whom he would "feel lost." Malcolm says that he is still able to express himself occasionally with his girlfriend but she gets jealous easily so he chooses to keep "most things" to himself.

Like Malcolm, many of the boys in the study used a language of vulnerability and intimacy when describing close or best male friends (e.g., "you feel lost without them") that I did not anticipate. Their use of this language surprised me given what I had learned from the research literature about adolescent boys, particularly those from the inner city. Even though these boys came into the interview office *looking* "hip-hop," cool, laid back, and macho (pants riding low on their hips, headphones from their Walkman around their necks, sneakers untied), they did not *speak* in such ways. Rather, they spoke about their pain, frustration, fear, and loss. When asked why he doesn't have close or best male friends, Shawn, who is actively involved in sports at school, explains to his interviewer in his junior year:

> I've got like a brick wall around me . . . gonna take a lot just to get inside me. . . . 'Cause I see many people out here, they be open [with others] and many people could find a way to break them apart. But I don't want nobody knowing me and being able to break me apart and do anything they want with me.

In his senior-year interview, Shawn claims that he is still struggling to get rid of his "suit of armor" with his male peers so that he can have "real friendships." Looking directly at me, Jamal says in his junior year: "I always don't label people as like my best best friend, you know. I don't put, you know, faith in people 'cause I don't wanna suffer." These sensitive and vulnerable responses challenged what I saw reflected in their pose and their clothes. Boys who typically have been portrayed in the research literature as primarily interested in *doing things* with other boys as opposed to sharing their thoughts and feelings[7] spoke to us about having or yearning for male friendships that "you feel lost without," "deep depth" friendships, friendships within which you "share your secrets" and "tell everything."

Albert

Albert, an athletic-looking Puerto Rican adolescent, reveals that while he has a slightly different perspective from Malcolm and Guillermo, he shares many of their beliefs about his male peers. During his sophomore year, Albert says matter-of-factly to Mike: "I don't have friends because I don't like walking around here, like I be hanging with people getting killed and I try to play it safe and stay home now." Boys commonly drew a connection between violence and having friends. They indicated that when they are with their friends or associates, they are more likely to get into trouble than when they are by themselves. Thus, the best option, they said, is to "maintain a distance" from their peers. Many types of fear prompted boys to distance themselves from other boys: fear of betrayal, fear of theft, and, presently, as Albert made clear, fear of violence.

When Albert, who has recently transferred to the school, is asked in his sophomore year if he would call anyone a close or best friend, he explains in a barely audible voice:

Now, no. . . . I'm lonely here, but I have to deal with it. I was trying to find one but—I was going to find a good friend, you know, like my first one that I had back in New York. I've met a friend but I don't know if they do things like that because I don't talk to them that much. You know, so I go to class and that's it. I don't talk to people, I just go to class, sit down, listen to the teacher, and when the class is over, go to another class, all day long. I never be talking to nobody.

Albert clearly feels isolated as he seeks, unsuccessfully, for the type of friendship he had in junior high school.

In his junior year, Albert says to Mike:

I got friends and everything, but I don't consider them as close friends, not now. *Why is that?* No, 'cause it's like I haven't known them that good. I know them this year and a part of last year, you know, so I don't know them good. . . . You know, some friends they show they can be good friends. You could show it but you have to see it a few more months, maybe a year, you know, to find out really good friends. . . . I would like a friend that if I got anything to say to him or like any problems or anything I'll tell him and he'll tell me his problems. . . . Some friends be your friend when you're not in trouble, when you have money or something. Once you don't have a lot of money or something they'll back off. But a real friend will stick right there with you. He won't back off.

Albert speaks about both his lack of and his desire for close male friends. He does not claim to want friends with whom to "do things," but rather to discuss personal problems.

Victor, an African American student, suggests a similar theme in his junior year:

Do you have a close or best friend this year? I wouldn't say . . . I don't say I would. 'Cause I feel that a friend is going to be there for you and they'll support you and stuff like that. Whether they're good and bad times, you can share with them, you would share your feelings with them, your true feelings . . . that's why I don't think I have any real close friends. I mean, things can travel around in a school and things would go around, and the story would change from person to person. Yeah, basically, I hate it, I hate it, 'cause you know I wouldn't mind talking to somebody my age that I can relate to 'em on a different basis.

The boys in the study, like Albert and Victor, frequently discussed their frustration at their peers' unreliable behavior and their longing for friends "that would really be there" and with whom they could share their "true feelings." They felt betrayed by the gossip of their peers and they sought refuge from the rumors.

When I interview Albert in his senior year, he looks tired and worn out. He tells me with exasperation that he still does not have a best friend:

Best friend, no. Just friends.
I'm interested to know what your thoughts are on why you don't have a best friend. Like wh—?
You know I can't trust—I don't trust 'em too much. I had a friend and he [tried to steal my tapes and my girlfriend] and, you know, [I] can't trust nobody else.[I have] kind of friends, you know, but to have another best friend, that would be pretty hard now, can't trust nobody else no more.

Although there were already indications in his earlier interviews that he was struggling to trust his peers, Albert's current experience of betrayal seems to have deepened his sense of distrust. Albert suggests an inflexibility that was common among the boys. Many of the boys, once their male peers had betrayed their trust on one or more occasions, refused not only to be close with those particular individuals but to trust any of their male peers. Thus, they effectively gave up the possibility of having a close male friend altogether.

Joseph, a Dominican student, tells me both in his freshman and sophomore years that he has a best friend with whom he has been friends for ten years. In his junior year, however, the situation has changed:

Do you have a close or best friend?
No. I don't trust nobody

You don't trust nobody? How come?

(Pause) Can't trust nobody these days.

Have you had bad experiences with people?

Yeah, especially this year.

Can you tell me about one of them?

Yeah, okay. Me and my friend got, you know, in trouble at school 'cause we broke the elevator.

Oh, you did?

Don't say nothing about it. And he went and told Mr. Talcott that I was the one who did it . . . nobody knew that we did it. So he just went and told him. He went ahead and told and I got in trouble. I got suspended for five days.

Joseph expresses anger at his friend for double-crossing him and hence will not trust anyone any longer. Experiences of betrayal do not register lightly for Joseph and for the other boys in the study. The boys' sensitivity to betrayal seemed acute and dramatic. Boys who are actively and implicitly discouraged in mainstream culture to have intimate, close male friendships[8] may become particularly intolerant of maintaining such friendships when they entail betrayal and loss.

In his senior year, Albert further explicates this theme of distrust:

Can't trust people no more. Before you could, but now, you know when you got a girl, and they think that she's cute, they still might go try to rap to her and everything. You can't trust 'em like before that they will be serious. Like that friend I had in New York, my best friend [the friend he referred to in his sophomore year], I could trust him with my girl, you know, and he could trust me with his girl. People ain't like that no more . . . back then you could trust.

Albert believes that when he was younger, trusting others was easier than it is now. He remembers his former best friend from junior high school (whom he mentions each year) as someone he could trust and whom, he says later in his interview, he could "talk to and he would talk to me, too." Albert's "back then," I suspect, indicates less the "good old days" in the clichéd expression than time at a younger age.

About girls, Albert says:

You can't also trust girls, you know it's not always the friend, it also has to be with the girls . . . they have the responsibility also if they are your girl-friend. But my girl told me about this friend that tried to pick her up. I could trust her, and when she told me, I was gonna fight with him but then she was like, no forget it. I was really mad 'cause I thought I could trust him and when I found that out, you know, that's when I found I couldn't trust him no more.

Although he is cautious about trusting girls, Albert is ultimately more will-ing to trust girls than boys ("You can't trust girls . . . I could trust her"). Albert's flexibility with girls, however, is never heard when he speaks about his male friendships: he cannot trust his male peers and he has made no re-cent exceptions.

When asked whether he misses his former best friend, Albert tells me: "I miss [him] a little bit, but not as much as before . . . I'm getting used to it." Albert may slowly be distancing himself not only from his former friend but also from his own *longing* for a close friend. The boys typically discussed, in their freshman or sophomore year, their desires for intimate and close male friends. By their junior or senior years, however, they had often given up, or at least almost given up, their search for such relation-ships. They told us they were getting "used to" not having such friend-ships, which may be a sign that they are beginning to forget their desires for closeness with other males—they are, perhaps, becoming "real" men.

Learning Not to Trust

A few of the boys claimed in their freshman and sophomore years to have close or best friends and did not mention having any reservations about trusting their peers. By their junior and senior years, however, they too began to indicate that they no longer had close or best friends because they did not trust their peers. The shift from trusting to not trusting occurred later for these boys than it did for boys such as Guillermo, Malcolm, and Albert.

Marcus

When Marcus, a shy student whose parents are from El Salvador, is asked by his interviewer whether he has a best friend in his freshman year, he says: "Nah, I got a lot of best friends. We fool around a lot, sometimes we're mischievous. Sometimes we have real big conversations, arguments, all that. But we always come back and we talk like friends again." Marcus explains that he can communicate openly with numerous best friends, even if it involves disagreements. "Talking" is a key component of his friendships. When asked if there is one best friend with whom he spends a little more time than the others, he says:

> No. I used to have one but he had to go to Florida. . . . He was our best
> friend for like about eight years. But then he had to go to Florida last year.
> *How did you get along?*
> Like if he needed something, we would give it to him, and if we needed
> something, he would give it to us.

Marcus's use of plural pronouns ("we" and "our") may indicate a hesitation or doubt on his part to identify this boy as particularly his best friend, or it may be a sign of a collective sense of identity. Nonetheless, the boy he describes was someone with whom he would spend more time than the others, and was more of a "best friend" to him than are his current friends. Marcus says, later in his interview, that he is more cautious about revealing his personal life with his current friends than he was with his former best friend (the one who moved to Florida).

In his sophomore year, Marcus says to Jamie, his interviewer this year, that he is part of a group of about three or four boys who have been close friends since first grade (the same group of friends from the previous year).

> *What makes these friends your closest friends?*
> Like they care like if one gets into trouble, they try to pull you out or they try
> to help you. They're all the same. Say they have problems at home, they
> sometimes go over, buy a pizza or something, go to the movies, try to
> relax, and help the person get that anger out. . . .
> *What kinds of things do your friends get angry about [besides problems at home]?*
> 'Cause I'm more the clown, sometimes I like to joke around on other people,
> but sometimes the joke goes too far and people get mad. Then they get
> hurt and other people get mad. But then we settle things out. . . . They
> told me myself sometimes [that I was making them mad]. We don't, like—
> we don't keep anything from each other.

Open communication and helping each other with difficulties are clearly important elements of Marcus's friendships. His choice of pronouns this year, however, suggests that he may not feel as much a part of his group of friends as he initially states (*"They* care like if *one* gets into trouble. . . . *They* have problems. . . . *They* sometimes go over, buy a pizza . . ."). He may be more ambivalent or uncertain about them than he is willing to directly admit to Jamie. Any concerns about his friendships, however, are not made obvious until his junior-year interview.

In his junior year, when I ask Marcus about having close or best friends, he says:

No.
No, and why is that the case?
I don't know. I don't 'cause I guess that person might not be with you for the rest of your life, so why bother telling that person.
Huh. So you feel like it would sort of be a waste of time in a way 'cause they might not stick with you?
Yeah.
Do you feel like, I mean it sounds like, and I don't wanna put words in your mouth, so you have to tell me whether this is true—but it sounds like there's a trust issue there. I mean like not really trusting the person will be around.
I mean it's not that I don't trust them—them being around, but you know, I'll tell them a couple of little things, you know. But I have some of my friends move out and stuff like that, and then I never speak to them again.

In contrast to his previous interviews, Marcus indicates here that he finds it too risky to have close or best friends. His problem, he explains, is related not to trusting others (he rejects my leading question) but to not believing that friendships will be maintained over time and distance ("I never speak to them again").

Has this made you sad a little bit [to lose contact with your close friends]?
No. You know, you think about him, you get to miss him a little bit, but then after a while you just forget him.

Along with Albert, Marcus suggests a sequence of coping with the loss of a friendship that first involves "missing" the friendship and then "getting used to it" or "forgetting" the friendship. Marcus's somber voice, however, indicates that he has not forgotten his close friends.

Tyrone, an African American student, also speaks about the difficulties of close friends "leaving" him. In his second-year interview, Tyrone says:

> No. Nah, it's like everybody I get close to, they either go away or, you know, so it's just like, nah . . . and you know I have friends that I chill with, you know, hang out with from time to time. But not ones that I usually do everything with. You know, how like you just have that best friend and it's always like—say it's like you and him? Stuff like that. Nah. I did, I really did but you know. . . . Me and this other kid took up for each other, everything just came together like, you know, it was like it was made to be . . . if I had a problem I could always talk to him 'cause he knew mostly all my family. I knew mostly all his family. And everything just worked . . . and they moved and, you know, ever since then it's just like nobody. . . . I don't want to get too close to somebody because I fear when I get close to people—the people I love have been taken away from me. And I just say, "Hey, I don't want to get too close to anybody 'cause I don't want to lose them." It just seems like I'm not supposed to have any good friend 'cause, the ones I have, they move or they die. I know it's a messed-up way of like thinking but that's the way it seems obvious to me. I've lost so many people in the past that were real close to me. I learn to take it and keep going.

Tyrone powerfully reveals that not only does residential mobility have terrible consequences for close male friendships but violence does as well.[9] Tyrone and Marcus also indicate that "losing" friends leads them to distance themselves from their peers in order to protect themselves from further loss.[10] These boys suggest a sensitivity to loss that is similar to their response to betrayal discussed earlier. Once a close or best friend betrays them, moves, or dies, they find it difficult, if not impossible, to find a replacement. Yet they have learned, in Tyrone's words, "to take it and keep going."

With further exploration, it becomes clear that his fear of friends leaving and not staying in contact with him is not the full explanation for Marcus's isolation. When I ask him if he thought he would have close or best friends if I could guarantee him that they would not leave, Marcus says:

No.

Why not?

I don't know. I wouldn't—I don't know—I just wouldn't. . . . I mean if I tell you a secret, you have to tell someone else, you know. So I just don't. I just keep it to myself.

Marcus, like the boys discussed earlier, believes that having a close or best friend involves trusting him to keep his secrets confidential and he does not believe he could find such a person. Marcus's responses are brief this year, which may be a consequence of his believing that not only are his friends untrustworthy, but that I, his interviewer, am also untrustworthy ("If I tell *you* a secret, *you* have to tell someone else"). He may not want to share with me if he believes that I will eventually break confidentiality just as his friends do.

When I ask Marcus what his current friendships are like, even if they are not close relationships, he says:

I have a friend right now who lives on my street. But I don't trust trust him, you know. Just joke about, you know, only tell each other what to do and stuff like that. . . .

How is this friendship different from the one you mentioned in your freshman year? [The friend who moved to Florida.]

'Cause they have different attitudes. One would talk about, you know, joke around but then he wouldn't bring it to nobody else and the other one is like the type of person that would tell at least one person.

The group of friends to whom Marcus referred in previous years are no longer his close friends in his junior year. Although Marcus provides no explanation, his reasons are likely due to his experiences of betrayal given his focus on this particular topic.

Near the end of his junior-year interview, Marcus says:

I don't trust trust nobody. You know, I just a little trust.

Why is that?

I don't know. I just think I always think that [my friends] won't be there when I probably need them a lot.

Confidentiality and reliability were, in fact, the two most important qualities of close or best friendships for all of the adolescents in the study.[11] The adolescents implied or directly stated that friends had to "be there for you" and had to keep secrets in order to be considered close. If friends failed on either account, they were demoted to an acquaintance or "associate" level.

When I tell Marcus that I find it sad that so many of the boys have difficulties trusting other boys, he tells me with a secretive voice:

> I believe that, I mean all I know is that, say if I was with these guys and these guys didn't get along with the other guys. But I'll have his back, and he'll have my back, you know. We know that already. If my friend was in trouble, I'll be there, backing him up, or if I was in trouble, he'll be backing me up. But that's not being trustful.
>
> *Why?*
>
> 'Cause maybe the next day, he might be the one that's joking and making fun of you.

In this eye-opening description of friendships and trust, Marcus reveals that someone who backs you up may not necessarily be trustworthy. He implies that although a friend may "be there" when he is in danger (i.e., he may protect Marcus when he is physically threatened), this type of dependability may not last, or may not ensure that this friend will respect him or protect him from embarrassment or feelings of vulnerability ("he might be the one that's joking and making fun of you"). Marcus appears to be drawing a distinction between physical and emotional protection. Marcus has friends who will physically protect him, but not friends who will be sensitive to his feelings, which, for Marcus, is the definition of trust.

Near the end of the interview, when I ask Marcus if he would like a trusting male friendship, he says: "I don't, I don't really care." Finding, perhaps, our conversation too difficult (given that it is about his lack of close friendships), deciding not to trust me any longer, or simply being unable to maintain his openness and vulnerability, Marcus withdraws from our conversation. He begins to claim, like Malcolm, that he does not "care" about having close friendships after he has implied that he would like such friends to "be there when [he] really needs them." Marcus follows his proclamation of "not caring" with a discussion of why, in fact, he has no interest in having a close or best friend: "Having a best friend would be boring because we would know everything about each other . . . there would be no surprises." While Marcus may truly believe this, I am skeptical about his apparent disinterest. Marcus may be trying to distance himself from his own desire to have close male friendships because he does not think they are possible. In addition, he may not want to continue openly communicating his feelings with me precisely because he "trust[s] trust[s] nobody."

The boys' discussions of trust and maintaining close relationships with other boys took on different shapes and forms both across and within their interviews. While most of the boys indicated that they experienced a shift from trusting to not trusting their male peers, the timing of this shift varied.[12] For boys such as Marcus, the change occurred during the high school years. For Guillermo, Malcolm, and Albert, the change took place before high school or during the transition to high school. By their junior or senior year in high school, however, almost all of the boys reported that they did not trust other boys. When asked about friendships, the boys spoke openly about betrayal, pain, and loss. The boys did not speak of wanting friends with whom to do things but to share their personal stories and confide their secrets. While they claimed to have had such intimate "chumships" when they were younger, these friendships disappeared as they grew older. Close relationships did not vanish, however, due to a lack of interest but rather to a lack of faith. The disappearance of such close male friendships leaves many of the boys acutely wary of their male peers, and seemingly lonely.[13]

Listening to Girls

Cautious Close Friendships

Marie

Marie, a strikingly beautiful adolescent whose parents are from the Dominican Republic, is interviewed for the first time when she is a freshman. Marie says her best friend of six years is her cousin: "I had like a lot of friends but like either I had a big argument with them or they like were two-faced or something, you know, and they were like good friends to talk to but then they weren't like totally good." Her cousin, however, stands apart from her previous friendships—she is the exception. While describing her close relationship with her cousin, Marie speaks about the potential perils of friendships:

> We haven't had the first argument yet and she's like—she doesn't lie to me and she's like—she's real. I dunno, it's like I could really, really trust her and could be sure about her. Sometimes people be like your best friend could be your worst friend because they know everything, you know. But I'd be telling my mother, "Oh, she's my best friend," and my mother's like—'cause my mother you know she had a lot of friends who did bad things to her—she'd be like, "Don't be telling everything to your best friend 'cause you don't know." But it's like some people tell me that—you know, I be like, "Oh, she's my best friend" [and they say]: "Don't really tell her everything. Can't really trust your best friends," and all this and that. But it's like I feel that I can because we've been [together] so long already.

Warned by her mother about trusting others (even her cousin), Marie explains that bad things can happen when a friend "knows everything." When I ask Marie about what she has learned in the past, she says she has learned "not to be so trustful" and "not to believe in everybody." What is striking about Marie's interview is that, although she is acutely aware of the potential of hurt and betrayal with best friends, she continues to have a best friend each year she is interviewed.

Unlike the boys, the girls in the study typically did not remove themselves from their relationships with other girls as a result of their apprehensions or concerns. Instead, they continued each year to find exceptions among their female peers.[14] The categorical "no" that was so commonly heard among the boys when asked about the existence of close or best friends was rarely heard among the girls. There was a flexibility in the adolescent girls' perspectives and actions that was not evident in the boys'.

Marie says her best friend is the same person each year. She likes her best friend because she is honest and she can tell her "anything." When she is asked in her sophomore year about the values she lives by, Marie tells me: "I don't want to be able to walk without the pride. People talk anyways, but I want to walk without having someone talking behind my back and saying something that is not true." Marie mentions her fear of betrayal by her peers each year alongside her discussions of her close friendships.

This fear of betrayal carries over into her relationship with her boyfriend. She tells me in her sophomore year that she does not want to "get too many feelings for him and end up . . ." (she does not complete her sentence). Marie says she has never "really" trusted a boy enough to let herself feel for him as much as she "has wanted." She repeats this theme in her junior year when she tells me that she does not want to get "too serious" with her boyfriend because she wants to avoid being hurt by him. Nonetheless, Marie has the same boyfriend each year she is interviewed. Unlike the boys, the girls' wariness about trusting their peers typically extended to their opposite-sex peers, including their boyfriends. Yet, like Marie, they commonly maintained relationships with boys.

Sonia

In her freshman year, Sonia—a vivacious, energetic, Puerto Rican student—says to me that she has a best friend about whom she feels good because they are "open" with each other. She admits, however, that she does not tell her "everything" because she finds it necessary to "hide things" that are too personal. In her sophomore year, Sonia explains:

> I have a friend. But I don't have a best friend. I don't think I ever had a best
> friend. My sister, I'll always consider her. We were talking about that yes-
> terday. Like you know, we thought we had so much best friends, but we
> never did. . . . It always boiled down to the same thing. Me and her are al-
> ways best friends.
>
> *Why do you think that you haven't?*
> Because I mean, a best friend is forever. And I never had a friend that's been
> there forever. I have close friends.
>
> *What makes your close friends close?*
> When I talk to them, they make me feel like I can really talk to them about
> anything. And I trust 'em as well as they trust me. I just don't give any-
> body my trust, but since I've known them for so long, it's like I can talk to
> them about anything. We just sit down in a group and we talk.

Sonia perceives best friendships in a seemingly idealized way—best friends are "forever" and, like a few of her female peers in the study, the only person whom she considers a "best friend" is her sister. Sonia, however, is also clearly a part of a trusting and supportive network of nonfamilial friends.

When I ask Sonia in her sophomore year why her best friends have not been there "forever," she responds by giving a nonidealized answer:

See, I'm not the type of person that if I have a boyfriend, I'm gonna devote all my time to my boyfriend. 'Cause I need my social life too . . . if all my attention would go to my boyfriend, my friends are gonna be like, "Look at her. She's leaving us for him." I don't like that, and I have friends that do that. They're caught up too much with their boyfriends and they forget about their friends. . . . I've had a lot of friends that do that. They don't call me.

Believing that friendships involve loyalty, Sonia emphasizes her own loyalty with her friends ("see, I'm not the type of person that . . ."). Sonia has had difficult experiences with female friends and, consequently, is unwilling to consider any of her peers a best friend.

Chantel says in her sophomore year that she has a best friend but is similarly wary of her female peers:

Diane is my best friend . . . I don't really know why she is my best friend. But, it's like—'cause she's always going through a lot of problems and stuff and it's like, she's always calling me and complaining and stuff. I'm like the only person that will deal with her, because everybody else is like, "I don't wanna hear that," and I talk to her all the time because I know if I was going through something like that, everybody would probably turn their back on me and stuff, except for her. Because she's the type of person that if I need to talk, she'll be like, "Okay," no matter how boring it is or whatever, she'll talk. So I know that I can depend on her and that I can trust her. . . . Everybody else is like, well, I think I can trust them, you know, but then when it comes down to me having a problem and stuff, everybody's running, you know, like, "Well, I ain't got nothing to do with it."

While she believes she has to be tolerant of her friend's behavior in order to maintain the friendship, Chantel says she finds this friendship important because she considers her the only one whom she can trust—again, her friend is the exception. Chantel repeats this theme in her junior year:

It's weird 'cause she gets on my nerves and we argue all the time and she does things—sometimes I don't even want to be bothered with her but she's the type of person if I really needed somebody, she would be there for me. You know, that's what I call a friend 'cause a lot of people—they—they'll be with you. They're fun to hang with. But yet when you really need somebody, they're not there. And every time I needed her she's there.

These girls seem resilient in their friendships and also perceive their friendships to be resilient.

In her third-year interview, Sonia echoes this pattern:

> Because, I mean, I have very close friends. I have a best friend. . . . She's in Puerto Rico. You know, she's real close to me, but like my sister—there are some things that you can't tell other people and you know you'd rather go to your sister. . . . And I go to her because I wouldn't feel comfortable telling other people, you know, like real deep personal things, I wouldn't wanna tell other people.
>
> *What is it about telling people that wouldn't make you comfortable?*
> I don't know, I just [coughs, silence]—I wouldn't feel right. You know, I just—there's something in me, I just wouldn't feel right . . . probably because I would be embarrassed.
>
> *What is it like with your close friends?*
> It's trusting, the relationships. We're honest, you know, it's full of honesty. And it's like we're sisters. I'm very close to them . . . but you know I would always consider my sister my best friend. I know for a fact that if I was to fall, she would catch me.

Sonia is hesitant to be entirely open with her close friends and even with her best friend and repeatedly states that her sister is her only "real" best friend. Yet she has close, trusting, and supportive female friends. Sonia constantly reminds me that while she has close friends, she too has been hurt and betrayed by close friends: "You never know who your friends are until you really go through certain things and you look out if they're there, then you know. Sharon forgot me when she met her boyfriend and you know you don't do that to so-called best friends."

Sonia, Marie, and Chantel and most of their female peers in the study repeatedly discussed their expectations and their actual experiences of betrayal by their female and male peers. However, they also described the one or two "exceptions" with whom they maintained close relationships. The girls did not cut themselves off from all close friendships after their experiences of betrayal, as did many of the boys, but sustained such relationships in the midst of their fears and experiences.[15]

Falling Out of Relationships

A few girls, however, suggested patterns similar to those heard among the boys. In their freshman and sophomore years, three girls spoke of having close friends but feeling wary of trusting their female peers. By their junior or senior year, they spoke of having no close or best friends and of trusting neither boys nor girls.

Felicia

Felicia, a soft-spoken African American student, says to Helena in her freshman year that her godsister is her best friend because they have common interests and goals for the future, "and it's like a person I can relate to other than myself." When asked what makes her life worth living, Felicia says: "I have people that care about me and friends that I can really trust." In her self-description, however, she indicates that not all of her friends can be trusted:

> *How would you describe yourself?*
> I don't like for people to—I don't like to get back-stabbed. Like, if you're helping somebody and then they turn around and they back-stab you, I don't like that.
> *Can you give me an example?*
> Like, when I was in the eighth grade. I had this friend and it was like she would talk to me about somebody else and then she would go back to the same person and then talk about me to that person. Then she would come to me and talk about that person to me. And it's like she would smile in my face, but behind my back it was a different story.

Unlike many of the girls who told such stories only when asked specifically about their friendships, Felicia spoke of being "back-stabbed" as part of her self-description—an indication, perhaps, of the depths to which this experience has affected her. Felicia, like Sonia, Marie, and Chantel, suggests in her freshman year that she has a best friend but she is wary of other friends betraying her. In her sophomore year, Felicia says confidently that she has a best friend (who is different from last year) and they do "everything together." Felicia tells me that her best friend "understands the things that I understand. . . . We're kind of like the same person . . . sometimes we don't agree on everything but most of the time we do." Felicia's relationship with her best friend this year seems, like last year, both intimate and supportive.

In her junior year, however, when I ask Felicia whether she has a close or best friend, she says with frustration evident in her voice: "No, I don't have best friends. I just have friends. That's it. . . . Nowadays you can't trust anybody." The wariness concerning trust heard in her freshman-year interview has been transformed into a general wariness about having best friends. As with many of the boys in the study, Felicia has moved from having a best friend to not having one because "nowadays"[16] she cannot trust people. Although Sonia had no best friends, she did have close friends. Felicia has neither.

When I ask Felicia about her best friends from her freshman and sophomore years, she responds only by saying that they are no longer her best friends. Felicia speaks about her inability to trust people throughout her junior-year interview: "You can't trust nobody . . . I know not to trust anyone no matter, you know, no matter who they are." Her repeated expressions of not trusting others "no matter who they are" suggest that Felicia may also feel distrustful of me and, therefore, less willing than in her earlier interviews to expose the intricacies of her thoughts and feelings regarding friendships. Felicia mentions that she has friends, but she would have to trust them much more to be considered close or best friends. She trusts her cousin "a little bit because she is family," but then says to me: "Well, then again, family do, you know, let you down, but you wouldn't expect it from your family."

With a deep sigh, Felicia says in her junior year that she not only has no close or best friends, she doesn't have a boyfriend this year either: "I'm not gonna say all boys, but boys are liars. They're unfaithful. You can't trust nobody. . . . Men are all the same. They are liars." Like most of the girls interviewed, Felicia's feelings of distrust extend to her relationships with boys. Felicia says that while she may trust her peers in the future, she currently does not.

Tyiesha

Tyiesha also spoke about close or best friendships in her first- and second-year interviews and then, in her third interview, states that she does not have close friends because she cannot "trust anybody." When I ask Tyiesha in her freshman year why she considers her friend of three years to be her best friend, she says: "I could tell her something and she won't tell nobody else. Like if it's real important or something and she tells me things and I don't tell nobody." Tyiesha says that although she and her friend "sometimes argue" with each other, they are usually friends again shortly afterwards.

While apparently able to trust her best friend in her freshman year, Tyiesha is more uncertain about trusting her boyfriend. By her sophomore and junior years, Tyiesha says she does not have a boyfriend because "boys are dogs." While Tyiesha suggests a shift in her feelings about trusting her female peers (as will be heard by her junior year), her distrust of boys stays the same each year.

In tenth grade, Tyiesha, once again, tells me about a best friend (different from the one mentioned in the previous year) whom she is able to trust and "tell her stuff and she doesn't tell nobody else."

Why is this best friend closer than the others?
She is more trustworthy. I really don't trust anybody that lives around my
way. They're phony.
What does phony mean?
If you tell them something, soon as you turn around somebody's coming
back telling you what somebody told you . . . when my friend tells me
something I don't go around telling everybody.

Although she has a best friend this year, Tyiesha finds it difficult to locate reliable friends. By her junior year, she has no close or best friends. When asked to explain why, she says: "You can't really trust people these days[17] . . . 'cause they're supposed to be your best friend and you tell her not to say something and she go back and say something." As in her previous interviews, Tyiesha continues to suggest that girls cannot keep secrets. This year, however, this sense of distrust has led to a lack of close friends: "Right now, I don't call nobody nothing."

In her junior year, Tyiesha explains that her current friends are people with whom she has fun but they are not close or best friends. In fact, she adds, she has never met someone whom she could trust enough to be her best friend. This response raises questions concerning the intimacy of her previous best friendships. Tyiesha's apparent loneliness this year may have led her to describe her relational history in ways that do not reflect how she felt at the time, or she may have misrepresented her friendships in her earlier interviews. Tyiesha says that presently she feels close to no one.

Reflections

Repeatedly and consistently, the adolescents in this study spoke about having difficulties trusting their same-sex peers. By the third year of the study, twenty-one out of twenty-four of the participants spoke at length about their feelings of distrust. They wanted to trust their peers but felt unable to do so. Although the boys' expressions of distrust were often more categorical (e.g., "I don't trust anybody") and more frequent than the girls', the boys and girls were equally likely to voice feelings of distrust.[18] A gender difference in the data was evident, however, in the adolescents' *responses* to their lack of trust. Almost all of the boys stated that they struggled to trust their male peers and were unable, consequently, to have close or best friends. In contrast, only a few of the girls suggested this pattern and, even then, only in their junior- or senior-year interviews. The girls described close, intimate friendships with other girls even though they, too, struggled to trust their same-sex peers. Violations of trust in male friendships frequently resulted in the termination of close friendships as well as the possible preclusion of future close friendships. The boys seemed to avoid intimacy in response to betrayal by their peers, whereas most of the girls appeared to pursue intimacy with friends despite their experiences of betrayal.[19]

Similar to previous research findings regarding adolescent friendships,[20] two important qualities in close or best male and female friendships were that one's friend would "be there" and would keep one's "secrets" confidential. Furthermore, clear distinctions were made by most of the adolescents among associates, friends, close friends, and best friends, and these distinctions were primarily based on the extent of trust in the relationship. In contrast to research findings that indicate that adolescent boys' friendships are focused on activities, autonomy, and leadership rather than on connection, intimacy, and shared stories,[21] the boys in this study described both current and hoped-for close male friendships as involving open communication and mutual sharing of thoughts and feelings. In their descriptions of friendships, only two of the boys and none of the girls emphasized the activities they "do" with their friends rather than what they "share" with their friends. The adolescent girls were more likely to report having close or best friends over the three years of interviews, but when close friends were described, the boys were almost as likely as the girls to describe their friendships in intimate and emotionally supportive terms.

The boys, furthermore, stated that they had experienced intimate same-sex friendships at a younger age (primarily in junior high school), and that they now longed for those earlier types of relationships. Although it is unclear just what those friendships were really like for these boys, they all remembered them to include open communication, mutual support, and nurturance.[22] None of the girls expressed a similar sort of yearning for an earlier friendship. Even the girls who distanced themselves from their female peers by their third-year interviews did not express a desire for an earlier type of friendship. While much of the research on friendships, including the findings of this study, indicate that adolescent girls are more likely than adolescent boys to *have* intimate, self-disclosing, and emotionally supportive friendships,[23] my findings also suggest that both girls and boys have equally strong *desires* for such relationships and may have had these types of friendships earlier in their lives. The girls have simply been more successful, skilled, or fortunate in finding and maintaining such friendships over time. When my analysis shifted from looking at what teens *had* (e.g., casual friendships that are not intimate) to what they *wanted* (e.g., intimate friendships), I discovered unexpected themes and patterns in their narratives.

Notably, almost all of the girls spoke about not trusting boys and only a few of the boys spoke about not trusting girls. Girls voiced many more fears about being in relationships with boys than boys voiced about being in relationships with girls. Bonnie Leadbeater, Joanna Batgos, and Judy Lin have suggested similar patterns in their research on young adult friendships.[24] In their study of 115 college undergraduates, males reported less open communication and emotional support with their same-sex friends than did females. When they examined opposite-sex friendships, however, the men were more likely to report having emotionally supportive and trusting relationships with young women than young women were to report having such relationships with young men. While in the present study only two boys spoke of difficulties having close, intimate friendships with girls, twenty-two of the girls and boys reported having difficulties attaining or maintaining emotionally supportive and trusting relationships with boys.

After listening to these adolescents speak about their friendships, I am left with three central questions: (1) Why did the boys have more difficulty than the girls maintaining close friendships, especially given that many of these boys desired such friendships? (2) Why did the theme of distrust of one's peers become more prominent as many of the adolescents reached mid- to late adolescence? and (3) Why did the majority of adolescents in the study report that they struggled to or were unable to trust their peers?

In order to address the first question, the larger culture in which these adolescents were raised as well as their individual experiences must be examined. Girls who grow up in a culture that encourages and validates emotionally close relationships with other girls (or at least does not discourage them from such relationships) may be more willing and motivated than boys to sustain close and trusting relationships *even* when they have experienced betrayals and other violations in their friendships. In addition, girls may learn to forgive others quickly in the name of being a good, nice, or, what Lyn Mikel Brown and Carol Gilligan call a "perfect girl."[25] Girls may learn to be more flexible in their relationships as a result of cultural pressures to be nice, kind, and good. While this flexibility or willingness to forgive may ultimately lead to positive social behavior such as intimate friendships, it may also undermine these girls' ability to terminate relationships in which they are not being cared for properly—a pattern suggested when some of the girls spoke about their relationships with boys.

Boys who live in a largely homophobic culture may find it hard to maintain such friendships with other boys *especially* when they have been betrayed by their male peers. Diane Raymond notes: "Indeed, homophobia is so pervasive and so powerfully internalized that individuals may 'voluntarily' abandon a close friendship rather than risk charges of homosexuality."[26] Boys may decide that given both society's ambivalent messages regarding close male friendships, their fear of "seeming like you're gay," *and* their individual experiences of betrayal, it is neither worthwhile nor safe for them to pursue such friendships. The shift from having close friendships during junior high school or the early part of high school to not having such relationships during high school may suggest that boys fall out of relationships with other boys right at the point in their lives when messages about the presumed link between manhood and heterosexuality move to the foreground. Distrusting and, consequently, not having close friendships may allow adolescent boys to distance themselves from their own culturally unacceptable desires for close, intimate male friendships. Furthermore, boys may be socialized to be less tolerant than girls of betrayal or acts that undermine their self-esteem, self-worth, or public image. All of these factors may begin to explain the seemingly acute sensitivity to betrayal evident among many of the boys.[27]

Cultural and social expectations as well as individual experiences and physical and sexual maturation may address the second question concerning the prominence of distrust of one's peers during mid- to late adolescence. Trusting one's same-sex peers may become increasingly difficult for both teenage girls and boys as they become involved in romantic relationships and begin to "abandon" their friends for their boyfriends or girlfriends or "steal" each other's romantic partners. Some of the boys and girls specifically stated that these were the reasons they no longer trusted their same-sex peers. In addition, teenagers may grow more wary of their same-sex peers when they reach mid- to late adolescence because their experiences of betrayal have multiplied. Adolescents' feelings of vulnerability and of self-protection may also escalate as their bodies mature uncontrollably. This heightened sense of self-protection may cause them to become increasingly cautious about trusting their peers who are also physically and sexually maturing, and becoming, perhaps, also more self-protective.

The third question regarding the prevalence of distrust among this particular group of adolescents may be addressed by examining the environments in which they live. Since many researchers note that trust is one of the most important ingredients in adolescents' friendships and betrayal a commonly perceived threat to such friendships,[28] it was not surprising that a pervasive concern among the teens revolved around the potential for others to betray their trust. It *was* surprising, however, that the adolescents spoke so frequently about not trusting any or very few of their peers.[29] Few previous studies of friendships have noted such high levels of distrust among adolescents.[30]

Reasons for the high level of distrust may lie indirectly and directly with the poverty, violence, racism, and homophobia that shapes and pervades these adolescents' lives. When asked about the reasons for the distrustful feelings among his male peers, Malcolm attributes it to his peers' wish to be "number one": "If, like, if somebody's downing me behind my back and somebody I know is with him . . . but to make them both feel good, I guess they both gotta go along with it." Wanting to be important, for boys such as Malcolm and his peers, may lead to betrayal which, in turn, causes distrust. While this pattern of betraying one's peers in order to feel important is likely to be evident in peer cultures across all environments, it may be more frequent among poor and working-class adolescents. These adolescents, bombarded with implicit and explicit messages from mainstream culture concerning their lack of importance in the world, may find themselves having particularly strong desires to "be somebody."[31] Such desires may lead some to strive for importance among those whom they feel they *can* be, namely, their peers. Their desires to feel important may override, at times, their loyalty to their friends. However, their longing for loyalty from and close bonds with their male peers is also evident in their interviews. "Downing" each other may not only result in feeling important, it may also enhance a bond between two friends ("but to make them both feel good, I guess they both gotta go along with it"). Being important and having loyal friendships are primary wishes for these boys. Yet these wishes may ultimately work against one another and cause the boys neither to feel important nor to have loyal friendships.

Everyday experiences of harassment and racism may also influence their abilities to trust their peers. The boys consistently spoke of daily harassment from the police, of being watched carefully in every store, subway station, school building, and neighborhood they enter (this topic is the focus of chapter 9). They are watched by adults both outside and inside their own communities. When an entire auditorium full of students in the high school was asked who had ever been stopped by the police, approximately 90 percent of the boys' hands went up. These predominantly ethnic-minority boys repeatedly told us stories of being strip-searched, asked for identification, and questioned by police when they were simply walking down the street. They receive clear messages about not being trusted by the world outside their homes. This lack of trust experienced on a daily, minute-by-minute basis is likely to have a profound effect on these adolescents' abilities to trust one another. As Richard Wright suggests in his novel *Native Son*, it is difficult for a person to learn to trust others if the society in which she or he exists systematically corrodes, debilitates, and dismantles that trust.

Examining the particular school where this study was undertaken may further explain the pervasiveness of distrust among the adolescents. All of the participants in the study attended a particularly large, underfunded, and chaotic inner city school that lacked any real means to create a community. As mentioned in the beginning of this book, upon entering the school each student goes through a metal detector, security guards patrol the hallways, and the school doors are locked after second period to prevent stragglers and criminals from entering the building. As Joyce Epstein and Nancy Karweit note:

> Negative features in a school environment—ridicule, discrimination, low expectations, stereotypes, repressions, punishment, isolation—may increase the dissociative quality of the setting and affect the thought processes and social behaviors of the students.[32]

Norris Haynes and Christine Emmons found that students' peer relations are greatly affected by the school climate: a reproachful, negative environment was commonly associated with distrusting and negative peer relations.[33] While none of the students in the present study specifically discussed this issue, the social relations of the adolescents who participated in the study are most likely influenced by the school they attend and where they attempt to make close friends. Like the larger community, the school environment in which the students spend 80 percent of their waking hours conveys to them that they are not trustworthy. It is not hard to understand how these messages of distrust could seep into their interpersonal relationships.

A final explanation for the prevalence of distrust found among students in this study may lie with the quality of the teens' relationships with their parents. Specifically, those who did not have trusting, close relationships with their parents may not know how to develop such relationships with their peers. They may have had no model from which to learn.[34] Yet, among those adolescents in the study who reported distrusting their peers, their feelings for their parents (or the adult with whom they resided) were as likely to be positive as they were to be negative. Some spoke about lacking trust in their peers but trusting their parents, while others spoke about trusting neither their peers nor their parents.[35] Some of the parents, however, specifically warned their children not to trust their peers. Such messages may reflect a belief system—considered common within many close-knit, oppressed communities—that those who are not part of one's family or one's extended family should not be trusted.[36] Shawn, an African American young man, says that he doesn't have close friends outside of the family because "I don't trust them. Don't trust other people. I was always brought up to trust the family first. . . . Family first." Such messages from parents and other family members may make it particularly difficult for adolescents from these communities to have close, trusting, nonfamilial friendships.

These stories of trust, betrayal, and desire among urban adolescents raise critical developmental questions. What are the implications for relationships among adolescents (both friendships and romantic relationships) if boys are more likely to terminate their close relationships in response to betrayal while girls tend to pursue intimacy despite betrayal? These types of gender-based responses may severely disrupt not only male friendships but also male-female relationships. Furthermore, what does this tell us about adolescent development if, as this study suggests, urban adolescent boys desire intimate same-sex friendships as frequently as their female peers? In addition, what are the implications for adolescent development if adolescents are not trusting their peers and if boys, in particular, are not finding the relationships they seek? Given the critical importance of friendships for adolescents,[37] these latter findings seem particularly disturbing.

While these findings may reveal patterns evident among adolescents from all walks of life, they may also be specific to the population studied. Researchers have, in fact, found significant ethnic and socioeconomic differences in the quality and characteristics of adolescent friendships.[38] In their study of friendships among 240 Mexican American, African American, and European American sixth and ninth graders (socioeconomic status was predominantly lower-middle to middle class), Jones, Costin, and Ricard found that African American males were more likely than the other boys in the study to reveal their personal thoughts and feelings with their male friends.[39] Furthermore, European American teens were the only ones who revealed significant sex differences in levels of self-disclosure in their same-sex friendships. In their study of 292 black and white junior high school children, DuBois and Hirsch found that the white boys in their sample were the least likely of all groups to discuss their personal problems with their school friends or to feel that they could rely on their best friend for help.[40] Gallagher and Busch-Rossnagel found, in their study of 311 urban low and middle socioeconomic status black and white adolescent girls, that middle-class white and black girls were more likely to share their beliefs and attitudes with their friends than black and white girls from low-income families.[41] Socioeconomic status, in their research, was a stronger predictor of the quality of friendships than race or ethnicity. These research studies and others suggest that friendships may differ substantially depending on the social and cultural context.

The findings from my study indicate that adolescent boys and girls from all different socioeconomic classes and ethnicities need to be listened to on their own terms. What would white, poor, working-class, or middle-class adolescents say about friendships if they were interviewed in an open-ended format over time (as few studies of white, middle-class youngsters have done)? Perhaps they, too, would reveal a desire for intimate same-sex friendships. My findings lead me to wonder if social science researchers have assumed that adolescent girls (and women) are *more interested* in intimate same-sex relationships because they are more likely than boys (and men) to *have* these types of relationships. We may have a firm understanding of what kind of relationships white, middle-class adolescents, in particular, *have*, but do we know what they *want* or *desire;* and, at least as important, do we know what they think they have *lost?* These findings regarding trust, betrayal, and friendships underscore the need to examine such questions with diverse populations, using research methods that allow adolescents to speak about what they have and what they want in their lives.

6

■ ■   ■   ■   ■   ■   ■   ■   ■

"I Never Put Anyone in Front of My Mother"

What would you say makes your life worth living?
Worth living? My mother. 'Cause she struggled. She struggled a long
way in her lifetime to get where she's at now. . . . So it's like, for
right now, her achievement—it really made me think that out of, out
of nothingness, you can make something out of yourself.
                                        —Victor, sophomore year

LIKE VICTOR, many of the adolescents in the study spoke with passion about the importance of their mothers.[1] They spoke about them not
only as women who were nurturing, supportive, and caring, but also as
women who showed them that they could thrive in the world despite the
difficult odds ("out of nothingness, you can make something out of yourself"). Their mothers made their lives "worth living." The boys and girls
discussed their mothers when they were directly asked about such relationships and when asked about themselves, their beliefs and values, their
futures, their role models, and their relationships with fathers, siblings, and
peers. While some of the adolescents spoke about the significance of their

mothers *and* fathers, they typically believed that their relationships with their mothers were most important. Furthermore, their stories of the influence of their mothers in their lives were delicately layered. Their reasons for and conceptions of their mothers' importance varied. These variations and similarities are described in this chapter.

Boys and Mothers

Jamal

Jamal lives alone with his mother. He has no siblings and his parents have been divorced for ten years. Until the week before his first interview, he had not heard from his father in six years. At school, Jamal is an athletic and academic star and is exceptionally popular among his peers. In his sophomore year, Jamal tells Mike that his father recently called to congratulate him on an athletic achievement:

> You know he had the courage to call me.
> *Was it good hearing from him after all this time?*
> It was a good talk. Like [he said], "Do you miss me?" and all that and I said well, after so many years, you know, you really don't miss him. There's my mother and I and we're sort of like best friends so it doesn't really matter if he's there or he's not there, because I have everything I want with my mother.

While Jamal says he doesn't miss his father, he also suggests, as he shifts from the first to the second person ("*I* said well . . . *you* really don't miss him"), that he is trying not to miss his father. Nonetheless, Jamal feels strongly about his mother and the support she offers him.

Throughout his sophomore-year interview, Jamal continually refers to his mother and the important role she plays in his life:

> *How would you explain the fact that you have grown up the way you have, that you haven't become one of the people who is selling drugs or using drugs. . . . That you've got all these things going for you? How do you explain that to yourself?*
> I explain it to myself like this: My mother took time, she's not soft, so they say—they say women can't raise boy children, but if the woman is right,

she knows how to raise her children right. So she raised me right and I guess she said through prayer and asking God and just taking a lot of time, asking me questions, and being straightforward with me, I got to be the man I am.

So you attribute a lot of it to her?

All of it, just about.

Challenging the belief, held inside and outside of his own community, that single women cannot properly raise male children, Jamal attributes his success almost exclusively to his mother. In light of the previous discussion of girls' ability to speak honestly in their relationships, it is noteworthy that Jamal identifies his mother's "straightforward[ness]" as the very reason for her success in raising him, and as the reason he is the *man* he is today. After speaking about his friends and girlfriend, Jamal says that out of all of his relationships, his relationship with his mother is the most important: "Yeah, I never put anyone in front of my mother. No way."

When Jamie, Jamal's junior-year interviewer, asks Jamal about his relationship with his mother, he says: "We're real close, we're good friends, we talk about things. . . . If I'm not sure of anything I'll just ask my mother and she'll just give me advice. Not real real personal personal things though." Jamal's close feelings toward his mother do not include sharing his most personal experiences but rather a mutual commitment and a willingness to solve problems together. This type of closeness was more common among the boys than among the girls. For the girls, being close to their mothers typically involved telling her "everything" or "most things." For the boys, the bases of their close relationships had more to do with respect and admiration than with open communication.

Later in his junior-year interview, Jamal identifies his mother as the person he most looks up to:

I want to get a little bit more of a sense of understanding of how and why she's been so important to you.

You know—you know one-parent family. The only person around is my mother so I have no father. So every time I need something I go to my mother. So if I need something done, I gotta go to my mother. If I need her help, I go to my mother. She's been there for so long.

As in the previous year, Jamal explains that his relationship with his mother is important to him because she is the only one on whom he can consistently depend.

In his senior year, Jamal, still a star athlete and student and still very popular with his peers, is again asked by Jamie to describe his relationship with his mother:

> We're still close, good friends, we talk. We have a good relationship.
> *So when you say that you're close to her, what does that mean to you?*
> It just means, you know, it really does not mean—it's just like—it's important to me and I'm thankful that we are close 'cause it's always been just my mother and so she's really important to me.

While Jamal strains to explain what he means by "close," he clearly values his relationship with his mother. Jamal's sense of closeness, once again, seems based primarily on his appreciation of her support rather than on being able to disclose personal experiences with her.

Further in his senior-year interview, when Jamal is explaining why he does not fight with other boys, he says that his mother has always taught him to be a leader, so he never "follows" when his friends start fighting with other kids. As he did in his sophomore year, Jamal attributes his ability to avoid trouble to the way his mother has raised him. He is clearly proud of her:

> *Who's the most important person in your life right now?*
> Mom.
> *Still Mom? It's been Mom every year. Why is she the most important person to you now?*
> Because, like I said, she's always been there for me and that's all I ever had. And so she's always my role model because they usually say they need a man around the house to raise kids. She raised me on her own, and I respect her and I thank her for that, so she's my role model.

Jamal continues to challenge the idea that children are raised properly only when adult males are present in the home. His mother, he insists in his interviews, was enough to ensure a good upbringing. In the last section of Jamal's senior-year interview, Jamie asks him how he has been able to be so successful:

> Back to the Mom thing. She grew me to be like, you know, she always said the same: "Make your bed hard, you lie down hard. Make it easy, you lie down comfortable." And I know she works so hard to get her house and I always wanted to get a house. She went to school—'cause originally she's from Trinidad—so she went to school and she got a degree and so I want to go to school and get a degree. I'm not around my father or anything and he doesn't support me, so I don't consider him a father anyway. Just my mother, so I figure I'm going to be a dad and I want to have a kid and I want to have the closest relationship with my son or my daughter and then I always wanted a house like the one that my mother worked so hard for, so I want to get my house too. And then she worked hard to get a degree from Trinidad and then I'm American and I want to get myself a degree too, so.

Motivated by his mother's hard work and educational and material accomplishments and expressing indifference toward his father that only thinly covers his anger and disappointment, Jamal aspires to be like his mother and unlike his father ("I want to have the closest relationship with my son"). For Jamal, his mother is an unparalleled source of support and inspiration throughout his high school years.

Albert

Albert, a Puerto Rican student who lives with his mother and younger sister, also views his mother as the most important person in his life during all three years of his interviews. Albert's mother left his father after many years of physical and emotional abuse. He had not seen his father for over a year at the time of his first interview. Like Jamal, Albert does well in school. At the end of Albert's sophomore interview, Mike asks him:

> *What makes your life worth living?*
> My mother. Like, I see her like she's been through rough times and I think about it. She's gone through all that and still she's alive. And so I think that might happen to me now, I could go through it too.

Along with the other boys in the study, Albert is motivated by watching his mother endure and takes her experience as proof that he, too, can survive and even excel.

In his junior year, Albert says to Mike that his relationship with his mother is slowly changing:

> *Why do you think it has changed [since last year]?*
> I really can't—I don't know. . . . I like talking to her, you know, it's like me and her get along a lot. It's not like as I get older I get separated. Like as I get older I get more—it's not like I get separated or nothing, I just get more closer to her.

Both Albert and Jamal directly challenge mainstream developmental beliefs about adolescents. Albert is aware of societal expectations concerning the need for adolescents to separate from their parents, but unapologetically explains that as he has grown older, he has only become closer to his mother.

Albert emphasizes in his junior year that he will always depend on his mother:

> *You always will [depend on your mother]? Tell me in what ways you see yourself always depending on your mother?*
> Talking about our problems still, you know. If I'm married and I still got a problem, I'm still going to call my mother to let her know what's happening. And to let her see what she thinks about it, what should I do about it.

Marvin, an African American student, says in his junior year: "My second sister, she's like independent and she doesn't need nobody. I feel I need my mother. I don't know about nobody else. I just need her around." While the adolescents in the study occasionally spoke about feeling independent from their parents, they typically described growing closer to and feeling more dependent on their mothers as they grew older.

When Albert is asked in his junior year if there is any adult that he looks up to, he says:

> My mother.
> *Why do you look up to her?*

It's like that same thing I said last year. She's been through a lot and still she'll keep on taking good care of us, not like other people who've been through a lot and it's like they can't handle it anymore [and] leave or do something stupid, you know. She just kept on right there taking good care of us.
Do you think that you'd like to be like her?
Yeah.

To explain why his mother is the most important person in his life, Albert says: "I see the way she suffered so much before like, you know, like all the stuff that she did before [throwing her husband out because he was abusing her] that she still keeps on right there, happy, always a happy life." Watching their mothers get through arduous times has a profound effect on the adolescents in the study. As Victor pointed out earlier, it proved to them that they too could be resilient. *Seeing* their mother "stay happy" through difficult times provided them with a model to which they could aspire.

In Albert's senior year, the themes concerning his mother are repeated. He admires his mother's ability to cope and states that she makes his "life worth living." Albert adds this year that he considers himself to be very much like his mother:

In what ways do you think you're similar to your Mom?
My character.
How is your character similar?
You know, I take it easy. I wouldn't get mad for everything. I control my emotions, you know. Not gonna pop it out to everybody.
You don't or you do?
No, I don't. I just stay, you know how it is . . . I stay calm. I don't get that hyper, you know, for anything. Like she does—something might happen, she takes it cool. I think I take it off my mother, you know. Same way my mother is, that's the way I am.

The ease with which Albert at eighteen years old identifies with his mother surprises me. Lacking any self-consciousness and sporting a Lakers baseball cap and a matching oversized T-shirt, Albert proudly tells me: "Same way my mother is, that's the way I am."

When I ask Albert in his senior year what made it possible for him to do well in school, he says his reasons have to do with his mother:

> *In what ways?*
> Like she could have been a mean mother, too, you know. Seeing things that were happening. Some mothers do become that way. Like, the husband'll beat her and then the son'll try to bother her and she'll beat on the son, you know, to get her anger off. She wasn't like that even though she would be angry sometimes, she would never take it out on us.

Having watched his mother being beaten by his father, Albert is clearly appreciative that his mother did not vent her anger on him. Albert, like Jamal and Malcolm, credits his mother alone for his success. Mothers were not simply supportive figures in these boys' lives, but their heroes and the cause of their strength.

Victor

Victor, the African American student whom I quoted at the beginning of this chapter, lives alone with his mother (his father died at the beginning of his freshman year). Unlike the three boys I have just described, Victor is struggling in school, his grades are poor, and he remains one grade below that of his age group. Like his peers, however, Victor states in his sophomore year that his mother is his role model. After Victor describes his mother, girlfriend, and friends, Helena asks:

> *What would you say is the most important relationship in your life right now? Of all the different ones we've talked about?*
> I'd say right now, me and my mother. 'Cause right now we're we—we never were this close. We're sort of like hand and glove now. 'Cause whenever she needs something, I be there for her. And she knows that now. And, um, whenever I need somebody . . . she'll be there for me.

Victor seems to enjoy a mutually supportive relationship with his mother that is *closer* than it ever has been before.

In his junior year, I ask Victor:

Which would you say is the most important relationship right now?
My mother. Me and my mother. Why is that? Because that's really the key
to—for both of us to really, you know, stay together. 'Cause like, what's
happening now people can't really live alone these days in our neighborhood 'cause a lot of things are going on. And there really is like—I want to
know where she be at a lot, and she wants to know where I be at a lot
'cause that really determines what's happening.

Victor's relationship with his mother is, in some ways, unique among the
boys in the study. While mothers typically supported and looked after their
sons, few sons reported that they, in turn, provided emotional support to
their mothers. Victor's and his mother's reliance on each other is strongly
influenced by their awareness of the dangers in their neighborhood. When
I ask Victor what his mother will do when he eventually leaves for college
as he has planned, he explains that his aunt will take care of his mother and
he will "come back as soon, as much as possible." In the future, Victor
would like his mother to live with him and his girlfriend because he wants
to make sure his mother is cared for and that she has "everything she
needs."

In his third-year interview, Victor, who is still struggling in school and
is not going to be able to graduate with his class, speaks once again about
his close relationship with his mother and the support he receives from her:

It feels a whole lot better in the house to know that you—that you have
somebody behind you supporting you . . . and my mom's making sure she'll
be with me every step of the way. And I appreciate that, 'cause I mean, that's
something that a lot of moms—a lot of mothers wouldn't do. 'Cause that
means that in some ways she's looking out for me.

In spending the entire first thirty minutes of his third-year interview passionately discussing the ways in which he is supported by his mother, Victor testifies to the central role his mother plays in his life.

When the boys spoke about their mothers, they commonly told stories
of being cared for and supported, of being inspired by them, and of being
increasingly dependent on and growing closer to them over time. They
saw their mothers as the source of their strength and motivation, their role
models, and as the most important relationship in their lives. They ideal-

ized their mothers but also learned concrete survival skills from them. It is interesting to note that while many of these boys spoke about the importance of their mothers, they also typically stated that they did not feel comfortable telling their mothers their "personal personal" thoughts and feelings. They felt close to their mothers but also, as with their peers, maintained certain boundaries in these relationships.

Girls and Their Mothers

Marie

Marie, a student whose parents are from the Dominican Republic, lives with her mother, father, brothers, and sisters. Marie does well in school, participates in many extracurricular activities, and holds an after-school job. She epitomizes success. When I ask her in her freshman year about her relationship with her mother, Marie says they are closer than they used to be.

> *What do you think has made you become closer?*
> Now that I'm going through puberty, you know, it was like I need—I need more of her. You know she's all scared. She needs to be more secure so she's like talking to me more. And, you know, getting—being closer to me.

Like the boys, the girls emphasized that they too feel closer to their mothers as they grow older. For Marie and her mother as well as for Victor and his mother, the desire for intimacy appears to be shared.

In her sophomore year, I ask Marie:

> *Of all the relationships that we've talked about so far—anybody that we've talked about—who do you think is the most important to you right now?*
> Like if I lose a person? My mother.
> *Your mother? And why do you think she's the most important?*
> Because she has went—she has gone through a lot with me. I mean, I don't know what I would do without her.

An individual's importance, for Marie and for Malcolm (as seen in his case study), is determined by remembering who had stuck by them and imagining who would be most missed if "lost." Marie states unequivocally that this person is her mother.

Marie, in her sophomore year, feels more comfortable sharing her personal life with her mother than last year: "it's like, 'cause I learned that— I mean my parents are the only people I have and I might have close friends that I trust, but my parents are always gonna be the ones there for me." Marie implies in this response that she is able to communicate openly with her mother because she can be relied upon for support—a belief that was standard among the girls. For them, open communication was the natural consequence of support.

When I ask Marie whom she would like to emulate when she is older, she answers: "[My mother] just like the way she is . . . she's understanding, she's funny. She's like—she has that humor, like teenager humor. I can go out with her and have fun, you know. Just like I could go with any other friend."

In her junior-year interview, Marie speaks at length about the passionate arguments she has with her mother. She frequently disagrees with her mother and will challenge her when she thinks she is wrong. However, she also tells me that her mother "understands" her more than before. Understanding does not imply a lack of disagreement for Marie but rather a sense of engagement. Like Marie, the girls in the study commonly discussed the conflicts *and* the close bonds they have with their mothers.

As she nears the time she will leave home, Marie finds herself feeling even closer to her mother than she has in previous years:

> I can speak to her now about certain things that I wasn't able to speak to her about before. . . . Now I've gotten closer, you know, I'm growing up and I'm doing all these different activities and she's like supporting me and everything. And sometimes my father just really gets—he—um—he treats me in a way that she gets mad and that's how we got closer.

While themes were not detected regarding relationships with fathers, fathers played a significant role in many of the teenagers' lives. Frequently, however, their importance lay in their role as the common "enemy" against whom mothers, daughters, and sons coalesced. Marie and a few of her peers in the study expressed gratitude toward their mothers for recognizing and responding to what they felt was unjust treatment by their fathers.

Like the boys, Marie also believes that her mother gives her courage:

I mean the thing that sticks out for me in your interviews is how you've had such a hard time with your Dad, and in some ways with your Mom too, but much more with your Dad. So you haven't had like a really easy home life at all, and yet you are doing all these things and you're a super achiever. You're involved in all these activities and I just wonder why that's true. Where have you gotten your strength?

My mother.

How has she given you that strength, do you think?

'Cause I don't want to let her down because she doesn't earn much on her job and she's always—she came here, she couldn't go to school and finish because of, um, she had us already. And she couldn't get a job, you know [because she did not have a work permit] . . . and she's been allowed to work for my father's family. And I just do it for her 'cause I want to give her a good life that she couldn't achieve. I just don't want to let her down.

Marie's desire not to disappoint her mother becomes the motivation for her achievements. She repeats, later in her interview, that she wants to "make it" because of her mother. Many students in the study stated similar themes—they wanted to succeed in their lives to honor what their mothers had done for them. Their motivation for doing well, or at least trying to do well, was not based on wanting to reap rewards from their mothers, but rather on wanting to "give back" to their mothers. Even the adolescents who lived with both of their parents implied that they had more of a desire to "give back" to their mothers than their fathers. Their reasons lay with their firm belief that their mothers have had more difficult lives than their fathers or, at least, they have made greater efforts on their behalf.

In all three interviews, Marie asserts that her mother enhances her confidence and is the most important relationship in her life:

Why your mother?

I don't know. She's just gone through so much for me. And she supports me and everything. She's always there for me. I don't know what I'd do if she—without her, you know?

Chantel

Chantel's interviews suggest similar themes. An African American student, Chantel lives with her mother and sister. Her parents have been divorced for approximately eight years and her father is remarried and lives close to Chantel. Chantel speaks about the inspiration provided by her mother and father and feels comfortable speaking freely with both of them. In fact, she admits to feeling more comfortable talking to her father because her father is more "accepting" of her than her mother. Still, Chantel, in her freshman year, says she is close to her mother:

> I can talk to [my mother]. We're close and everything. In a way we're like sisters 'cause like I talk to her like—you know mothers and everything, they always like, "How you doing in school?" Instead of that, I just go up to her and be like, "You know what happened in school today?" I like talk to her and it's more like it's just like an everyday thing. So we're more like friends than mother and daughter.

Chantel tells lengthy stories of her mother's interest and participation in all aspects of her life: school, friends, and boyfriends. Her sense of closeness with her mother appears to arise from, or at least be enhanced by, their open communication and her mother's active involvement in her life.

In her sophomore year, Chantel describes her parents as she did in her previous interview. Her role model this year is her mother:

> If there is anybody, I'd have to say my mother, 'cause she's like—I don't know, she's like—she's real independent. She's just the type of person that when everything's—like right now, she got laid off and stuff. But it's like when she first got laid off, I was scared. I was like, "Oh no, we're gonna lose the house, we're gonna get kicked out," and all that stuff and she was like, "Don't worry about it, everything's gonna be okay." At first, she's a little grumpy in her own way, but she just keeps, like, going on, like, "That's okay," you know, "I'll be all right." I don't know, she's just—she's real strong. Like anytime something like gets ready to knock her down she's just standing there like, "I can take it." . . . I don't really see any weak points in her. She can—it's like she can take anything, you know. She deals with everything. It's like she's real smart and stuff. I have to say, I probably do look up to her.

Chantel's admiration of her mother, like that of so many teens in this study, is based on her mother's ability to endure during difficult times. Chantel's moving and passionate portrait of her mother's ability "to stand there like [she] can take it" is echoed by Sonia, a Puerto Rican student who lives with both her parents. Sonia, in her junior year, tells me that her mother is her role model:

> My mother—she hasn't given up, she's still going on. I see what, you know—she tells us what she went through. She dropped out of school when she was in the eleventh grade and now she went back to school. And now she's trying harder to make it up there. And that's something that I'm very proud of and I see her and I look up to her a lot. You know, for not just stopping there even though it took her this long, she still kept going. You know she's very determined.
>
> *Do you think you are as determined as your Mom or Dad?*
>
> Even, even more because you know, like I could see what my mother went through. I could see it, and I know it's hard. So I could never see myself as giving up.

What is striking in these stories of admiration, pride, and tenacity is that so many of the adolescents, even those in the ninth grade, appreciated their mother's ability to cope with difficult circumstances. Directly experiencing their mothers' obstacles was not necessary (as I had assumed from my own middle-class adolescence) for these adolescents to understand what their mothers had accomplished. At a very young age, they understood what their mothers were up against and what grit it took to cope with such adversity. Remarkably, none of the adolescents seemed to take their mothers for granted.

During her sophomore interview, Chantel says that her relationship with her mother is the most important, followed closely by her relationship with her father. She repeats this in her junior year, but she spends more time talking about her relationship with her mother:

> We still get along with each other. She's like a friend instead of like a mother. . . . It's like talking to a sister instead of talking to a mother. We have a good relationship sometimes. Well, you know, we argue like everybody else. But I don't know, I don't know, it's different. Everybody's like, "I wish I had your mother."

In emphasizing that her mother is not like "a mother," Chantel distinguishes between a presumably distanced and more authoritative parent and her own parent. Chantel, like Marie, describes the friendship with her mother as well as the conflicts. She freely, and in great detail, describes the exchanges she and her mother have during specific arguments and then tells me what she most admires about her.

When asked directly what she likes about her mom, Chantel says:

> She's independent. . . . It's like she doesn't depend on anybody to take care of her. It's like she's on her own. It's like everything she does, she doesn't—if she's in trouble, she never leans on anybody else, "Can you help me?" It's like—like when she was laid off, she didn't, you know—I know a lot of people that were laid off and stuff, they always went to somebody else: "Oh, I need this. Can you help me?" And my mother, she was just struggling by herself. And it's like since it's just me and her together, it's like she doesn't need anybody to take care of her. I like the way she carries herself. I don't know. Everybody tells me I act just like my mother . . . very independent. . . . Don't wait for everybody to do for you 'cause you'll have nothing.

Chantel not only admires her mother's independence but believes that she shares this quality. The girls in the study often appreciated their mothers' independence or wished their mothers were more independent (none of the boys suggested this theme). Repeatedly they suggested that they had learned from their mothers or other women in their family about the importance of not depending on others for financial or emotional security. They sought independence especially from men and were fiercely proud of their own and their mothers' autonomy.[2]

Chantel ends her junior-year interview saying that while her father is significant in her life, her mother is particularly important:

> If my mother left me, I would have so many problems, I mean, she like kind of holds me together. She keeps me from having a lot of problems that I know I would have 'cause if my mother wasn't there, I mean I would feel like I would have nobody. Even if my father was there, it's not the same 'cause it's like, you know, you live with your mother and that person's gone, I would have to adapt to a whole new lifestyle living with my father . . . and my life wouldn't be possible if something happened to her, if she wasn't here.

While stressing her independence, Chantel believes she needs her mother. Her desire to be independent does not compel her to distance herself from her mother but is, instead, proof of her identification and intimate relationship with her. Chantel feels no contradiction between her valorization of independence and her admiration and dependence on her mother.

Reflections

The importance of mothers in the lives of black and Latino children has been discussed extensively over the past two decades.[3] Less research has been devoted to the ways in which poor or working-class adolescents from various ethnic backgrounds speak about their relationships with their mothers. In the present study, the adolescents discussed the continuing importance of this relationship in their lives. They did not describe their mothers simply as important figures but as *the most* important figure in their lives, as the source of strength and determination, and, for several of the teens, as their very reason for living. Their mothers' persistence and fortitude made them role models. Similar findings were also reported by Gloria Joseph in her study of relationships among black mothers and daughters. She says:

> The daughters showed tremendous respect, concern, and love for their mothers. The positive feelings that were expressed did not imply that all was sweet, kind and loving between them. Rather, what was expressed was an undeniable respect and admiration for their mothers' accomplishments and struggles against overwhelming odds; in her economic ability to make ends meet; her personal relationship with men; raising her families as a single parent or head of household; and encouraging them to be independent and get an education. The mothers were role models for their daughters.[4]

Mothers in the present study were portrayed by the girls and boys who lived with both parents or with only one as deeply caring, supportive, and inspirational. The boys typically felt close to their mothers and took great care to emphasize the importance of this relationship. They did not, however, typically share their personal thoughts and feelings with their mothers, although some, like Victor, stressed that he anticipated discussing such topics as marital difficulties with his mother later in life. The girls, in contrast, typically felt both close to their mothers and comfortable talking with them about most, if not all, of their concerns, experiences, and problems. Both the boys and girls, however, spoke about their mothers with equal intensity and passion. The extent to which they shared personal stories and experiences together did not appear to be associated with the strength of their feelings for their mothers.

The adolescent boys' discussions of their mothers were more idealized than the girls. The girls were more likely than the boys to discuss their fights and disagreements with their mothers and were seemingly more likely to challenge them. However, the adolescent boys forcefully challenged the widely held notion that male children need male role models in the home. They believed, articulated, and demonstrated through their words and their achievements that their mothers had alone raised them to be mature and caring people. The girls also credited their mothers with much of their own success and spoke of their admiration for their mothers' competence, strength, and independence. Several relationships between mothers and daughters were "like sisters" or friends and allowed the daughters to assume roles as support providers as well as receivers of support. The adolescents spoke freely about depending on their mothers currently and in the future, and their *increased* sense of closeness with them over time.[5] They were uninhibited and proud to let their mothers be part of their worlds and they actively resisted separating from them.[6]

Remarkably, the adolescents seemed to understand their mothers' experiences and appreciate their contributions to their own well-being. I do not remember having this perspective at their age, nor have I heard such stories from middle-class adolescents.[7] The middle-class, primarily white adolescents I have interviewed in previous studies were more concerned with not letting their lives be "ruled" by Mom or Dad or both than with protecting and "giving back" to them. Growing up under oppressive circumstances may lead adolescents to greater empathy and understanding of their mothers' struggles than a more privileged background might afford. Poverty and racism may result in highly visible coping strategies, and mothers, experiencing such oppression, may work hard to let their children know of their difficulties and their coping strategies so that their children are better prepared for the future.[8]

A reason for the importance of mothers among many of the adolescents is clearly related to the specific ethnic communities of which they are a part. Gloria Wade-Gayles states that in black communities, "praise for our mothers is the refrain of church songs, the text of sermons, and the subject of wise sayings passed from one generation of Black women to another."[9] Earl Shorris[10] claims that in Latino cultures, motherhood is honored and respected and associated with strength, perseverance, and patience. African American as well as Latino adolescents are likely conveying messages (to their interviewers) and living the lessons about mothers that they have absorbed from their respective communities. The valuing of mothers may also stem from the adolescents' socioeconomic circumstances. As part of a social class where living a comfortable and healthy life is not taken for granted, the person who makes such a life possible (at least during adolescence) will clearly be important. For these adolescents, their mothers have not simply raised them, they have made it possible for them to live.

Another plausible reason for these adolescents' strong feelings toward their mothers may lie with the problems many of them had in maintaining close friendships with their peers. As a result of their lack of intimate and trusting friendships, their mothers may be the only ones whom they can really trust or who will "be there" for them. Strikingly, the two boys who rarely mentioned having difficulties trusting their peers were the two whose mothers had died when they were young. Without mothers, these two boys may have been more motivated to establish close peer relationships. Or perhaps these two boys did not have a trusting and loyal relationship at home with which to compare their friendships.

Notably, the adolescents who spoke about the importance of their mothers were better off academically and more socially integrated than those who felt less passionately about them. These teens were typically on the honor rolls, in extracurricular activities, and were not involved in high-risk activities. Their relationships with their mothers may be a critical factor in their resilience. However for those few adolescents who felt passionately about their mothers and who struggled in school, their deeply connected relationship with their mothers may explain why, for example, they still remain in school.

As these adolescents described themselves, their role models, their futures, their values, their school, and their lives, I was able to hear—both in form and in content—the importance of their mothers in their lives. Had this discussion of maternal relationships been carried on in isolation, without questions about other parts of their lives, I would not have understood the extent to which they perceive their mothers as part of, and indeed fundamental to, their very existence. By asking about their worlds, I was able to come closer to understanding what their lives "feel like and what they mean personally."[11]

7

■ ■ ■ ■ ■ ■ ■ ■ ■

Maintaining a "Positive Attitude"/ Fearing Death

AS THE ADOLESCENTS spoke about their futures, about what they want to do and be in the years to come, I heard hope, excitement, anxiety, and pessimism. Some told us that the only thing they live for is the future. Others saw no future for them to anticipate. Among these voices I heard recurring motifs: themes of optimism and of death, of hope and of fear. The adolescents believed they could reach their ambitious goals through hard work and persistence. They maintained a "positive attitude." At the same time, however, they were tremendously afraid of failure and of death, invoking insecurities about financial well-being and basic survival. They knew only too well that they are at much greater risk for health problems and of an early death as a consequence of violence or poor health care than their suburban, middle-class peers. Like Malcolm and Tyrone, they have "lost" friends and family members through illnesses and drive-by shootings. They live amidst poverty and devastation and have numerous peers who have dropped out of school, have become teenage parents, or have joined gangs. They are justifiably worried that the fate of some of their peers will be their own fate. Remarkably, however, these adolescents expressed *both* a belief in the "American Dream" and a real fear of meeting a violent death. They had optimistic *and* grave expectations. Contrary to what many social scientists have suggested,[1] these adolescents were neither hopeless nor optimistic about their futures; they were both. These seemingly contradictory perspectives were a central theme in the teens' interviews.[2]

Listening to Marie and Gayle

Marie

Marie, from whom we heard earlier when she spoke passionately about her mother, does well in school and belongs to a singing group that regularly rehearses and performs in clubs around the city. In the ninth grade, Marie says she admires her brother and her godmother because they "think positively about the future." They encourage her to think of the possibilities her future holds instead of the potential obstacles. While she is aware of such obstacles (her father repeatedly reminds her of them), she tells me she does not want to "dwell" on them.

"Thinking positively," a theme that emerged in Marie's interviews and in those of her peers, had many definitions and consequences. Marie explains to me that "thinking positively" does not mean being blind or naive to the "negative things" in life. In fact, it is people with "negative minds" who do not think realistically: "Some people that have like their negative mind—like my uncle—he's such—like a playboy, and he's like, 'I ain't going to get AIDS.' They don't even think that they could get it." Marie stresses the importance of "positive thinking." Yet this mindset does not prevent her from seeing and understanding the realities of her world.

Marie's desire to be "positive" is heard when she speaks about her future, her relationships, and also, surprisingly, when she speaks about the death of a cousin. Marie says she is "really hurting" over the recent murder of her fifteen-year-old cousin who was shot over a case of beer. She says she "cannot help" thinking about him. After speaking in detail about her anguish, Marie suddenly changes her tone and tries to find a redeeming element in this senseless murder:

> And my cousin, he probably . . . that probably wasn't his destiny. . . . And then again they say he had—everybody has a mission on earth—and it's true because they say that he had a mission. He died and now everybody's like,

all the Spanish people and everybody, they're like real close. Like he's had—his death has brung unity—like a lot of unity with people. And it's made, you know, made people drink—think—more, um, positive and be more aware and be more careful. 'Cause not even in your own house you could be safe, you know? . . . It's brung, well it's brung unity to a lot of people. You know, people will be more careful what they do, how they act.

Initially telling me that she does not believe that her cousin was meant to die, Marie quickly shifts to describing the positive impact her cousin's death has had on her community. But in a telling slip of tongue ("it made people drink—think—more positive"), Marie implies that just as she can understand "the negative" while focusing on "the positive," the outcome of her cousin's death on her community was both positive and negative. "Thinking positively" did not necessarily involve the denial of pain or frustration, but a willingness to view such events through multiple lenses.

Marie and her peers' insistence on "thinking positively" suggests a *need* to think in this way. When Albert is asked about his fears about his future, he says: "I just feel real comfortable. I got the positive attitude . . . so I'll get there even though I've got struggles. I'll get [to the future]." Maintaining a positive attitude was considered a way to overcome or work through difficult situations. Some of the adolescents stated that they believed their "attitude" would directly affect their long-term fate: "thinking positively" would lead to positive outcomes and "negative thinking" would have negative consequences. A few stated that if they lost their positive attitude, they would lose their reason for living. "Thinking positively" was not considered a trite cliché for these teens but a critical strategy for living.

Marie and I continue to discuss her future in her freshman year:

When you think of your future, what do you think of?
[Pause.] Being successful. I think of like having [sigh] a big house like, you know—not all work but not all play either. You know, like have fun in my life.
What do you most hope for in your life?
That I reach my goals. That's about it 'cause there's nothing else to life but the future, you know? . . .
What's the first feeling you have?

I feel I can do it. . . .
Okay, what are some fears about the future?
That it might not turn out that way. That my mother might pass away soon. That [pause] I dunno—that I may not, you know, be able to prove my parents wrong [Marie's father doubts her potential], or if something happens, 'cause you can't really prevent things from happening sometimes.

Marie is not simply hopeful about her future but this hope and optimism is the force that propels her life ("'cause there's nothing else to life but the future"). At the same time, Marie has specific fears of being powerless to chart her own destiny. By the speed of her replies to my questions about hope and fear, Marie intimates that she is closely attuned to both her feelings of optimism ("I feel I can do it") and to her sense of dread ("that it may not turn out that way").

Believing that "you can't really prevent things from happening sometimes," Marie suggests a theme of unpredictability and cautious realism that was repeatedly heard among her peers. Her fears lie both with external circumstances ("my mother might pass away soon) as well as internal ones ("I may not be able to prove my parents wrong"). During his junior year, Joseph tells his interviewer what he fears:

> That I take the wrong way. I don't know, be a drug dealer and all that. Have no future.
> *Is this a real possibility?*
> I don't know. It's only a fifty-fifty, you know. I might go the right way or the wrong way.

Joseph is a good student who says he has never taken drugs in his life. Yet he worries about making destructive choices in his future, or about going down a path he has not chosen. Alfredo echoes Joseph's anxieties about his future actions: "I think the pace that you're going now, you can change at any moment. You can change from now 'til tomorrow, you can be somebody bad." Samuel voices a similar apprehension in his senior year. But his fears lay more with bad things happening *to* him rather than *by* him:

> I've been up late some nights. I'm like, "What if something goes wrong here?" 'Cause the future is so uncertain, you know. I mean sometimes the

best-laid plans go frustrated. So it's like, "What if I get kicked out of school for some reason?" Certain things in life just happen like that, there's really nothing you can do about it.

Samuel, who does well in school and is well liked by his teachers, believes there is a chance that he will be expelled. Samuel's, Alfredo's, Joseph's, and Marie's responses suggest a keen sense of not feeling in command. They believe negative things can happen *to* them (e.g., Samuel), *by* them (e.g., Joseph and Alfredo), or *to and by* them (e.g., Marie). Their vulnerability, however, is not associated with feelings of hopelessness. They do not believe that their efforts will go unnoticed. In the midst of discussing their fears that "things can just happen," these students fiercely maintain their "positive attitudes."

When I ask Marie, in her freshman year, what her past experiences have taught her, she says:

> I have learned not to be so trustful and to believe in everybody . . . 'cause I used to have a lot of friends that would really put me down. I told them all about—sometimes I think that I should just live my life and forget it, 'cause I'm gonna—'cause, life is a child of death. You know? And it's like, in order to—to—to live, you have to die. And it's like you're going to die some day so why don't you just live your life and stuff? Some people think the other way. I want to work but I want to have fun, too.

Moving from a discussion of betrayal and death to having fun, Marie suggests her strong urge to think positively. Her sense of her own mortality ("life is a child of death"), in fact, motivates her desire "to just live [her] life and forget." Acutely attuned to the very real possibility of an early death, the kind of death experienced by her cousin, she wants to enjoy her life.

Marie once again insists on "thinking positively" in her sophomore year when she tells me about a friend who was shot in the foot at the subway station after school. The news media, she says, paid no attention to the brutal event. Marie angrily contrasts this public disinterest in her friend's suffering with the newspaper's lengthy coverage of an incident where the principal of her school was held at gunpoint in school by a student:

> Nobody really cared about what happened [to her friend who got shot]. She could've been gone, you know, for no reason. Maybe because she was black

. . . I don't like thinking like that but maybe it is that way [however] when it happened to [the principal]. Yeah, it's like whoosh, it's like it was on the newspaper everyday. He was in the news everyday. I was like—it's true because you have to look at the positive side, you know 'cause I don't think negatively. You have to look that he's—he's a principal and it's the first time that it happens in this school system that a principal got assaulted so it should be big, you know. So it's like—can't really just say, "Oh, because he was white."

There is an unsettling quality to Marie's emphasis on "positive thinking" in the middle of her story of perceived injustice. She is clearly angry about the media's indifference to the shooting of her friend but tries, in midsentence, to justify the attention given to the principal's story because she does not want to "think negatively." She states tentatively that the media's lack of attention to her friend's trauma may have been racially motivated, only to quickly withdraw and deny this connection. It is possible, of course, that her shift in focus was due to not wanting to offend me (because I am a white adult who might feel protective of the white principal), or due to a quick revision of her opinion on the incident in midstory. Yet her emphasis on "positive thinking" throughout her interviews suggests that her response is, at least in part, self-censored in the name of "positive thinking." While a positive attitude may be a coping technique for Marie—it may help her mitigate her fury—it may also silence her more angry feelings. This attitude may, consequently, lead to inaction and passivity when action or reaction is called for.

Marie repeats this shift from the "negative" to the "positive" when she speaks about her future. Although this shift does not seem as double-edged as the one cited above, it is equally noteworthy:

When you think of the future, what do you think of?
Oh, it's scary 'cause all this violence going on now. And I—and I just wonder if it's gonna get worse or if it's gonna be better. 'Cause I've like—I've gone into church now. And I mean I've really gone into it. 'Cause the other day, I bumped into a friend of mine . . . she said that Satan is the one taking everybody away. And all these young people, you know, he's making them do all these bad things. I think it's true that Satan is just taking everybody away like that.
What do you think will happen in your future?

Working and getting a lot of money. I'll get married later on after I finish college and stuff. And helping my mother. I want to—I want to buy her a
house later, stuff like that. That's what I see.

Within the space of two questions, Marie's outlook, the tone of her voice,
and the gestures of her body abruptly transform as she moves from a discussion of *the* future, that even includes Satan, to speaking about *her own*
future. Marie and her peers in the study spoke about the frightening, even
chilling, events happening in their neighborhoods—the violence that is
killing their friends, families, and acquaintances—and about being successful in the future. Their optimism openly contradicts the hopeless image
that academics and journalists frequently attribute to this adolescent population.

Victor similarly distinguishes between a general and a personal future in
his sophomore year:

When you think about the future, what do you think about?
The way things are going, I can't—I really don't see no future. Not really.
    Not the one I want to see—I want—I want to have. I want to see peace for
    the future, but that—that—that's one of them, like an impossible dream.
How does that make you feel when you think about the future?
It makes me sad. You're gonna just be frustrated a little bit 'cause it's like,
    there's a lot of, there's a lot of smart people out here not doing anything
    with their capabilities.
What do you see happening in your future?
Myself? I see myself with a—a nice family, um, very financially set, have my
    mother living with me, and maybe she has everything she needs. . . . Make
    sure my aunt's living with me . . . and plus my wife wouldn't mind 'cause
    that's my girlfriend now. And she wouldn't mind. But I just see us all liv-
    ing together just happy.

The split between what Marie and Victor expect for the future of their
communities and even the world, and what they expect in their own futures, may be a coping strategy. They realize that the world in which they
live has the potential to limit their future possibilities. Yet they also understand that if they are going to sustain their determination, they must maintain hope about their own lives. They *must* believe that there will be a dif-

ference between their own futures and the fate of so many of their family members and peers. What would it mean for teenagers such as Victor or Marie to believe that their futures would reiterate the ones they see around them?

When Marie is asked, in her sophomore year, what she fears most about her future, she says:

> The violence. It's getting bad now. People are getting killed . . . kids can't go outside. I know my neighborhood used to be kind of quiet. And now across the street every day there's a shoot-out. There are shoot-outs every day. The kids can't go outside. They gotta stay in their house in the hot weather or go somewhere else because they can't be around their own neighborhood.
> *Do you think your thoughts about the future have changed over the past year?*
> [Pause.] Yeah, I think, I don't know, I think I've been looking at things more positive. I don't think I've been looking at things in such a negative way.

Chantel shares Marie's perspective about the future:

> *When you think of the future, what do you think of?*
> Probably—no—I know I'm going to college. I want to go to college and be a lawyer or a doctor. I'm not sure. I also want to be a singer. I think that's probably my first goal. I can see myself being successful 'cause in a way, I can't wait. I keep saying, "Dang, I wish I was there right now."
> *What do you hope for in the future?*
> I just hope that, you know, everything goes good for me. Like I hope nothing happens to my mother, my father—especially me—I don't want anything to happen to me. And now—you know, you don't know what's going to happen. I could be dead tomorrow. That's why I don't argue with my mother or nobody. I try and keep it "okay, okay" 'cause you know, you never know if you're going to see them again. . . . And a lot of people that died and stuff are my friends. You know, I turn around: "Oh, shoot, look at all my friends dying and everything."

Contrary to my expectations that discussions of violence and death would be accompanied by feelings of hopelessness or, at the very least, a tentativeness about one's own future, the teens' stories of violence and death were heard in concert with "positive" visions of their future possibilities. Although some of the adolescents, such as Chantel, felt that death[3] was more of an immediate threat than others, they did not allow these depressingly reasonable fears to prevent them from making plans and having great expectations.

At the end of her sophomore-year interview, I ask Marie what values are important to her, and she tells me: "I always want to be positive." As in her freshman year, there is an urgency in Marie's expressions of positive thinking that suggests that if she did not think in such a way, she would incur terrible consequences. The numerous "negative" events in her life (her cousin having been shot, her mother's illness, the continual risk of physical harm to herself, her friends, and her family) may force her to focus on the "positive" for fear that the "negative" will ultimately invoke depression and despair. "Thinking positively" seems to be Marie's way of maintaining strength in the face of tremendous adversity.

I ask Marie in her junior year:

You sound as if you are thinking more pessimistically about your future this year?
Yeah, you know everything is falling apart. You know it's like this whole world is falling apart.
So you think that's made you feel more—
In a way it's made me want to make it even more. But then again I don't know. I want to make it even more now because of that. To try to change that. It just makes me sad to see all these things. Every day I see all different things.

While Marie appears more affected by the troubles in her community than in previous years, she still maintains her optimism and, in fact, is inspired to "make it" by the difficulties she sees around her. Marie ends her third-year interview by telling me that she wants to be a role model for younger girls through her singing and her involvement in the youth activities at her church. Because of the devastation in her community, Marie says, she is determined to make a difference.

Marie's "positive attitude" has various meanings, depending on what she is speaking about, when she is speaking, and perhaps with whom she is speaking. Her outlook allows her to deny or "forget" her anguish, disappointment, and anger. It also permits her to acknowledge the difficulties in the world while maintaining hope about her own future. Sometimes her "positive thinking" seems troublesome—when it appears to silence her angry thoughts and feelings—and at other times it seems uplifting. Throughout her discussions of having a "positive attitude," "thinking positively," or simply having hope, Marie demonstrates her tactics for success and, perhaps, for survival.

Gayle

Gayle, Marie's peer, reveals similar beliefs. An African American student who is on the honor roll and is also involved in extra-curricular activities, Gayle says in her sophomore year that she is hopeful about accomplishing her future goals. She also tells me soon after this optimistic statement: "I pray to help me wake up the next morning with no hurt, harm, or danger." Gayle suggests, as did Marie, that she wavers between feeling hopeful and fearful.

Gayle admires people when they are able to maintain a "positive attitude." Her role model is her uncle:

> Like when we, okay, when we have funerals and stuff like that, he's always the one that has a positive outlook on everything. And everyone else is thinking negatively about life and everything, and he helps bring everybody—he helps bring a positive attitude towards things in life—to the people who are down really bad.

Gayle says she admires those who think positively because they are able to get through painful experiences without giving up or becoming hopeless. They provide inspiration for others. During difficult experiences, a "positive attitude" may help teens put one foot down after the other.

In her junior year, Gayle begins to suggest a more problematic aspect of positive thinking that was also suggested in Marie's interview. In the previous year, Gayle had spoken about the strategies she took to avoid men whom she found potentially threatening. This year she tells me about her new "attitude":

> I used to watch a lot of movies and about, um, how all the men would rape girls and stuff no matter who they were. You know, I used to see them in

movies how uncles and stuff would rape their nieces or daughters and stuff and that's when I started feeling uncomfortable.

And do you still feel this way?

I don't even let it bother me anymore.

How would you describe the change?

It's just different. I don't know. I guess I have a more positive outlook toward it than I did last year. . . . 'Cause last year I used to just say, "Well I don't—I don't like to be around men. I don't like to talk to my father. I don't like to do this." I just was thinking negatively. And now it's just I have a more positive attitude towards it.

For Gayle this year, having a positive attitude involves not "letting" her fears bother her. Like Marie's statement about living one's life and forgetting, Gayle tells me "you have to learn to forget things." The question that immediately arises after hearing her say this is: What is Gayle forgetting and is this forgetting psychologically and perhaps physically dangerous for her? "Forgetting" in the name of having "a positive attitude" may prompt her, at times, to neglect her own need to protect herself.

Gayle offers further evidence that she is trying to "forget [her] fears" in her junior year:

'Cause you never know when you might get shot or whatever.

Do you think about that a lot?

I don't think about it. I just think about a lot of people that I know that get shot. I know like a lot of people that got shot and killed.

So how do you deal with that?

Well, I don't get upset or anything about it.

I mean does it affect you when you go out at night?

I never take the bus at night. When it starts to get dark, I don't take the bus.

You don't take the bus. It's too scary.

It's not the idea of being scary. It's just I don't take the bus in the night. I don't walk down nobody's street in the night. I don't do it. 'Cause you never know what happens.

Switching back and forth from implying that she is afraid to denying such feelings, Gayle suggests that while she actively takes precautions in response to her concerns (she does not neglect her own need to protect herself), she is ambivalent about acknowledging her fears to me and, perhaps, to herself. Given Gayle's repeated discussions of the importance of having a positive attitude, this ambivalence may reflect both her desire to maintain a positive stance and her comprehension of the realities of her circumstances.

Like Marie, Gayle's seemingly "positive" outlook may lead her to deny to herself and to others that she is frightened or worried. It may even prevent her from taking the proper precautions. On the other hand, her "positive" outlook may also enable Gayle to take care of herself. If she were to dwell on her fears about being shot or about being attacked at night, for example, she might lose her ability to move freely in the world—it might immobilize her. With her positive attitude, she may feel empowered to act independently and spontaneously.

At the end of her junior-year interview, Gayle is asked:

When you think of the future, what do you think of?
I think of me living in a nice house with a family. Having a steady job. Everything just the way I want it to be.
Do you think that's going to be a reality, having everything you want?
If I make it that way.
Do you think you will?
Yeah.
Do you feel like you think about the future much?
I try not to. I try to live every day as it comes.
Why do you think you have that philosophy?
'Cause I might not be here tomorrow. I might die or something, so I try not to say, "This is what I want to do in the future." Okay, I'll say, "My goal is to do this." But I'm not gonna say, "Well I want to do this," or "I hope this is like this." I don't say that.
And why don't you say that?
Because you never know. You might not be here tomorrow. . . .
What do you think makes your life worth living?
The attitude that I have about life.
What do you mean your attitude?
My outlook about things in life. Like when I walk out in the street, I'm not gonna think I'm gonna get shot or whatever.

Telling me about her expectations of success, her future and present orientation, her worries that she may not live another day and her positive "outlook" that attempts to forget this concern, Gayle suggests that she has very real fears about the future but, once again, resists thinking about them. She maintains a positive outlook—an "attitude"—that makes her life worth living and, perhaps, more livable.

By her senior year, Gayle's discussions of her concerns and worries are more frequent, her discussions of having a positive attitude are less common, and she begins to sound an ambivalent note about her chances of achieving her goals:

> *When you think of your future, what do you think?*
> I think of going on to grad school. And maybe getting a job and a family, I guess.
> *What do you want to go to grad school for?*
> I want to be a lawyer, but I don't know.
> *Do you think you'll actually be able to be a lawyer?*
> Yes, if I make it. I can make it happen if I don't drop out of school. . . . I know a lot of people that wanted to become lawyers and they actually dropped out 'cause they said it was getting too difficult. I told them that I was not gonna drop out. . . .
> *What do you think you fear most about the future?*
> Life itself. . . . Life is getting difficult, it's getting rough. It's not getting easier in this day and age that I'm living in. Everything is getting worse. . . . I hope to finish grad school. That's what I want. 'Cause if I don't finish grad school then I didn't really accomplish anything. That's the way I feel. I wouldn't have accomplished what I wanted to accomplish. . . . I wouldn't have reached my goal.

While Gayle has goals and is set on achieving them, her apprehensions about her future are also evident ("*maybe* getting a job . . . if I make it . . . if I don't drop out of school. . . life is getting difficult"). Gayle's uncertainty, however, may have been provoked by my own uncertainty about her future ("Do you think you'll actually be able to be a lawyer?"). On the other hand, I may have been responding to her own sense of doubt. As Gayle and Marie grow older and prepare to enter the adult world, they become increasingly wary of the obstacles, challenges, and troubles before and around them. Consequently, they seem to find it more difficult to maintain a positive stance. However, even though their positive attitude is deflated, it has not disappeared. Both Gayle and Marie suggest in their third-year interviews that thinking positively is still an integral part of their lives.

For Marie and Gayle, thinking positively means "seeing the positive side" to negative events, not denying (but possibly forgetting) negative possibilities, and not dwelling on one's problems. Sonia, a Puerto Rican adolescent, conveys a similar perspective: "I love my life. Even though, you know, there's always problems there, but you always have to go on. When you have problems, you try to fix them. If you don't, you just go on. Can't dwell on things for the rest of your life. I don't." In her article on racial identity formation among black adolescent girls, Janie Ward states that a coping strategy used by the girls she interviewed included not "dwelling on" events that challenge one's self-worth and value. "Thus when messages of white society say 'you can't,' the well-functioning black family and community stand ready to counter such messages with those that say, you can, we have, we will."[4] This strategy may be necessary for black adolescents as well as other adolescents who, because of their social standing, live under oppressive circumstances and find themselves immersed in a society of negative messages and "attitudes."

While Marie, Gayle, and Sonia's positive attitudes may be, in part, an adaptive inclination, it also has some troublesome aspects. "Thinking positively" seemed to encourage forgetting or denying the actual existence of obstacles and risks. In their attempts to be positive, adolescents may mute their anger or rage. Such silence, in turn, inevitably leaves intact the very relationship, system, or social structure that produced their worries and anger. Sonia says, in fact, that her desire to see the "good side" has led her to deny "real" problems:

I have this tendency that—if I see a hole in the wall, I want to cover it up. No matter how big—how big the hole is, I want to cover it up. And there's always cracks in the hole that keep getting bigger and bigger and bigger. And the wall would just tumble down. No, I never wanted to see that way.

In her relationship with her boyfriend at the time, Sonia was so determined to see only its positive elements that she found herself overlooking his mistreatment of her: "I [saw] a hole and I want[ed] to cover it up." Maintaining a positive attitude may be essential for coping. However, it may also discourage girls from protecting themselves.

Listening to Malcolm and Tyrone

Malcolm and Tyrone, like Marie and Gayle, intersperse their discussions of death and violence with discussions of optimism and hopes about their own futures. Unlike Marie and Gayle who spoke continuously about having a positive outlook, however, Malcolm and Tyrone's "positive attitude" was evident primarily when they spoke about their futures.

Malcolm

Malcolm tells Mike in his freshman year that with his rap music he tries to deliver "positive messages"—those messages which convey the importance of working hard and not looking "back too much 'cause you done wrong then. Just look forward to what you can do now." "Thinking positively," for Malcolm, is about having hope and not lingering over the past. About the future, he says: "I'm just gonna go in school as long as I can, just keep thinking positive." However, he also points out that he spends a lot of time worrying about the effects his own death would have on his mother. He says, "I don't think it all ahead. I just take it one day at a time. Right now, I'm taking the present." Like Marie and Gayle, Malcolm blends optimistic, more future-oriented statements with cautious, more present-oriented thoughts.

In Malcolm's sophomore year, when Mike asks him about his future, he says once again that he takes "one day at a time":

> Because I don't ever know what might pop up, you know. Therefore, I don't try thinking too far ahead 'cause the way things are today. I don't try to think too negative, but you gotta think in the right perspective where you're at, you know, where you're living. You know a lot of people getting killed, especially innocent people, for no reason. You gotta think like, "Well, I could be one of those people so why should I sit here and just wait for this to happen." Make a name for yourself while you're here. So, therefore, people can remember you for not being lazy, drinking beer all the time. They could think that you were trying to do for yourself, trying to make a name, trying to get out.

Malcolm's wish to "take one day at a time" stems from his concern about bad things happening in the future ("because you never know what is going to pop up"). He explains, however, that being realistic does not mean being hopeless or "negative." In fact, being realistic motivates him, as it did Marie, to succeed. Malcolm's awareness of death induces him to pursue his goals. Another student, Shawn, reiterates this belief:

> I think of my future as, for now, being a bright one 'cause I have so many av-
> enues that I can do. I want to take up music. I like to sing and stuff. I like
> to play basketball. I'm very smart so I know what, wherever I'm going I'm
> gonna excel in the classroom. I know that definitely.
> *What do you fear most about the future?*
> <u>Whether there's really gonna be one.</u>
> *What do you mean?*
> <u>'Cause, I mean, there</u>'s so many things happening out here. And I mean, even
> though you don't feel like your life should be taken today, somebody
> might think your life should be taken and bullets have no names. And the
> area, the high crime area that I live in. . . . And there's nothing you can re-
> ally do about it but sit back and see if the fools gonna either kill each other
> off, understand that it's senseless and stop. But until then you're gonna see
> numerous accounts of people who are dying and stuff. And I don't want to
> be one of those people. I have a lot to do in life. I have a lot of plans to do
> in life. I personally, I like life.

Just like Malcolm and Marie, the possibility of an early death enhances Shawn's desire to pursue his goals. Shawn, Malcolm, and Marie assert a belief, theorized in existentialist philosophy, that a knowledge of death allows for the articulation of plans for the future or throws them into relief.[5] However, for Shawn, Malcolm, and Marie, unlike for most existentialist philosophers, death is not an abstract concept in the future, it is an immediate threat that haunts their everyday lives. While these students appear to hold two contradictory beliefs, they reveal in their interviews that their beliefs are not contradictory at all—the presence of one (the awareness of death) strengthens the other (a positive attitude).

Malcolm says during his sophomore-year interview that he tries not to think of the things that could get in the way of doing what he wants to do in the future. "If there is, I just try to walk around it or through it or whatever." When asked what makes his life worth living, he says:

> Just the fact that I feel I know I can make it. That I have the strength and the whatever it takes to succeed. Really, that's really what makes me feel like, "Yeah, my life is worth living." 'Cause if I was doing bad in school and I felt there was nothing I could do about it, I feel that there would be nothing else really going for me. You know, I would probably be drinking more, whatever.

Malcolm's optimism stems, in part, from his confidence in his abilities. Jerome, in his senior year, says: "It makes me feel positive because there's things I know I can do. I know I can cut hair, I know I can draw." Knowing how to do things and that one has "the strength . . . it takes to succeed" makes it easier for them to feel "positive" about their futures.

In his junior year, Malcolm tells me about the impending death of his sister (already mentioned in chapter 3) and his hopes for his own future. With death even closer than before, Malcolm's positive attitude persists. He "really wants to make something of [himself]" so that he can help his mother, particularly since his sister will not be there to help. When asked this year about what makes his life worth living, he says: "Because I'm doing well in school. You know, there's so much positive coming out of what I've been doing. That makes me feel good. . . . To be alive and stuff to be around and to show the others." His school performance plays a large role in his outlook just as it did in the previous year. It allows him to appreciate his life and foresee a "positive future."

Tyrone

While Tyrone shares the optimism of the others, his life circumstances suggest fewer reasons for such optimism. Tyrone has been held back in school and was arrested for theft just before he entered high school. In his freshman year, he says he lives by the motto: "I only live once and in this lifetime it's best to have all the fun you can 'cause you never know in this moment when you'll go. So you live each day to the fullest." Tyrone's appreciation of his life is heightened by his knowledge of its tenuousness.

In addition, he believes that his positive outlook will lead to positive outcomes:

When you think about the future, what do you think of?
The best. I think—I strongly believe that if you think positive, you will
achieve. So there's no doubt in my mind that I'm gonna—I'm gonna ac-
celerate to the top and when I grow up, I want to be somebody, a role
model. I want to have people looking at me and going, "There's someone
I want to be like or listen to him 'cause he knows."

For Tyrone, "thinking positively" is a strategy to "make things happen."
Although he speaks about being held back in school and of being arrested, these topics are absent from his discussions of his future. He
may not see or may not want to see these events as relevant to his future.

In his interview during the following year (he is still a freshman), Tyrone speaks about the many losses he has experienced lately. His younger
sister and his cousin have recently passed away: "I learn to take it. I learn
to take it and keep going." He emphasizes his ability not to linger on his
losses. "I just realized it's the harsh reality of life, and there's nothing you
can really do about it. You just gotta deal with it." Moments after this discussion, Tyrone says:

Well I feel that I'm going somewhere in life instead of going nowhere.
When you think of the future, what do you think of?
Better days, I can see better days.
What do you see happening in the future?
Me going on with life and going to be somebody. Making good money and
having a house and hopefully having kids.
How do you feel when you think about the future?
Happy, 'cause I know deep down I can achieve what I really want.
What are your—do you have any fears about the future?
No, 'cause I don't know what it holds so I really can't be scared of it.
You don't know what it holds, but you have hopes for it?
I have hopes for it. I have great hopes. A lot of hopes.
*Is there anything that you can let yourself think about that might be a frighten-
ing thing that you wouldn't want to have happen in the future?*
I don't really know. I don't look at my future as being dull or boring that it
would come back on me, and things wouldn't happen as good as I hoped,
but I just don't know.

Resisting my leading question, Tyrone wants to be optimistic. In contrast to his peers, however, he seems to refrain from discussing his fears for the future (although he implies that boredom is a frightening prospect for him). In light of his recent arrest and his performance in school, the content of his fears may feel too close to his lived reality for him to discuss them with ease. Along with his belief that "thinking positively" will have positive consequences, he may also believe that thinking "negatively" will lead to negative outcomes.

Tyrone insists in his third-year interview that he will be "one of the few black males that will make it" in the world. "Instead, when they'll be like 50 percent is here, 60 percent is there, they will be like that 10 percent [who succeeds], I'll know that'll be me." Tyrone's intense determination not to "be a statistic," when in fact his school performance is already "a statistic," suggests a preoccupation with the possibility of meeting the same fate as some of his male peers (although far fewer than 50 to 60 percent). His overt optimism may be an effort to contain this potentially debilitating fear.

Reflections

Listening to Marie, Gayle, Malcolm, Shawn, and Tyrone, surprising patterns emerge concerning how they perceive their lives and their futures. While adolescents have typically been described as either "hopeless" or "optimistic" about the future,[6] the teenagers in this study suggest the possibility of holding multiple and seemingly contradictory perspectives.[7] They state that they will achieve their goals if they work hard, and, in the same breath, discuss the violence and death they experience in their current lives and which they fear in the future. They believe they will accomplish their goals but that their lives are constantly at risk. They believe that if they work hard enough—if they try and "really want" something—they will succeed in their pursuits. Like "the Brothers" in Jay MacLeod's[8] study of urban adolescent boys and the working-class youth in Victoria Steinitz and Ellen Solomon's study,[9] the teens in the present study believe in the "American Dream." At the same time, they also believe in an unpredictable and uncontrollable future and are acutely aware of the pain, loss, and danger in their own lives and in the lives of those in their communities. They emphasize the importance of having a "positive attitude" and speak about the death and violence in their communities and the possibilities of "all of a sudden" becoming a drug dealer or a school dropout. These adolescents have great hopes for themselves and are deeply concerned with what the future may bring.

The adolescents in the study suggest a split consciousness about their current lives and their future prospects. The feminist philosopher Sandra Harding[10] has asserted that women typically have a "split consciousness"[11] in their understanding and analyses of the world because they view the world from the inside, as participants and agents, as well as from the margins to which they are socially and economically confined. The girls and boys in this study evince a similar "split consciousness" in their discussions of the possibilities of an early death in the midst of their optimistic discussions about their futures. These students apprehend their complex experiences and invent ways to thrive in response to their realistic views of the world. They speak from the margins about the brutal reality in their communities—a reality that they feel is out of their control. They also speak about hope from the inside. In fact, they tell us that their marginal status compels them to maintain this "positive" insider view. These teenagers are inspired to act because they know that their lives may end prematurely or that "things can just happen." The hope and fear detected in their interviews are not contradictory at all. They are weaving together their life experiences and their future dreams and creating strategies for everyday living.

As noted previously, while these positive attitudes may have beneficial effects, they also reflect an individualistic approach that has the potential to silence "negative" feelings and lead individuals away from collective action when such action is needed. Jennifer Pastor and her colleagues note in their studies with urban girls of color that such individualistic strategies are common: "Yet, individualistic strategies cannot change the ongoing oppression of surveillance sanctioned by police and the state, nor can it transcend harassment from men, misogyny from (and toward) other woman, or low expectations from teachers."[12] The individualistic strategies of positive thinking and being responsible for their own fate, as articulated by Marie, Gayle, and Sonia, enhance these teens' hopes for their futures while decreasing their awareness of their commonalities with others in their communities.[13] Positive thinking helps them cope and dream and also silences them and leaves them alone to work on "their attitude."

The adolescents, as revealed in this chapter, actively engage and struggle with creating values, messages, and beliefs that will help them flourish. With a "positive attitude," the adolescents believe they can plan, hope, and dream for their futures in the midst of "all the bad things." Not finding, perhaps, a collective call for action,[14] these teenagers focus on themselves as their route to fulfillment and success. For them, the "American Dream" is shot through with experiences of an unforgiving reality. Yet they are working hard (on themselves) allowing neither this mythic and powerful "dream" nor an equally powerful but all too tangible reality to gain the upper hand.

8

"Slacking Up" in School

How do you feel about how you do in school?
I'm lazy. I mean, the work's not hard, but I'm lazy and don't do my
   work.
Why do you think you're lazy?
Slacking up, I guess . . . last year I used to always get B's, nothing less
   than a B. I'm just slacking up this year. I'm just tired. You burn out
   usually this time of year anyway.
Yeah. What are other reasons you think you're burning out?
I dunno. I'm just lazy, I guess. It's not hard. I'm just lazy. Just don't
   want to do anything. . . . So, long as I pass, I'm satisfied.
Do you think if you really tried you could do well?
I probably do well next year. You know I have to. But now, I'm just
   lazy. I just, I'm not really serious about school . . . I just do work
   just to pass.   —Christine

CHRISTINE, a sophomore enrolled in all advanced-level classes,
states in this passage that her "laziness" is to blame for her lower grades
this year. Milagro, who is not doing as well in high school as she did in
middle school, also attributes her poor grades to her "laziness . . . it has

nothing to do with the school itself." In fact, most of the students in the study blamed themselves for their academic struggles. When speaking about their school performance, they rarely spoke about the quality of their education, their teachers, the school administrators, their families, or their peers. They spoke almost exclusively about themselves. While this focus on the self may not seem particularly remarkable, it attains significance when placed in the context of the actual school they attend. As described earlier, their school—an underfunded, police-monitored high school that houses almost twice as many students as it has room for—is not a place in which learning can easily take place. Yet the students in the present study, like the urban poor and working-class youth in other research studies,[1] blame themselves for their academic performances. No matter how much we pushed them to tell us why they were not doing as well as they wanted in school, they insisted that the problem lay with their own "laziness" and weaknesses. At times, "laziness" was viewed as a seemingly permanent "trait"—something that could not be changed—and at other times as a variable and fluctuating condition. Laziness and self-blame, however, were consistently and repeatedly the bottom line.

Taking Full Blame

The students who specifically stated that they were "lazy" included both those who excelled in school and those who were not doing well academically. Malcolm, who does well in school, speaks about his "laziness" in a way almost identical to Chantel, who typically receives C's and D's. As we heard in his case study, Malcolm, who recently held numerous jobs to help his mother pay the rent, explains: "I'm gonna tell you straight, I'm lazy. 'Cause I don't really like to work." During this freshman interview, Malcolm adds that he wants to get better grades in his classes so he will be able to "impress" potential employers but sees his "laziness" as an obstacle. In his sophomore year, Malcolm says:

> You know I haven't been doing as well as I want to because I do get lazy
>   sometimes and I be like, "Oh, I do this tomorrow, I do that tomorrow."
> *I hear you saying like you wanna write, get into shape, do well in school?*
> Yeah, I want to, you see. I'm more lazy, it's all in my mind. 'Cause I know I
>   could do it. But see, I'm like kind of lazy 'cause I be like I don't

progress that fast. Then when I think about it in my head, I'm like, "Damn," you know, "Let's get out there. Let's start doing it." I always try to put things off a day later and stuff, and the next thing you know it's the next month.

Like Christine, Malcolm does not perceive his "laziness" as a permanent trait but rather as a changeable quality within himself ("It's all in my mind. 'Cause I know I could do it"). While this stance may inhibit or prevent feelings of hopelessness for Malcolm,[2] the fluid quality of his "laziness" is precisely what frustrates him. He believes he *could* change but has difficulty changing.

When Mike mentions that he saw Malcolm's name on the honorable mention list, Malcolm says with pride that he received a medal for being on this list. He then immediately adds that the reason he is only on the honorable mention list and not the honor roll is that he is getting a C in math. Malcolm acknowledges his success but, at the same moment, and as we have already seen in his case study, is sharply critical of himself: "I try to listen when I'm in class and think about certain things. 'Cause I do get lazy when it comes to like reading the whole section like I said, I do [homework] while I'm at school. I'll say I'll do it at home, then when I get home, I just get lazy. It's just that I gotta get out of this lazy mood."

In his junior year, Malcolm says proudly to me that he has been on the honor roll all year. When describing himself, however, Malcolm says: "I'm determined but I feel that I lack—I do have self-discipline, but only so much. It doesn't push me far enough." Although he does not use the term "lazy" this year, Malcolm continues to state that he is not satisfied with the amount of effort he puts into his daily activities. When speaking about school, he focuses primarily on what he should be doing that he is not doing, or what he should not be doing that he is doing. During these discussions of his school performance, he never mentions unfair teachers, chaotic classes, difficult or easy homework assignments, bad or good schools, friends distracting him, or overly strict or lenient parents. Malcolm only speaks about himself.

When Tyrone explains to Helena why he has to repeat his freshman year, he says: "I don't really regret nothing I did . . . it happened 'cause of me. I can't blame [being held back] 'cause of someone else, it happened 'cause of me. So since it happened 'cause of me, I shouldn't have no regrets. I shouldn't feel sorry. If you do the crime, you do the time. So you just gotta do what you gotta do." Eva says: "I should be getting A's but I play around a lot." Gabriela states: "I don't know what I'm doing so I would say just forget it and don't do it." Tyiesha tells me she doesn't "try hard enough." Marie says: "I have to get my mind more focused on school." Jamal and Marvin say their grades have to do with their "laziness." Guillermo says his low grades have to do with his "attitude." "Teachers always say it's not their fault they gave us an F or something. It's probably my attitude." This repeated self-blame is troubling for me. I expect the students to discuss the abject conditions of their school, the overcrowded classrooms, the lack of ventilation that makes breathing difficult, the burned-out and uninspired teachers, administrators, and students, the gun-toting students, the mutual abuse by students and teachers. I want them to acknowledge the "external"[3] factors that must affect their ability to focus and to achieve in this school. While "internal" factors certainly play a role, there is no doubt that their achievement is also profoundly affected by the numerous negative aspects of their school. Focusing on their own weaknesses, however, may feel like a more effective strategy for improving their school grades than focusing on "external" or institutional factors that they may feel powerless to change.

Samuel, another African American student who does well in school, claims to be "lazy" and says his lack of A grades is the result. As I interview him in his sophomore year, I cannot help but ask him leading questions concerning the cause of his school performance:

How do you feel about how you do in school?
I do all right. I feel okay about it.
So, like, do you think you could do better?
Oh, yeah, I could, I could do *much* better. Yeah.
How come you don't do better than you do?
Well, like my coach tells me, I'm lazy. You know. I guess that's the main
   thing. I'm lazy, yeah.
And you believe him?
Yeah. Yeah, I am lazy. Yeah. [Laughs.]
Why do you think you're lazy?
I dunno. I just don't feel like doing things and I don't do them.

But do you think that it all has to do with you being lazy or do you think that part of the reason may be with the classes or with the teachers or anything like that?

No, it's basically me being lazy. Yeah, yeah.

Even with my encouragement to extend his critique beyond himself, Samuel does not budge. He firmly states, in accordance with his coach, that the responsibility for his struggles in school lies solely within himself.

In his junior year, I ask Samuel once again how he is doing in school, and he answers:

I'm doing good. . . .
What kind of grades did you get this year?
I got B's, I got an A, yeah, mostly B's. . . .
How do you feel about your grades?
Pretty good. I could've done better.
Have your grades changed from last year?
Oh yeah, they're better than last year.
And could you do even better?
Oh yeah, I could do better. . . .
Why do you think that you're not doing better?
I'm a little lazy, you know. And I—I had like fun in my class. I play around a
     lot. That's me. I don't even do reading. . . . Yeah, I do homework in
     school.
What does "lazy" mean to you?
Well, I just don't do a thing I'm supposed to do when I'm supposed to do
     them. I just put them off. I just like forget it. I'll do it later. I believe I can
     change my work ethics really in time. And I plan to change them, you
     know, next year. But it's just that this year, that's how things are.

Like Malcolm, Samuel believes not only that he is a "little lazy" but also that his "laziness" is within his power to change. Samuel, however, does not seem bothered by his "laziness." His belief in the mutability of his lazy behavior appears to provide him with a sense of security that he can and will change.

In his senior year, Samuel begins to offer another perspective:

I mean, how did you do in school this year?
I did well. This is my best year. Yeah, when I really needed to do good.
Are you on the honor roll?
Yeah.
That's excellent.
Like three times.
Three semesters?
Yeah. Well I had no other choices this year. I want to get into a college.
  School was fine, it wasn't hard or anything.
You don't think it was hard to get on the honor roll?
No, it wasn't hard at all.
Do you think the teachers challenged you?
No, not at all, it was very soft. They're not pushing us at all. I mean that's
  how I see it. That's partly the reason why I did bad [in previous years]
  'cause it was so easy. I just didn't even do it. I was like, yeah, I would just
  turn it in at the end of the year and do well on the finals and pass for the
  year. That's what I basically did.

Samuel's belief that it's not "hard" to get on the honor roll may be shared by other honor roll students who maintain that they are "lazy" in school. The perceived lack of academic challenge may lead them to believe that being on the honor roll, or any academic achievement for that matter, is not evidence of hard work or of *not* being "lazy." In his discussion of un-demanding teachers, Samuel begins to provide more of an "external" as-sessment of his school performance. He suggests that his "laziness" was, in part, a *reaction* to an academic situation and not only the *reason* for his academic struggles. His "laziness" was a response to an unchallenging cur-riculum ("it was so easy") that, in turn, caused him to neglect the work that was required. Samuel implicitly challenges how the other interviewers and I had conceptualized "laziness." Once an adolescent stated that "lazi-ness" was the reason for his or her grades, we assumed such a response needed no further explanations. We typically did not ask them why they were lazy (although we did ask them about other factors that may influ-ence their grades). Samuel reminded us, however, that "laziness" is not a personality trait, but often a response to a frustrating "external" situation.

Unfortunately, the importance of understanding the reasons for laziness became evident to us only during the end of the third-year interviews. Had the teens been encouraged to explain why they were lazy during each of their interviews, they might have extended their analyses of their school performances to include factors other than themselves.

Chantel repeats some of the themes suggested by Samuel, Malcolm, and Christine. She does not, however, do as well in school as they do. In her freshman year, I ask Chantel:

How would you describe yourself as a student in school?
Lazy. I don't have problems. It's just that, I dunno, sometimes I just don't feel like doing work, so I just don't do it. But in my head I'm like, "What are you doing? You know you're smart." In English I got an F because of homework. That's my main problem. When I go home I just want to go to sleep because I'm so tired all the time. And I just get lazy. I turn on the TV and everything.
What grades do you usually get?
A's and B's usually and a couple—maybe one or two C's.

In her sophomore year I return to the topic with the following question:

How are you doing in school this year?
Hmmm. Well, I'm doing pretty good in all of my classes except Algebra, I mean, I just wasn't doing my homework.
How do you feel about your grades in general?
They can be better, 'cause it's like I'm just lazy, that's my problem. I don't like to do homework and stuff like that, so that like messes me up, because of it. I was in elementary school and when I was in middle school, I was on honor roll straight through. Got into high school last year, and I was like—I was close to honor roll, but I had like one D or something like that and then, I just never got on the honor roll, 'cause I kept getting D's, just like barely passing, 'cause I was being lazy.

In her junior year, Chantel tells me how she is doing in school:

Well [laugh], I'm doing better than I was doing last year. . . . I'm not doing as good as I can be doing. I don't know why, I'm just lazy. It's like I'm real smart when I'm in school, I know what I'm doing. But it's like bringing home the homework. When it comes to homework, I don't wanna—it's like, when I'm in school, I deal with school, when I'm home I don't wanna deal with school. It's like hard for me to, like, I don't know—my mother—I think it's really 'cause I'm lazy, because some days I can do my homework. . . . Soon as I got to high school, I was like, "Whoop, time to be lazy," which is the worst to be lazy, you know.

Given Chantel's description of her laziness, I am tempted to interpret her "lazy" behavior as simply the product of not liking to do homework. It becomes increasingly apparent, however, that Chantel's laziness has been due, at least in part, to relational difficulties:

And this is my junior year and I'm like, "You gotta straighten up, you gotta straighten up." . . . So I was like, I got here and when I first started off [in my freshman year], I was okay, but then I just started, like I don't know. Soon things like my father, like when I started having problems. I let other things get in front of school. And I didn't—I didn't care anymore. 'Cause I know I was coming to school for a while and doing no work, I just sat there and was like I didn't want to deal with nothing. When I was having problems with my father, and then I had broke up with my boyfriend. I didn't care, I didn't want to do nothing. . . . Didn't do homework, didn't even do the work in class. And I was getting bad grades. . . . Last term was my worst term, 'cause that's the term I was like, "I don't care." I just didn't care anymore, I just came to school and like "shh." And I was like, "Get yourself together, do your work."

While her discussion of school during her junior year eventually moves to a recognition that her "I don't care" or lazy attitude may be linked to her interpersonal problems, she provides an entirely different story (like Samuel) when asked directly about the reasons for her laziness in school:

Some classes are interesting, some classes are boring. And it's the interesting classes that, you know, it—it has a lot to do with—everytime I say it has a lot to do with teachers, my mother will be like, "No, it doesn't. It has to do with you kids. You got a bad teacher, who cares if the teacher's boring, you're still supposed to learn," which I agree with. But I'm the type of person, I need to be motivated. Because if I go into a class and she's going, "wa wa wa wa," I'm not going to be motivated.

Stemming, perhaps, from her mother's dismissive attitude, Chantel initially struggles to tell me that she sees her performance in school affected by the quality of her classes. Seeing and hearing that I do not have the same reaction as her mother and sensing that I want to hear more about her thoughts concerning her teachers, Chantel speaks of those teachers who have made a difference in her school performance:

> He's the best teacher, I mean, I was doing so good in his class. I was doing good, getting A's in his class . . . until we got a substitute. Now I got a C in his class, you know what I'm saying? It's like, almost like the teacher counts . . . all we do is worksheets . . . he's not really doing anything but going over worksheets with us.

Chantel's examples of how teachers "count," told only *after* she was asked repeatedly to explain her laziness, suggest that other students who claimed to be "lazy" may have told their interviewers only part of what they knew, felt, or experienced. They may have shared Chantel's experience of being challenged by parents when they criticized their educational setting, and learned that when speaking to adults, it is best not to reveal such controversial thoughts. This situation, however, was clearly not the case for those students who firmly resisted overt prompts by their interviewers to broaden their internal analyses. Like Samuel in his sophomore year, Jamal flatly denies that his lack of motivation has anything to do with the quality of his education: "I'm just lazy."

Following her brief discussion of her teachers in her junior year, Chantel flips back into her self-critical stance:

> The thing is, the work that I'm getting is not hard. I mean, I could pass it like that, like it's nothing. But it's me. It's like, I sit there and I think, in a way in the back of my mind, I know I could do this. So I don't really try, try. I don't really know why I act like that, but it's like if I'm bored, I just sit there and I'll look. And I'll just sit there and sit there, won't do the work, and I'll start falling behind.

Chantel claims both to understand and not understand why she "acts this way" ("I don't really know why I act like that, but it's like if I'm bored, I just sit there"). Like Samuel, she implies that she is not inspired in her classes and is, therefore, unmotivated to complete the work. At the same time, though, she believes that the problem lies primarily within herself ("but it's me").

Sonia, who struggles in school, also suggests this pattern in her freshman year:

> I'm doing okay. I'm trying to—well, this last quarter, I'm trying to do better. 'Cause you know if I don't do better, I have to go to summer school.
>
> *I mean, how would you describe yourself as a student?*
>
> I'm all right. I'm not that good. I'm okay.
>
> *Why don't you think you're better?*
>
> I'm lazy. I just—I dunno—I mean, I know that I should be a better student because you know you have to pay when you don't do things the right way. You pay later on.

Repeating a well-established belief ("you pay later on"), Sonia is certain of the consequences of her laziness. She believes firmly that there is no need to look farther than her laziness to understand her school performance.

When she is asked how she is doing in school in her sophomore year, Sonia says:

> I'm doing pretty okay. I should be doing better this time. I had the baddest— I had a D in math. . . . My attendance messed me up. I got lazy. So I had like an F in dance.
>
> *In dance, and then how about the other classes?*
>
> I got B's and an A.
>
> *Why do you think you got a D in math?*
>
> 'Cause there were certain things in there that I really didn't understand.
>
> *Why do you think you don't do as well as you'd like to?*
>
> Sometimes I get just so lazy. I don't like to study. I hate studying. But now, it's like I'm studying more. . . . 'Cause, you know, I'm just tired of getting bad grades. I mean the one thing I'm doing bad in is math. I could, if I really try, I could really, you know, do things, understand things. But I guess, I'm—I'm the lazy type of person. I'm just like—I hate studying, doing homework. I don't have a problem as long as it's not hard, you know?

While Sonia provides a reason for her laziness (she doesn't understand the material) during this sophomore-year interview, her reason is once again focused on herself. Sonia seems unsure about whether her "laziness" is fluid and changeable or static and permanent ("I *got* lazy . . . *sometimes* I get just so lazy . . . I'm the lazy *type* of person" [emphasis added]). Unlike her peers, her uncertainty about the quality of her laziness seems to translate into feelings of hopelessness. She admits, in this interview, that she has thought about leaving school because she gets "so frustrated" with herself.

In her junior year, Sonia discusses her laziness and her struggle with the material in her math class: "Math is just killing me." She begins to indicate, however, that her laziness stems from external factors as well as her own lack of understanding of the material. Yet it takes some insistent questioning on my part for Sonia to elaborate on such detail. It is clear when one listens to audiotapes of me asking the adolescents about their school performance during the third-year interviews that I was determined to have them provide a critique of the school:

> *I mean, you know, it's interesting because I think every year I've interviewed you, you talked a little bit about how you're feeling like you're lazy and I'm just wondering—because I don't see you as a very lazy person. I mean, I see you having just a lot of energy. And I'm just wondering why particularly around school do you feel lazy? Why is that?*
>
> I don't know
>
> *What do you think?*
>
> I don't know. Because of all—it gets boring sometimes [laughs]—I don't know, you know? And so, I get like, you know, I fall asleep in class sometimes. So like when I get out of school, I'm energetic, you know.
>
> *Yeah, I see you as very energetic.*
>
> Yeah, that's because this—this—this building is so closed in, you know. There's no like air coming in. It's like it drags people down or something . . . [my grades] they've gone down a little more. . . . The problem was in the first term, I was working every night til ten o'clock [at a local pharmacy]. So I would come home so tired that I wouldn't even think about homework. I would just go to sleep, then wake up, then go to school. And then, I was still tired because—you know, every day three to ten o'clock I was working like 35 hours a week sometimes. . . . So finally I just don't do it anymore.
>
> *So, do you still work?*

> On the weekends I do pharmacy [15 hours per week] and during the week I
> work at the junior high as a peer counselor [ten hours per week].

At the very moment when she says she does not know why she is "lazy,"
Sonia tells me precisely why. Like Chantel and Samuel in their third-year
interviews, Sonia explains her "laziness," after much probing and pushing,
by describing external factors—work and the school environment—that
keep her from concentrating in school. Once again, the importance of understanding "laziness" as both a cause of poor performance and as a reaction to internal and external conditions is underscored. Had I not insis-
tently asked Sonia to explain her laziness in school, however, I might not
have heard her institutional critique and her account of her overburdened
work schedule. Prior to my leading questions, she made no mention of her
school or her work schedule. Without the establishment of a safe relationship in which open critique is encouraged, Sonia and her peers may not be
able to overcome the cultural imperative of individual responsibility to express their outrage and frustration with inadequate institutions and demanding work obligations.

Balancing Perspectives

While most students focused primarily on themselves when discussing
their school performance, a few consistently implicated—without the interviewer's encouragement—themselves *and* others. Felicia says:

> I like school, I like being around a lot of people.
> *What do you think about the work?*
> Some of it's all right but then I hate like when the teacher be talking about
>   something and I don't understand it and they try to explain and I still don't
>   understand it. And everybody be like, "Oh. Oh, that's how you do it?" and
>   I'm still sitting there, like, "How do you do it?" and they still be explaining.
> *So you feel like the teachers don't give you enough attention to explain stuff to you*
>   *or—*
> No, it's not that. It's just sometimes they don't explain it clear enough for *me*.
>   And everybody else catches on.
> *So what is that like for you?*
> It's hard.

Without prompting, Felicia suggests that both she and her teacher are the reasons for her struggles (*"they* don't explain it clear enough for *me"*). Strikingly, a willingness to provide such critiques were particularly evident among those who dropped out of school during the study. These students seemed to know that the institution they attended was not providing them with the tools and the support they needed to succeed. Understanding these limitations, as other researchers have noted about urban dropouts,[4] may lead these students to despair about their future educational possibilities.

Alfredo and Mary, both of whom had dropped out by their third-year interview, intersperse their discussions of their school performances with comments about their own and their school's shortcomings. In Alfredo's freshman year, I ask him how he is doing in school:

> I was doing bad, and I knew I was doing bad, but I just felt like I couldn't start over, because I started the school year in another high school. Then they transferred me here, so they gave me incomplete grades and I was like, "Geez, what is going on? Where are my grades?" . . . So that messed me up in school so I was like it was too late to start over [at his new school]. I couldn't pick up on the things they were doing because they started already over here.
>
> *Do you think there were other reasons why you don't do better than you'd like?*
> It has to do with that [the transfer], and it has to do with myself. You know, I have to put my mind on things you know, I just like to have fun sometimes.
>
> *Why don't you think you try harder?*
> I feel like if I try real hard, because when I do try hard, it puts a lot of pressure on me and I get angry. I don't like the teachers and I start thinking, "I don't have to do this if I don't want to." I know it's going to be more frustration [when I try hard].

Alfredo, without much probing, tells me the reasons for his poor performance in school. He understands it as an interplay between what has happened to him (the transfer), his teachers, his own personal struggles (not to put too much pressure on himself), and his desire to have fun.

In his second-year interview, Alfredo tells me he is doing terribly in school:

So what is that about?

I could do my work. And when I do it, it's always—I always get a good grade for it. It's like when I'm in school, I don't know, me and [my friend] starts talking to me. You know, I'm ready to talk and start laughing.

So then you don't pay attention? Do you think your classes are interesting?

Some of them are. But some of them are boring. You go to the same class everyday and you just do the same type of work every day. Like biology, I like [this] class. She's about the only one I like. And last year I had the same problem. The only class I liked last year was science. . . . We used to do different things every day . . . but like classes like Reading, you go inside, read a story with the same person every day. That's boring.

That's boring? So will you just not show up?

No, I'll go but I won't do nothing sometimes.

Moving back and forth between seeing his own, his friend's, and his teacher's role in his "terrible" performance, Alfredo offers a well-rounded understanding of the dynamics of his academic achievement and the problems that beset him.

By his third-year interview, Alfredo has dropped out of school:

I think school . . . wasn't for me [laughs]. 'Cause like I would start good in the beginning of the year . . . and like the rest of the year I would start going down gradually. It was like—it was always like that with me. 'Cause I was in [an alternative school affiliated with the school in which the study took place]. You know I just used to chill out there all day 'cause you know nobody didn't force you to do anything. They give you so much freedom that if anything happened, you have to blame yourself. So that's what happened in my case. I was like school is not for me. . . . One day I stopped going.

Why weren't you doing well?

Just couldn't pull myself to focus on school work. I mean, they would hand out an assignment and want it done like on a Friday. And I couldn't get it done so it like would make me feel like oh, tsk, just pressured. . . . I wasn't using my smartness for things that I liked to do. I didn't like, you know, having an assignment and just sitting in class writing about whatever, whatever so forth. . . . And there just some people that have strong, you know, more willpower than others and I guess I'm not one of those people. I have willpower for certain things but it wasn't for school. There wasn't really nothing that captured my interest.

Unlike his earlier interviews, Alfredo puts blame primarily on himself in this interview for not doing well in school. His perspective, however, appears to be partially attributable to the attitude within his new school ("they gave you so much freedom that if anything happened you have to blame yourself"). Notably, the unstructured nature of the school exacerbated his self-criticism. Alfredo speaks of feeling pressured, uninterested, and having little willpower for school. When asked directly, however, about school-related factors that may have influenced his decision to leave, he presents a critique of his school:

Like, do you think it had to do with the teachers? It had to do with the subjects that you were being taught? What do you think?
—[Interrupt.] I think it had to do with all. It had to do with all of that. The subjects, the teachers, the everything. Everything that had to do with school. Having those assignments due every week. And I don't know. . . . The school—it was bad. Especially in that school I felt like a guinea pig. 'Cause it's like it's a new school first of all . . . they do all kinds of weird things they don't do here [at his old school in which the interview was taking place]. . . . No, the teachers were good, but I don't know. We had—I was tired of hearing the same things every year, in every grade. "You're so smart, why are you not doing good?" and it seems like that was a routine for all teachers. I was getting tired of them saying that all the times. I felt it got to me in two ways. In one way I was like, "Damn, I'm smart. Why am I not doing good?" And it got to me in another way that I was like, "Why they keep telling me this? I already know." I started thinking too much . . . getting stressed out.

Although Alfredo continues to suggest that his decision to leave had to do with his own internal struggles, he also perceives the school itself as a part of the problem. In the end, however, he seems particularly angry with himself for believing the praise of his teachers yet continuing not to do well.

Mary, while discussing her decision to drop out after her junior year, provides a balanced critique of both the institution and herself:

Tell me about why you felt you couldn't stay in school?
I don't know, I don't know. These public schools are filled with violence and things. You know, people getting shot in the next classroom. It is not an environment for learning, you know what I mean. I just wasn't gonna risk my life to go to school. To me it wasn't that important.

What do you think about the actual education, putting aside the violence, what did you think about the actual school?
In these public schools? Well, by the time they got the rowdy class to sit down, the period was over.

You just felt like it was pointless?
Yeah. I was like going to school to take your life in hand, to sit there and have them try to get the class together and once they did, it was time to leave. It was just like, this is wasting my time as well as the teacher's. . . . There was another thing—I knew a lot of people in this school, I had a lot of friends. I had friends who would just bring you down, I'll tell you that much. . . . You know it would be like, "Oh, well, we can cut this class today. We can always make it up tomorrow." But there's always—there's never a tomorrow. . . . "We'll cut class today. We'll go to class tomorrow. We'll cut class the next day." It's endless and it's useless 'cause you're just wasting the teacher's time and your own.

Voicing a perspective about the school that I expected to hear among most of the students, Mary describes why she dropped out of school. Not only were her friends enticing her away from her classes but the larger context—the violence surrounding her—and the rowdiness of the classroom environment affected her ability to learn.

Reflections

As is clear from the stories discussed in this chapter, the teens in the study maintain mainstream cultural values about individual responsibility and effort. While some of the students were willing to extend their analyses of their school performance to include family, school, work, and peer-related factors—especially when they were encouraged to do so by their interviewers—many of the students were not. Instead, most of the adolescents unyieldingly maintained that their difficulties in school were primarily or exclusively due to their lack of effort, motivation, abilities, or understanding in school.

Some implied that their laziness was a fluid quality rather than a static personality trait, and this belief seemed to prevent feelings of hopelessness. They believed they could change their "lazy attitude" and achieve academic success. The few students who suggested that their laziness may be more permanent ("I'm just the lazy type of person") were more at risk for dropping out of school. Furthermore, some of the students reminded us, especially by their latter-year interviews, that laziness is not simply an explanation of behavior but may also be a reaction to internal and external conditions. These students challenged our implicit understanding of what it means to be "lazy."

Those few students who provided, without being prompted, an external analysis of their school performance spoke about problems with their teachers, administrators, family members, other students, and the school building itself. They also typically had the most difficulties in school. As other researchers have suggested, alienation from school may heighten students' sensitivity to the external factors that influence their learning process.[5]

While many of the findings in this study provoke, move, and sadden me, these particular findings regarding school performance and self-blame disturb me. My experiences of working in this high school for five years, of walking down dismal hallways to windowless classrooms, of eating the junk food available in the cavernous cafeteria, of observing dozens of classes where teaching rarely occurs (with, of course, some exceptions) made me wonder how anyone could stay motivated and focused in such an environment. Yet what I know and see in this school is not discussed, for the most part, by these adolescents.

During my time working and conducting research at this school, I have repeatedly seen teachers spend entire class periods having their students fill out worksheets rather than actively engaging with them about the class materials. I have heard about and seen teachers arrive fifteen or twenty minutes late to their fifty-minute classes and apologize because they were in the bathroom, they had a meeting, they had to talk to a student, or they had to move their car. Sometimes they did not even apologize. I have also seen students imitate such behavior and then proceed to ignore or openly challenge a teacher's reprimands. I have repeatedly seen students in the hallways yell at their friends in classrooms and ignore the teachers' attempts to stop them. I have watched teachers reading a book or a newspaper during class while the students slept, threw notes, or chatted among themselves. I have heard students and teachers yelling at each other, calling one another "animals," "fat slob," "slut," or "bitch" in the classroom or in the stairwells. A few teachers spoke to the students and to me about disliking the students, and about the school having been "much better" when the entire student body was made up of white boys during the 1960s (currently the student body is less than 10 percent white). Some of the teachers appeared to be "teaching down" to their students, lowering their expectations and, consequently, the academic achievement of their students. A fellow counselor at this school was shocked to sit in on an "advanced" math class for freshmen and listen to math lessons she remembers being covered in her elementary school. The low-level classes, however, are not always the result of low expectations. Students often enter this high school just barely able to read or write, let alone do advanced math.

During my time at this school, I also heard history teachers lecture to their predominantly African American and Latin American students about the inventor of SPAM while the students looked on with puzzled expressions, perhaps wondering, as Malcolm did, why the invention of canned ham is more important than a basic survey course in African American or Latin American history. Although there is a group of excellent teachers at this school who seem to inspire and motivate their students, the majority seem "burned out," discontented, and frustrated with their jobs. I witnessed some teachers—especially the new ones—put tremendous efforts into trying to create cohesive and supportive environments for their colleagues and students only to be met with hostile and resentful responses from the school administrators, teaching staff, and the students themselves. This school is clearly not an environment, as Mary says, in which learning easily takes place. This fact, however, was rarely noted by the students.

Given the strong emphasis on individual effort and responsibility in mainstream culture, the findings presented in this chapter, while troubling, are not surprising. Messages about individual effort and responsibility can be seen on the bulletin boards, blackboards, and other public spaces in and outside of this high school. These students have been taught through movies, television, school, and, perhaps, by their families to believe—and they do believe—that "with hard work and determination anyone can succeed" (the poster hanging in a guidance office). The corollary of this belief is, of course, that those who do not succeed have only themselves to blame. Not only are these students adhering to mainstream beliefs regarding the association between effort and success, they are also accepting the stereotypes of themselves that surround them—the stereotype of the "lazy inner-city teenager." These stereotypes are an integral part of their lives and, as Sonia suggested in the beginning of this book, have a profound impact on their sense of self. They resist these stereotypes, while at the same time they believe them.

What does it mean when students who attend such a dysfunctional school attribute their struggles in school to internal factors? What will it mean for them if they do not see that they are being asked to learn in an environment in which very few people could flourish and which most middle- and upper-class Americans never see, much less experience? Jay MacLeod, who detected a similar self-blaming tendency among the urban working-class boys he interviewed, notes that

> the achievement ideology [i.e., anyone can achieve with hard work and determination] must be replaced with ways of motivating students that acknowledge rather than deny their social condition. When used to cultivate discipline by highlighting the eventual rewards of educational attainment, the achievement ideology is neither effective at drawing obedience and attentiveness out of students nor conducive to the development of a positive self image among working-class pupils.[6]

Messages that promote individual responsibility *and* ignore or actively deny the role of external forces (low expectations, inadequate education) do little to change the conditions that make it almost impossible for poor or working-class students to succeed in school. Such messages lead these students to look only within themselves to solve their problems when, in fact, only a broader strategy will equip them to solve them.

Yet perhaps, as Samuel and Chantel suggest, the students know about the poor quality of their education, and they also know not to make a fuss with authority figures who promote the idea of individual effort, responsibility, and success. These students may consider it too risky, given their experiences with their parents, teachers, and other adults, to criticize their school to these very same adults. If this is the case, how can we, as adults and educators, persuade them to express their concerns so we can learn from them about what is taking place in their classrooms and schools? How can we encourage individual responsibility, effort, *and* open critique and reflection on the quality of their school experiences?

Such institutional critiques, however, may create a sense of hopelessness among the students if they are not followed up with action.[7] If students are encouraged to see and discuss the problems in their school, they may lose their motivation to work hard when they realize that such effort may not make much of a difference. Yet if students continue to blame only themselves and if their parents, teachers, and counselors continue to allow them to do so, their schools and the policies that mold them will not be forced to change. Encouraging these urban students to see the problems and to communicate their concerns regarding the quality of their education needs to be followed up with active attempts by educators, psychologists, parents, and policymakers to create learning environments in which students are challenged, properly guided, and, consequently, motivated to do their school work. While telling students to work hard and take individual responsibility is important, allowing students to decontextualize their learning process serves only to mask and perpetuate the school's existing problems. Urban students need to expand their analyses of their school performance beyond their own "laziness"—beyond the stereotypic beliefs about them—and educators, psychologists, policymakers, and parents must be ready to respond.

9

Racism, Sexism, and Difference

AFTER THE FIRST YEAR of interviews, I sat down to listen to the audiotapes of the interviews and to think about what was and what was not being asked. Immediately I was struck by the absence of questions concerning discrimination and oppression. Here we were interviewing black and Latino, poor and working-class boys and girls whom we considered oppressed and who were selected, in fact, *because* they were oppressed and consequently not being heard. In the second year of interviews, we attempted to address this situation by asking the students whether they felt that their "race, ethnicity, or gender would make it more difficult for them to do what they wanted to do in the future."[1] Reviewing their responses after these interviews (which were mainly about their determination not to let anything get in the way of what they wanted to do), we realized that we were not asking the right questions. We were asking a watered-down or safer version of what we really wanted to ask. In the third-year interviews, we headed straight to the heart of the matter. We asked the adolescents whether they experienced racism or sexism, what these experiences were like, and whether they expected to have such experiences in the future. As a result, we began to hear their stories of discrimination. For the boys, these questions typically triggered lengthy responses about their direct clashes with racism. For the girls, these questions commonly led to responses about their awareness of the reality of racism but their lack of or infrequent brushes with direct experiences of discrimination. Both the boys and girls, nonetheless, found common ground as they spoke passionately about their determination not to allow discrimination to block them in the pursuit of their goals.

Once race/ethnicity and gender were introduced into the conversation, we had to ask one of the most obvious questions. During the third-year interviews we asked the adolescents how the interviewer's race/ethnicity and gender may have affected their responses during the interviews. While some students believed that the *gender* of the interviewer made a difference, few felt that the *race* or *ethnicity* did. In fact, they often believed that such a question was tantamount to asking whether they were racists. They were quick to tell us that the interviewer's warmth, understanding, and general empathic abilities as well as his or her age were all more important than his or her race or ethnicity. Their responses contradicted my own assumptions about the role race/ethnicity played in the interviews.

The purpose of this chapter is different from the aims of the previous chapters. While earlier chapters discussed specific themes that I detected when the adolescents spoke about their worlds, the current chapter is driven solely by my wish to present the adolescents' responses to questions about discrimination—an experience that I believe permeates their lives. Given that I conducted this study with firm assumptions about the oppression of these adolescents, it seemed critical to present their perspectives on this topic.

Experiences of Discrimination

Do you think that you experience racism in this society?
Yes, I do. I have a few incidents I experience but I'm over that. I know there's the bull-headed people that'll always be racist and there's those—I look at it like everyone's equal. No one's greater than the next one. Even though someone's always going to think they are.
Can you give me an example of when you've experienced racism?
All right, like I went in a store—I went in a store in—me and my friend we went in a store. We was in the aisle looking for things and, like, white kids, they came in the store and they just walked around. We're not stealing stuff but the guy is watching *us*. You know what I mean? And I'm like,

"Why you sweating us? You know, what's the point? I got money right here." Boom. Or like one time—all right, here's a good example: I went into a store—I went into a twenty-four-hour store and I picked up a piece of gum. I had my dollar out. My friend said, "Put that away. I'll pay for it." So I put my dollar back and I was just holding the gum and he's [the sales clerk's] like, "Are you going to pay for that?" You know that pisses me off. I'm like, "I ain't trying to steal.". . .

Are there ways in which you feel that being black affects your day-to-day life?

Yeah, like in my neighborhood. I could walk in a certain part of the neighborhood and just because I'm black they'll say I look like someone or they'll automatically assume I'm down with this gang or that gang.

While Tyrone's initial response is tentative and evasive, the minute Helena asks for an example he rapidly proceeds to give several detailed accounts of racist incidents that have clearly angered him. Tyrone may want to "get over" such experiences, but the tone of his voice suggests he has not. When the boys were asked about experiences of racism, they typically sounded much like Tyrone. They did not pause or hesitate, they leaped into their personal stories of racism.[2]

In his senior year I ask Guillermo, a Bolivian American student, about his experiences of discrimination:

Do you worry about being discriminated against?

Well, right now I see that there is a lot of racism. In the future I hope there is nothing left.

Do you feel like you have experiences of being a victim of racism?

Yeah, yesterday. After I got out of school, I went downtown, right? First I went to wait for a friend and there are a lot of Hispanic guys and gangs down there. And some of them are my friends, okay. I was just saying hi to them and then I went to downtown. I came back from downtown and my friend I was waiting for, he was there already. So I was talking to him when this man, I think he was Irish, I don't know, he was white, he came to me and he asked me for my name. He said he was going to arrest me for being there.

And what did you say?

[He was] a detective. He said that I was waiting there fifteen minutes, right, and I wasn't even there for five minutes. There were other kids, some white kids waiting down there, that were waiting there before I went to

downtown [sighs] and they were in a crowd too. And we were four people
and he comes to tell us that he's gonna arrest us. And I say, "Why?" and
he says, "Because you've been hanging around here," and I say, "Okay."
So what happened? So he arrested you?
No, he just took my name and all that. But I know that if he wants to arrest
me, he better bring some papers saying something like that I cannot be
hanging around there . . . I didn't like that. I don't like that. And you
know Rockville [a neighborhood in the city]? You live around there?
No, no, no. But I know the neighborhood.
Those people are racist too. I mean, if black people go there, or Hispanic,
they be looking at you like you are some kind of dog. And the other day I
went to look for a job in a white place and they said that they were not hiring. And they were saying [at the front of the store] that there were open-
ings. So anyway, so I asked 'em for an application, right? And I went like
three times, asking for the same thing, if they had a place for me. When I
went the fourth time, they had a white p—, a white boy working there.
Obviously newly hired?
Yeah, 'cause they had taken the ad down.

As with Tyrone, stories of racism come easily for Guillermo. It is noteworthy that these boys were willing to tell stories about white racism to
white interviewers.[3] While Guillermo modified his language ("white p—,
a white boy . . .") and checked to make sure he was not about to speak
poorly about *my* neighborhood ("You live around there?"), he and the
other boys told us searing stories of blatant acts of white racism. Their
openness may indicate their comfort with discussing potentially difficult issues with us, especially by their third-year interviews. It may also indicate,
however, that they share these stories with whoever is willing to listen. Our
expectations concerning their lack of comfort and our subsequent tentative questions regarding the topic of discrimination during the second year
of interviews may have been more a reflection of our own lack of comfort
with hearing stories of obvious injustice at the hands of white people than
with an understanding of the issues that are easy or difficult for the adolescents to discuss.

Marvin, an African American student, says he has experienced job discrimination: "Right, I be going to a store that are hiring and they be like,
'We're not giving out applications.'" Jerome, also African American, tells

Mike about white cops arresting him and his friends for bothering a group of white teenagers when, in fact, the group of white teenagers provoked them with racist remarks. Marcus, a Dominican American student, says to me he experiences racism "all the time," and proceeds to tell me about being harassed by security guards when he was waiting for the subway (a common experience for the boys). Samuel, an African American student, says to me that he has had "people call me all types of names—black this, black that. . . . I think racism goes on a lot more than everybody thinks." For Malcolm, being in certain places enhances the likelihood that he will experience racism: "*Have you ever directly experienced racism?* At certain places, like if I go somewhere." For these boys, experiences of racism are common.

Listening to the adolescent girls in the study, a remarkably different pattern emerges. Only a few of the girls told us that they have been the victims of racism, and one said she only experienced racism as a young child.[4] While all of the girls acknowledged that racism exists in the world ("I've seen it on Oprah," says one African American girl), their stories of racist incidents primarily involved boys or, occasionally, other girls.

When I ask Marie about experiences of racism, she says:

Everybody's killing each other off. People don't really see it. But it's like everybody's dying. They're all black and Hispanics. You know, and everybody takes it as another thing. The other day I was so mad. This guy from here got shot in the face and the cop he just walked over all slow taking his time and then to the walkie-talkie, whatever, he says, "You have another black one—"

That's awful.

"—got shot in the face" and that was it. I was like, "What?" and he was just taking his time. They're all like that.

He was a white cop?

Mm-hmm. They don't care. There's a lot of discrimination against blacks and Hispanics.

Do you think that you have ever personally experienced discrimination or racism?

I don't think so.

How about in school, so you think you've ever experienced discrimination at school?

No.

Marie and her female peers repeatedly stated that while they have witnessed racist acts, they have not been the direct victims of such acts themselves.

When I ask Gayle, an African American student, whether she has ever experienced racism, she says:

> I haven't yet. I'm like real cool with everybody. I see a lot of people, I don't blame them, okay? Like if you're on the train or something and a whole lot of black kids get on—not to be harsh on black people or whatever, but if they get on the train then other people would get frightened. I would get frightened too. If you see a whole bunch of black boys get on the bus or on the train, you would get frightened. I seen that happen. But I feel that you shouldn't be afraid of them because they're nobody. They're only human like you are . . . it's like just because they're black or whatever, don't—don't think that they're gonna kill you or whatever.
> *Do you feel like someone's been racist against you ever?*
> Not—not yet.

Gayle has seen racist behavior, knows that racism exists, even responds in ways that she deems racist ("I would get frightened too"), but tells me that she has not experienced bigotry or discrimination "yet." Her response suggests, however, that she anticipates such experiences in her future.

When I ask Felicia, an African American student, whether or not she has ever experienced racism, she says:

> No.
> *You don't think you ever have?*
> No.
> *Do you think you ever will?*
> I probably will, probably as I get older and out into the business world. I just never run across it. If I have, it must have been, you know, behind my back, but it wasn't like to my face.

Christine, also African American, reveals a similar belief:

> *Have you experienced racism?*
> If I had I haven't known about it because I'm surrounded by basically black people so the only time I really encounter white people is in school or

from shopping or something. . . . . I haven't experienced it but I'm sure I
will.

Why do you think you're sure you will?

Because of the way people are and the way people—people's thinking. You
know, so I have to be experiencing racism and sexism. But I haven't experienced it yet.

These girls are well aware "of people's thinking" and even suspect, as Felicia does, that they might be discriminated against "behind [their] back."
However, stories of racist experiences did not roll off their tongues.

Only four adolescents, two of whom identified themselves as white, felt
that racism is not and will not be a problem for them in their lives. While
Sonia believes that her Puerto Rican community is discriminated against,
she does not experience discrimination herself:

Where I live around here, it's, you know, everybody's skin is black. And there's
white and there's Spanish. . . . I don't feel discriminated against at all.

You don't at all?

No.

Alfredo, a Puerto Rican adolescent, says he experiences racism but only
when he "looks" a certain way. He does not perceive his experiences to be
based on race per se, but rather on the image he chooses to present:

Do you feel like that you do experience some racism, though, in this city?

Yeah, only when I dress up like a hood though [laughs], I think it's more of a
hood type thing, you know. But like if I dress up, you know, wearing a suit
or something, shoes, nice pants and a shirt or whatever, you don't really
see much of that. People pretty much accept you. . . . But if I have, you
know, sneakers and long pants, that's when the people look at you.

Alfredo, whose light complexion contrasts with the darker ones of most of
his peers, believes he can easily manipulate how he is perceived by others
and, thereby, avoid acts of racism. This belief, however, was unique among
his peers.

Unexpectedly, none of the adolescents gave examples of personal experiences of sexism and only a few girls stated that sexism may be a problem

for them in the future. "Maybe . . . I don't know," Marie says in response to my question about whether or not she will experience sexism as she grows older. When Mary, an Irish American adolescent, is asked about the existence of sexism, she tells me:

> I mean it's not always equal, if men can do it, why can't women do it? We probably do it twice as good.
> *Has anyone tried to stop you from doing anything because you're a woman?*
> No.

Eva says that "being black and a woman, that's the two hardest things." Eva, as we will hear in her case study in the next chapter, is a politically astute student who devotes a large portion of her senior-year interview to discussing racism and sexism. Eva and Mary are the only two adolescent girls, however, who acknowledged the negative impact of sexism.

Overcoming Discrimination

The majority of the girls and boys, however, felt confident that neither racism nor sexism would present insurmountable obstacles for them in the future. They spoke repeatedly about overcoming or "not letting" discrimination interfere in their lives.

When Albert is asked in his second year about whether or not his ethnic background will get in the way of what he wants to do in the future, he responds:

> Sometimes, 'cause I'm Puerto Rican. But I'll still keep on fighting, you know. I don't think about it, just keep on fighting my way through. 'Cause mostly it's 'cause some racial people they just don't like Puerto Ricans. So I don't think about it. Just keep on fighting my way through.

When Jamal is asked the same question, he says:

> Nah, not really.
> *You said, "not really," but you didn't say it very convincingly. Do you feel like you really won't have any obstacles in your way?*
> I think I can do it, but you know you're always going to run into somebody who's like racist or prejudiced or, you know, they already have in their

mind that they're going to hire a certain person and stuff like that. You're always going to run into stuff like that so. . . .

Do you think you will really get what you want anyway?

Yeah.

Both boys expect to experience racism, but Jamal doesn't seem to believe it will prevent him from attaining his goals and Albert will not allow this understanding to discourage him. In my questions with Jamal, I reach for the response I expect. Yet Jamal maintains, albeit somewhat tentatively, that while he may experience racism, it will not hinder his ambitions.

Malcolm expresses similar views but provides more details about the strategies he intends to use when confronted with racism (this quote was previously cited in his case study):

How do you see being black having an affect on what you would do in the future?

Well, it depends on how the person sees me—if they see me as black and, therefore, won't speak to me at all, I feel that it's just gonna make things even more difficult. But if they see me as black and don't like me too much, you know . . . but if they speak to me, I feel like I can influence them in some way to make them understand I got the quality. I could do the job. I give it my best, you know. I'm gonna be here on time. If you wanna put it all hard on me, you know, if I'm late or whatever, I'm fired. If you wanna put it like that, then, you know, I'll prove myself. That's what I'm saying.

Sounds like you expect that people will be a little bit racist, prejudiced, because you're black?

Yeah, so, you know, I'm not . . . gonna come off all like, "Forget you," start yelling. I'm just gonna try to be like, you know, if they won't see me 'cause I'm black that's just gonna make it hard on me but I keep trying to get in there, but it depends on where it's at. But if they see me and know I'm black, they be like, "All the blacks in here" whatever, and they, therefore, try to make it harder for me, then I'm gonna try to give them my best to show them that I'm gonna stick with it. I wanna show them I got brains and stuff.

Malcolm is aware of the difficulties he may experience because of his race but also believes that, if given a chance, he can "prove" himself to others and, ultimately, challenge racist stereotypes.

Eva reports similar feelings:

> I'm proud to be who I am and I feel as though I just want to make a differ-
> ence. Like I know that right now in class everybody used to think that I was
> all like this around school, bad, you know. But I started writing poetry, and
> I shared it with them. And they was like, "Oh shoot, she can write and all
> that." And they were surprised. I don't know, I just know I'm not gonna use
> [being a black woman] as an excuse, as in not trying. That's just gonna make
> me try harder and, you know, do better.

Eva sounds optimistic that just as she was able to alter her peers' percep-
tions of her, she will be able to transform other people's opinions of her.
Sounding a note that reminds me of the adolescents' "positive attitude,"
Eva believes that racism and sexism will only make her "try harder and
. . . do better."
Eva continues:

> I'm proud to be black and everything. But I know, I'm aware of racist acts
> and racist things that are happening in the world. But I use that as no ex-
> cuse, you know. I feel as though I can succeed. . . . That's no excuse being
> black. In fact, I think that being black is good. I'm proud to be black but
> you also gotta face reality and what's going on, you know. Black people are
> not really getting anywhere in life. But I know I will. . . . I just know I will.
> Well, I'm determined to. I mean if someone else up there who's hiring isn't
> willing to help, what can you do? You know? But it's not an excuse, but you
> gotta do—sometimes you gotta do what it takes to survive.

Eva is both aware of the "reality" and refuses to be discouraged by it. Strikingly, she identifies with her black community and distances herself from it
("black people are not really getting anywhere in life. But I know I will").
She resists being a victim ("that's no excuse being black") but this resistance leads her away from a collective struggle and toward an individual
one.

Similar beliefs and strategies were heard by other girls in the study.
Shakira, an African American student, says: "I don't think about that
[whether or not racism or sexism will pose an obstacle], I don't think
about it's a black thing or it's a white thing . . . it's nothing. If you
gonna get it, you gonna get it. If you're not, you're not. I mean, you
cannot blame people for what you don't get." Mary also condemns the

stance of victim when asked whether or not sexism will be an obstacle for her in her future: "No, I won't allow it to happen. I'll do anything that I have to. If I have to go through a wall, I will." These girls have seemingly taken hold of popular beliefs about the dangers of being a victim and the benefits of individual effort and made them integral parts of their understanding of themselves, their struggles, and their positions in the world.

Marie, a Dominican American student, tells me:

> I'm Hispanic and you don't see—like all the Hispanics, all they [white people] think is, "Oh, they're pigs. They do this, they, you know, they did drugs." You know, like they have all these negative things. So—and a few doctors up there that are Hispanic, and I like that. So I want to—I mean out of a hundred you might find two that are Hispanic. So it's like I want to make it because of that. I want to show that we're worth more than that if we try. I want to be a model to these other kids, you know.
>
> *Do you think it's a fair society or unfair?*
>
> Unfair . . . I don't know, it's fair and unfair. Unfair because there is a lot of discrimination and it's fair because you know you get a lot of opportunities to be whatever you want to be.
>
> *Even being Hispanic you think you do?*
>
> Yeah, you can if you want to. You can make it because you know you have the opportunity of becoming whatever you want. They give you the opportunity to study, the opportunity to go to a decent college. But sometimes it's hard even though they give you an opportunity to do it, but it's hard. You have to face certain obstacles . . . sometimes you might get discriminated against in school.

Marie expresses both the culturally reinforced optimism ("you get a lot of opportunities") and the "realism," as Eva called it ("all they think is, 'Oh, they're pigs'"), which was typical of the youth in the study. While she suggests that the structure of opportunity may be a bit more complicated than she has been taught to believe ("But sometimes it's hard . . . you have to face certain obstacles"), she believes she can "make it." She is intent on challenging the stereotypes of her community and is determined to give back to her community by becoming a role model.

Jamal also wants to be a role model:

What does it mean to you to be a black man in this society?
Being a black man and not being on drugs, not in jail and going to college,
it's like one of the chosen few. And then it feels like it's my duty as a black
man to go to college and do as best for myself, you know, just to be like a
role model because there's so many of us you know. . . . Statistics show
that there's more black men in jail than in college, which shouldn't really
be. So, you know, now I'm the chosen few. So I have a job, it's really like
I'm the only one out of all those guys so this is just my chance and I'm
going to do it.

Knowing the particular difficulties he faces as a black man, Jamal is determined to be a success and, in fact, feels a responsibility to his community
to be successful.

Sonia speaks about challenging the stereotypes of her Puerto Rican
community:

Because at school, you know, you talk about it [racism]. That's why I feel I
always have an image to put up. Because I think, you know, a lot of people
that have talked so bad about Spanish people. You know, that they get pregnant too soon. And it is true because a lot of Puerto Rican girls they have,
you know, they've made people talk like that about them. . . . You know,
"Oh, they get pregnant soon. They're all on welfare." And it is true . . . and
that's where I come in. It's like I don't want people to think that about me.
'Cause you know I am gonna make it far, and I'm not gonna let anything
stop me. 'Cause if I do, then I'd get, "Oh look, what we all talked about was
true." . . . That's why, you know, I have this, I'm gonna go to college. I'm
gonna graduate. I'm gonna have a career set for myself and then I'll think
about making a family.

Sonia's affirmation of racist stereotypes ("they've made people talk like
that about them . . . and it is true") and determination to prove these beliefs false suggest that she, like Eva and Jamal, uses these stereotypes as a
backdrop from which to differentiate herself. She will be different from her
"Spanish" peers. She will be, as Jamal says, among the "chosen few." This
belief appears to strengthen her ambitions as well as the ambitions of many
of her peers.

A Question of Difference

While asking the participants about their experiences of racism and sexism during the third-year interviews, it became clear to me that we needed to ask if they felt that being interviewed by a person who was not necessarily their same gender or from the same ethnic or racial group affected what they told us.[5] Although I realized that the adolescents might find it difficult to be honest with us, I wanted to know how they would respond if we raised the question. I wanted to bring the race/ethnicity and gender of the interviewers into the conversation.

I ask Albert, a Puerto Rican student:

> *Given that I am a different ethnicity, that I'm a white woman interviewing you, do you feel like that has an impact on the interview? . . . I mean, do you think it would have been different had I been a Puerto Rican man interviewing you?*
> No, it would be the same way, how I answered the question, same way like with you.
> *You think so really?*
> Yeah.
> *Really?*
> Yeah.
> *And why do you think that it wouldn't have made a difference?*
> 'Cause I, you know—it's we all the same human beings, there's nothing different even though we're white, black, Puerto Rican, you know. Still the same human beings.
> *So you think—and if it had been in Spanish, you think it would have been—*
> Yeah, the same way.
> *The same way. I mean, you would have expressed yourself probably a little differently I can imagine.*
> Yeah, a little bit, but you know the same way I'm doing it now, you know, same way.

Albert's insistence that race, ethnicity, gender, and language do not make a difference in his interview, even when I actively encourage him to respond differently, initially surprises me. What becomes evident, however, is that my question about difference is commonly interpreted by the teens as a question about racism. Albert seems to believe that had he stated that my race or ethnicity "made a difference," he would be admitting racist feelings ("we all the same human beings, you know there's nothing different").⁶ Admitting that difference makes a difference is a risky assertion in a society that specifically ignores or minimizes difference in the name of racial, ethnic, and gender harmony.

Jamal, of West Indian parentage, says in response to Jamie's question concerning whether or not Jamie's ethnicity or race (white) had any affect on his interview:

> No.
> *Hasn't effected the way you answer any of the questions—you don't think?*
> No.
> *Why not? Do you think?*
> Because I mean this society is not like all black. You know, everyday I work, I work with like all white people. All my teachers are mainly white. I have some white—one of my—at one point a white guy was my best friend. 'Cause we grew up from young. Something like, you know, just a guy being white doesn't mean really much to me.

Sounding exasperated by Jamie's question ("Because I mean this society is not like all black"), Jamal appears to believe that Jamie is asking him whether or not he is racist. He responds by pointing out, though hesitantly, that he once had a white best friend. Jamal suggests that since he lives in a world of white people, being interviewed by a white man could not possibly make a difference. Difference, once again, is interpreted within a framework that does not allow for difference—especially racial or ethnic difference.

Samuel, an African American student, states that my race, ethnicity, and gender did not make a difference for him in his interview because either way "[I] would have been a stranger to [him]" and, therefore, "it would not have mattered." For Samuel, familiarity is the critical factor that determines what he communicates to me. Shakira, also African American, voices a similar belief:

> *Helena interviewed you as a white woman, and I interviewed you as a white woman. Do you feel that the fact that we are white influenced you in any*

way in terms of how you are? Like what you tell or what you decide not to tell me?

No, because I don't know you. You don't know me. Whether you was black or white or whatever, blue or purple. You don't know me still. You see my face, you got my voice. Still don't know me . . . and whether you was a black woman, Spanish, whatever. Information still the same. You still don't know me.

I mean you don't think the fact that if I were a black woman though—that there would be some sort of more of a—you would feel more at ease to be more yourself?

No, regardless I'm always myself. I could talk to anyone. As long as I like you. I don't like you, I won't talk to you. So, I don't like you if I don't talk to you [laughs].

In a matter-of-fact tone of voice, Shakira states that my lack of "knowing" her was the important "difference" for her. She directly asserts that what she chooses to share with me is firmly grounded in her opinion of me as a person irrespective of my race or my gender. Eva agrees:

How do you feel like—I mean if I had been a black woman, do you think you would have been different in any sort of way?

No, I come off as is to anyone.

You really think that?

Yeah. Anyone. Like I told you before. You could be a president or whatever. If I feel strongly about something, then I'll come straight out, and if you don't like it, that's your business. . . . Like if you offended me in any way, you know, I would just walk out. I would say, "I'm sorry, but I don't like the way—," I'd just walk out. Whether you were a black woman or a white woman.

Both Eva and Shakira maintain their identity as young women who freely express their opinions. However, they also believe that their personal impression of me as an individual overrides any concerns or beliefs about my race or ethnicity.

When I asked Tyrone if being interviewed by a white women affected his responses, he says: "Yeah, like I said, I'm not prejudiced against no one, racist against no one. It would make no difference. I talk to you like I talk to anyone else. You know, except for like people in my age bracket, you know, I talk to them different 'cause, you know, they don't really understand as well." While my race/ethnicity and gender did not appear to make a difference, my age did and, by implication, my ability to understand him. For Gayle, the important factor in the interview was my gender:

> *Do you think it's affected your interview at all to be interviewed by someone who is white?*
> No.
> *You don't think so. I mean, do you think in any way if I had been a black woman* [Gayle is black] *that wouldn't have sort of changed a little bit how—*
> No. To me it doesn't matter what color you are. I don't—I wasn't brought up to not like white people or Hispanics or black people or whatever culture it is. I was not brought up that way 'cause I was around a mixture of people when I was growing up, so to me it doesn't matter. I don't think nothing of that. . . .
> *How about if I had been a man? Do you think that would have made a difference?*
> About the sex part, yes [giggles]. Other parts, no.
> *So for you it made a difference that I was a woman?*
> Yeah.

As also heard in Albert's, Jamal's, and Tyrone's interviews, Gayle interprets my question about *race* as a question about *racism*. The adolescents appeared to believe what American society wants them to believe and what Ruth Frankenberg calls a stance of "color and power-evasiveness":[7] race and ethnicity are differences that should make no difference. Gayle says, however, that my gender is a difference that made a difference.

Marie was the only one who stated, although quite tentatively, that my ethnicity made a difference for her:

> *Do you think that the fact that I'm a white woman—do you think it had an impact on the interviews that you've done with me? You don't think so? So you think it would not have been different had I been an Hispanic woman? The way, you know, the way you would be in interviews?*
> No. Maybe it'd be like pretty more close because I could say, "Oh, where are you from," you know, like that. But that's all—that's about it. That's all.

Okay, so it may feel a little close and also possible you could speak Spanish?
Mm-hmm.
So that would be sort of a connection?
Yeah.

Marie tells me, with much encouragement on my part, that had I been Hispanic she would have been able to connect with me in different ways— possibly feeling closer to me. Remarkably, Marie was the only adolescent who gave the response I had expected from all of the adolescents in the study.

Reflections

As other studies of adolescents of color have found,[8] this study indicates that adolescent boys of color are more likely to report personal experiences of racism or discrimination than their female peers. Given the pervasiveness of racist stereotypes of specifically urban, ethnic-minority adolescent *boys* and the consequent apprehension many adults inside and outside of their communities feel in response to them, these findings are not surprising. Stories abound among the boys in the high school of being harassed walking to, from, and in school by police and security guards. They speak of being "eyed" suspiciously by salespeople when they walk into a store, or by passersby when they walk down the street. These adolescent boys know that most, if not all, of the suspicion and harassment they experience is in response to their gender, skin color, and most likely their social class. The urban girls of color reported fewer direct experiences of racism than boys. A reason for this finding may lie with the fact that the racism that is directed against these girls may take subtler forms. The racism that pervades girls' lives comes in the form of negative stereotypes (as Sonia stated: "They get pregnant soon. They're all on welfare"). These stereotypes may not lead to discrete incidents of racism such as police harassment, but they are a form of bigotry of which these girls are very much aware. Even if they claim that they have never directly experienced discrimination, these girls are actively responding to these racist stereotypes as they aspire to be successful.

The girls and boys were, however, equally likely not to perceive sexism as an obstacle for themselves or for their female peers. Sexism in the world of adolescence may be insidious and difficult to "see." Like racism for urban, ethnic-minority girls, sexism may come in the form of pejorative beliefs about girls and women that do not necessarily result in overt acts by shop owners, police officers, or even teachers. Research has shown, however, that such degrading beliefs often do result in overt acts of sexism in the schools.[9] Yet girls and boys may not interpret particular sexist experiences as sexism per se. Sexual harassment, for example, experienced by a majority of school girls from all socioeconomic levels across the country,[10] may not be interpreted as sexism if sexism is exclusively understood (as it appeared to be in this study) as girls not being allowed the same opportunities as boys. While girls and boys may be regularly affected by sexism, the youth in this study did not believe, for the most part, that this concept had much relevance for their present or future lives.

Whether they perceived racism or sexism or both to be obstacles in their lives, the majority of the teenagers believed they could overcome or "fight" the odds. They challenged stereotypes and wanted to prove to others within and outside of their communities that they could succeed despite discrimination. Like the common stereotype of the "invincible adolescent," the adolescents in this study tended to perceive themselves as invulnerable when they spoke about dealing with racism and discrimination in their futures.[11]

When I turned to inquire about the role of race/ethnicity and gender in the interview relationship itself, I did not expect what I found. I began these interviews with the assumptions that the interviewers' ethnicity, race, and gender would make a difference in the interviews. Although I realized that a multitude of factors influence the willingness of adolescents to speak openly with adults, I firmly believed that the racial, ethnic, and gender differences and similarities between the interviewees and the interviewers would have an impact—both positive *and* negative—on our discussions. I also expected, perhaps naively, that adolescents would be able to communicate to *us* why and how these factors made a difference. I was surprised to find that acknowledgment of racial/ethnic differences for these teens meant racism. Despite our insistent style of questioning, the adolescents, for the most part, would not budge. They stated resolutely that they were not racist and that, therefore, the race or ethnicity of the interviewer did not make a difference. Some adolescents, however, did believe that the gender of the interviewer made a difference. They also explained that our age, understanding, familiarity, and acceptance were more important for them than our race or ethnicity.

It is plausible that for some of the adolescents, our race and ethnic differences were differences that made little difference. Yet it is likely that our white identities inhibited them from discussing their real thoughts and feelings about when, where, and how race or ethnicity makes a difference. Clearly, adolescents may choose not to honestly express their thoughts about race and ethnicity to those very people who represent the racist and oppressive cultures about which they are being asked to reflect.[12] Furthermore, they were answering a different question from what I was asking and, consequently, it is unclear what their responses would have been had they understood my interpretation of the question.

Listening to their responses, however, I also found myself wondering if race, ethnicity, and gender made more of a difference for me in the interviews than for the adolescents. Reflecting on my own processes throughout the three years of interviews, it became clear that the racial, ethnic, social class, age, and, with the boys, gender differences between myself and the adolescents made me, at times, more cautious. At other times, these differences made me more aggressive in my questioning, probing and pushing more because I did not assume that I understood what they meant. With the boys, in particular, I asked many questions and, consequently, often heard richer and more detailed stories from the boys than from the girls whose stories were more familiar to me. The racial, ethnic, social class, age, and gender differences led me both to ask more questions and to be more hesitant in asking certain questions, particularly those about race and ethnicity, than if I had been interviewing teens with whom I shared similar backgrounds or gender. My determination *to get* the adolescents to admit that the race, ethnicity, and gender of the interviewer made a difference may have been motivated more by my desire to validate what I believed—that their race, ethnicity, and gender (and age and social class) made a difference *for me*—than by a desire to discover what they believed.

When I engaged with the adolescents in discussions of discrimination and difference, I heard both that race/ethnicity makes a difference (they experience racism regularly or expect to in the future), and does not make a difference (in the context of the interviews). Like their discussions of their futures, the teens' perspectives on discrimination and difference were both from the margins and from the inside. They knew about rampant racism, and they were deeply optimistic that they would be able to overcome such barriers. They were fully aware that race/ethnicity makes a difference, but they did not want it to make a difference. They resisted the values of mainstream culture while accepting them wholeheartedly. Irrespective of these tensions, however, the teens repeatedly suggested that they are continually creating strategies to cope as effectively as they can with the very real challenges they confront.

INDIVIDUAL LIVES

Part II

I began this book with Malcolm's story, and will end it with Eva's. Like Malcolm's, Eva's story reveals some new patterns as well as those that have been discussed in earlier chapters. Rather than merely repeating these patterns, however, her story contextualizes them. Eva's interviews reveal, for example, how outspokenness relates to having best friends, and how optimism about her future intertwines with her perceptions of discrimination. Her story also demonstrates how each of these themes can be understood within the larger context of an individual's life. While excerpts from the interviews were presented in each of the thematic chapters, they focused only on the themes being described. Eva's and Malcolm's stories show us how these themes fit into full and rich lives. Eva also discusses beliefs, values, and attitudes that were not themes in the interviews. Her story, like Malcolm's, is unique and compelling. My primary goal in chapter 10, as it had been in the chapter on Malcolm, is not to provide interpretations (as I did in the thematic chapters), but to present a life in progress over three years. While we are quick to interpret or note the themes in the data, we often forget to slow down and simply listen to a story told by a teenager. Here is Eva's story.

10

■ ■ ■ ■   ■   ■   ■   ■   ■

Eva's Story

WITH HER HAIR pulled tight into a barrette behind her head, Eva, a strikingly beautiful black adolescent girl with clear, soft skin and an athletic body, walks into our interviewing room in the spring of her sophomore year. She is going to be interviewed for the first time by Helena. Unlike many of her peers, Eva does not appear awkward or nervous as she confidently collapses into the chair and waits for Helena to turn on the tape recorder.[1]

Born in Trinidad, Eva has spent most of her life living with her aunt and uncle in the United States. She presently lives with her mother, who moved to the United States from Trinidad a few years ago. Eva explains to Helena that she only recently decided to move in with her mother because she wanted to get to know her younger sisters better (both of whom live with her mother down the street). She also thought that her aunt was favoring her own daughter over Eva. Eva's father had moved to the United States when she was young, but at that time Eva chose to stay with her aunt and uncle because she didn't feel close enough to her father to live with him. Eva's father currently lives nearby and they see each other frequently. She has seven brothers and sisters (two more siblings, one of whom was her twin sister, died when they were babies). She says she has many half-brothers and sisters ("so many, I don't know") because her father has had numerous girlfriends. Her mother isn't steadily employed but occasionally tailors clothes, and her father works as a manager of a local sandwich and bakery shop. Eva says that she receives no financial support from her parents and works to earn all her spending money.

Eva's Sophomore Year

Helena begins her sophomore-year interview by asking Eva about her relationship with her mother:

> *How would you describe your relationship with your mother?*
> Down the tubes, I don't get along with her at all. Not— nope—I don't get along with her. It's not that I haven't tried. I put my 50 percent in. We don't get along.
> *Why not?*
> I don't know. We just don't get along. She don't like me. I can't say I hate her, because I don't hate her. I just can't—I just don't like her.

Her mother, Eva says, continually "picks" on her about her late hours and her frequent absences from home. Eva explains that she and her mother argue so much because they did not live together when she was younger and, consequently, they are just now getting to know each other. In this brief assessment of why she and her mother do not get along, Eva reveals what will be a pattern throughout all of her interviews. Eva consistently suggests that she understands not only the nuances of her relationships, but also the relational nature of her difficulties. She is angry at her mother but blames neither her mother nor herself for their problems. Instead, she understands their problems as a product of their past and current relationship.

She and her father, Eva says, get along "great":

> Like we talk about things. Like, you know, when I'm staying with my mother and we're having conflicts and he always gets involved, because my mother makes him get involved. She would, like, say [to him], "You need to talk to her because when I talk to her, nuthin' gets through to her," . . . so he tries to talk to me and when he talks to me we have an open mind. I listen to his side and he listens to mine. And the reasons I did whatever I did, you know, and I like that.

Eva appreciates the mutual respect and openness in her relationship with her father. Her father's respect for her is revealed, she says, in his ability to admit to her when he is wrong, which her mother does not do. Eva does not feel respected by her mother:

> I believe in you give a little respect, you get some back. That's the problem these days in the world, grown-ups like they think children should respect them but they don't show any type of respect in return. What comes around goes around, no matter how old you are or how young you are. And my mother don't seem to understand that . . . like she said, "Two grown-ups don't live under the same roof, so one got to go. That's it."
> *So she said that to you about you?*
> Yeah. I'm going to go.

While Eva claims that she is planning to leave her mother's house, when pressed by Helena she admits that she will probably not move out because she does not truly believe that her mother wants her to leave. She adds that her father would be angry with her if she left her mother's house: "My father was like, 'Where you going? . . . You're not leaving, you're staying right there, you are not going away,' so I stayed." Eva has chosen not to live with her father because she enjoys her sisters' and brothers' company at her mother's house and thinks that she would be lonely in her father's "huge house." Eva appears conflicted about but, nonetheless, committed to living with her mother.

Eva gets along with some of her brothers and sisters. Her closest relationship is with her ten-year-old sister: "[It's] the goodest relationship I ever had . . . she understands me." Her twelve-year-old sister, she says, wants to "be like me . . . she plays basketball and tries to do everything I do, has the same type of clothes and stuff." Her mother considers Eva to be a bad influence on her younger sister because her sister gets suspended from school just as frequently as Eva did when she was younger. She strongly resents being blamed for her sister's troubles.

Tamara, Eva's best friend, attends the same school and is in the same grade as Eva. She is her best friend "'[c]ause when I'm having problems I talk to her, I go over her house, we cook food together . . . and we do a lot of things together." Some of their shared activities include community service and going to a local college Upward Bound program. Eva attributes her success in school to her best friend's encouragement. Her friendship with Tamara remains an important relationship for Eva throughout her high school years.

Eva had a boyfriend a few months ago with whom she broke up because he cheated on her. At first, she did not want to believe her peers' reports of her boyfriend's infidelity but gradually came to realize that they were "speaking the truth." "I overlooked what people said; I trusted in him and I found the truth, so trust really works, if you believe in it." Strikingly, Eva explains that her *trust* in her boyfriend eventually led her to see that he was not telling the truth.

Eva says she had sex with this ex-boyfriend because "I loved him, and at that time I thought he loved me, so I thought it was right, so I did it." Although she continued to go out with him, she stopped having sex with him when she found out he was lying to her about "certain things" (before she realized he was also cheating). I suspect that Eva may have difficulties taking care of herself in her relationships with boys. Although she ultimately ended this particular relationship, she did so only after repeated experiences of her boyfriend's "lying" and "cheating" and after her friends consistently told her about his bad behavior.

When Helena queries Eva more on the topic of sex, Eva begins to reveal her ability to speak her mind:

What was it like for you to do it and then to stop?
For me to stop? No, I don't think you should—that question should be asked because it's not as though I'm doing it like it's a job. If it's love, it happens, it just happens, it's not something you plan, like the theory about on your honeymoon, you're supposed to, you know, have sex or whatever. I don't believe in that, and I'm not going to follow that.

Unlike her peers in the study who only conveyed their dislike of particular questions indirectly, Eva directly expresses her concern with Helena's question (although she attempts to soften the critique by shifting from the active to the passive voice). It becomes increasingly evident that Eva often speaks her mind not only in her interviews, but also in her relationships with friends, family members, and, by her senior year, with her boyfriend. Eva is firm in her views and in her refusal to follow rules and conventions of behavior in which she does not believe ("I don't believe in that, and I'm not going to follow that").

Currently, she would like her friend Deshawn to be her boyfriend, but she says that they do not want to "rush into anything." "I think that's good because you have to be friends before you be anything else." Eva sounds more interested in having a romantic relationship with Deshawn, however, than he is in having one with her: "He's not my boyfriend, but I think of him as my boyfriend, but he's not." Eva considers her relationship with Deshawn the most important relationship in her life:

You say you look up to him. Why is that?

The way—he has this amazing way of going about things he's really into. For a teenager, you know, he doesn't let himself get into anything that he can't handle himself and he's just so intelligent. He's real smart, and I like that in a guy. Like, you know, the things teenagers do, they get drunk and all that. He is a peer counselor, so, therefore, he's not into all that. And so that's why I admire him.

Eva was one of the few adolescents who identified peers as the people for whom she holds the greatest esteem. She mentions her particular regard and respect for at least one of her peers each year she is interviewed.

Describing herself, Eva says: "I have a lot of potential, I'm very active, a lot of potential and I know I'm smart. Smart and competitive—competitive. And I'm very trusting—trusting and loyal, you know. I'm real, yeah." She likes herself and explicitly recognizes her strengths:

I'm not like normal people. If you see a pencil—if you put this pencil on the table, you'll see a pencil and accept it. I'll go around and say, "Yeah, I see a pencil, but why is the pencil there and who put it there." Most people would just see a pencil: "So what, a pencil," like that. That's how I go about solving problems, too. You know, that's it.

Eva is intensely proud of her curiosity and her ability to ask questions. Each year during her interview, she describes herself as smart, competitive, and curious about her world. Her pride in her curiosity was unique among the adolescents. Eva considers asking questions and trying to get beneath the surface an essential part of her approach to the world.

She also thinks it is good not to be "normal" because "I think if I'm doing something positive and using that in a positive way, then it's good."

You feel different from other people?

Very, 'cause it seems like most people today all want to do what other people want to do. I like stay to myself. If a whole bunch of friends said, "Yeah, we're going to the movies this weekend," and I really didn't want to go, I wouldn't just say, "Yeah, I'm going to be with them and not really enjoy myself." I would say, "No, I'm going to the library and reading up on my culture," you know. And that's like, I just like to be like that. If I don't want to do something, I don't do it. I don't like to be pushed or pressured into doing anything.

Distinguishing herself from her peers, Eva boasts of her nonconforming behavior and of her independent mind. She resists peer pressure although she does not resist, as evidenced in her discussion of her best friend and role model, being influenced by the attitudes, goals, and actions of her close friends.

When Helena asks her about current drug or alcohol use, Eva says that while she has smoked cigarettes in the past, she currently smokes neither cigarettes nor marijuana and only occasionally drinks alcohol:

Why do you not drink alcohol more?

'Cause great things are expected of me, not just from—I'm not saying as family-wise, because they don't really know what I'm capable of doing, because they never take the time to notice. But you know, I'm an athlete and your coach wants you to do it. When I did that [got drunk at a party], my coach and my teachers and my friends were really disappointed in me. And I was kind of disappointed at myself, but I think that one time because I was having a problem with something. Let me stress this, I didn't do it because my friends were doing it. Like I said before, if I say no, I mean no and no means no. I just did it just to do it. I stopped.

Eva's confidence and pride in her independent mind are evident in this passage as she tries to convince Helena that she thinks for herself. When Helena asks why she does not use drugs, she says, "If I don't like something, I don't continue doing it." Eva repeatedly insists that she is not one who follows the crowd. She is willing to admit her own vulnerability ("I was kind of disappointed at myself . . . I was having problems"), but is also adamant about being perceived as an independent, strong, and proud young woman.

Eva is getting B's in school in her sophomore year. She believes she is capable of higher grades because "school is easy if you put your mind to it. The work, it's not hard, but, I play around a lot. I may sound serious, but I still have fun, hanging around a lot." Eva was doing considerably worse in middle school and in her freshman year in high school. She began to do well when she took up basketball. In fact, she says, the required grade point average to play basketball is what first motivated her to do well. As a result of basketball, she eventually made the honor roll:

> The team always competes for honor roll. Me and my friend Tamara, we always competed: "Oh I bet you will get the honor roll," or, "I'll get the honor roll this term and you won't." You know, betting on it and things like that. I know it sounds nutty, but we do it.

Notably, Eva seeks to excel in school not only because it is demanded of her but also because her friend *challenges* her.

Since she entered high school, Eva has begun looking at education in a different way:

> *What do you mean when you say you look at education in a different way?*
> Before, you just go to school to get out of your parents' way, get a little free time, and now, now I love school now. But I hated school [in middle school]. Now I love school, and if we have a school vacation, I'll drive by the school—
> *Really?*—
> —like once a week.
> *What is it that you love about school?*
> Maybe it's because of my friends, even though I can still see them, but my friends, and the teachers are good. It's not that hard. I think it's not hard.

Since Eva receives a great deal of support (from coaches, teachers, and friends) at her school and is doing well as a student and as an athlete, it should not be surprising that she "loves" school. I am nonetheless surprised at her absolute and unequivocal affirmation of her school—the same one that I perceive having so many problems.

Do you think that how you do as a student will have an effect on your future life?

Of course. Yeah, if I work now and in my college years and do what I have to do, then later on in life I won't have to struggle and work so hard. I can just relax, you know. Be, not wealthy, because I don't think money— money's not important, but I'm saying, it's inside the head, understanding things. So if I work now and do what I have to do, like they say, like your mother says, "You do your chores, and then you get to go out." You know, do it, get it over with, and life is easy, you relax. You won't have to be thinking about retirement when you're eighty, you can be thinking about retirement when you're younger.

Although Eva describes her family as "very poor," she does not place much value on the accumulation of wealth. She has a larger vision about her future, which includes getting an education, learning, and working hard. Like so many adolescents in this study, Eva believes that working hard early in her life will inevitably reap positive outcomes, but her personal twist is that knowledge counts above all. "Understanding things," working hard, and "relaxing" are her future goals.

Eva would like to attend a predominantly black college and, after graduation, become an actress and an owner of a clothing boutique:

When you think about the future, what do you think of?

Me. [Laughs.] I think of me, and my friend Tamara, my best friend Tamara, owning a business right next to one another—right next to one another and competing like we always plan. I'll have a store right here and she'll have a store right there. I think she's going to have a hair dressing store, while I have a fashion store, and after work we'll go and work out and then go take our acting class, like that.

What is it about competing?

Me and her, I don't know, I like it.

What do you like about it?

The satisfaction, I don't know. I just like it, not winning or losing, well, I do like to win. I try my hardest to win, but you know, I don't take losing as hard as most people do. I just see it as an opportunity to get better and try to catch up to that person that beat you. [Laughs.]

As we have heard before, Eva enjoys competing with others, especially with her best friend, Tamara, with whom she imagines a lively and interconnected future. Competing is not only a source of enjoyment for her now, but is a key element in her image of her future. For Eva, competition does not exclude cooperation, encouragement, or affection.

When asked what she hopes for in the future, Eva says: "I'm not so much as into looking for marriage or anything. I want to be a working woman. And later on in the future I hope to have one child, maybe two, a boy and a girl." While it is not clear how Eva understands the association between marriage and working, it is clear that marriage is neither a primary nor a particularly attractive goal for her and is not linked to having children. The girls in the study typically conveyed such beliefs: they wanted to have children but were ambivalent about getting married. Marriage was perceived as risky and potentially confining, whereas rearing children was typically considered joyous for the most part. Their beliefs about marriage were most likely a reflection of those held by their mothers, many of whom were single and raising children on their own.

When Helena asks about any possible fears or apprehensions about the future, Eva says:

> The future, yeah. I think a lot [about my fears of the future] during class. I'm thinking about that, about all the killings and bad things and I'm afraid that, you know, all these young kids not knowing what they're able to do. Their lives being taken away. I think about all that gang violence down here, the drugs.
>
> *So you are afraid of those things, what those things can do?*
>
> I'm not really afraid of it, because I think if you know about something, you can't really—you can't be afraid of it. I'm not afraid of it, like drugs, I'm not afraid of drugs. Drugs can't do nuthin' to me. Only I can do something to me, you know. And guns, guns don't kill people, people kill people, so I'm really thinking about the people.

By reframing Helena's questions (*"What those things can do. . . .* Drugs can't do nuthin' to me. Only *I* can do . . ."), Eva suggests, once again, the

importance of individual responsibility. She believes she is entirely responsible for what she does to her body. Her emphasis on independent thinking and action, heard repeatedly among her peers when they spoke about
their futures, school, and the issue of discrimination, underscores the extent to which she has been influenced by mainstream values and the ad-
vertising that promotes them ("guns don't kill . . .").

Eva, however, is also deeply embedded in her relationships:

What makes your life worth living?
I'm happy that I'm living because my grandmother, I love her dearly. There's
    Tamara, my little brothers and sister, even though I am going to say this,
    because it's true, even though I try to deny it, but I know deep down, I do
    love my mother, Deshawn, all my friends, my father, really.

Eva expresses her feelings of love even for those with whom she is in constant conflict. Although she believes that her friends and her coach support
her more than her family ("family-wise . . . they don't really know what
I'm capable of doing because they never take the time to notice"), Eva has
strong attachments to her family.

In this sophomore-year interview, Eva appears self-confident, highly articulate, critical, intellectually independent, and deeply connected to her
peers. She believes that she will accomplish what she wants in the future.
Each year, most of these themes become stronger and more pronounced
for Eva (although her self-confidence seems to decrease slightly in her junior year). While listening to her, it remains unclear for me how Eva is able
to hold a job during the summer, participate in sports, get good grades,
and have numerous friends when she experiences little support from her
mother at home. Her admission that she loves her mother "deep down"
even though she does not "like her" leads me to suspect that her mother
may provide more support than she is willing to admit. Her peers, teachers, and coaches, however, may also furnish her with enough support to
thrive even with her difficulties at home.

Eva's Junior Year

This year, Eva starts off the interview with Helena saying that although she
still lives with her mother, she "really" has three homes—her mother's, her

father's, and her aunt and uncle's: "When I'm having problems at one place, I just go to the other house." Most of the time, however, Eva lives with her mother.

When asked what changes have occurred with her mother since last year, Eva says she is more independent this year because her "mother trusts [her] more." However, when Helena asks her directly to describe their relationship, Eva tells a slightly different story:

> Same as it was before. . . . You know, I go home, do my homework. Go in my
> room. Then leave.
> *And then leave? Where do you go?*
> To the park or to the library. Nothing bad. But she always thinks I'm going
> out somewhere bad or hanging out on the street.

Although, according to Eva, her relationship with her mother has improved since last year, there is "still not much said" nor is there evidence of increased trust between her and her mother. The source of her mother's mistrust is unclear throughout her interviews.

Eva says she still has a good relationship with her father because she believes that he "understands" her more than her mother.

> My mother always thinks that I'm doing bad stuff. My father doesn't think
> that. You know, I bring [athletic] trophies and stuff home and I show 'em
> to my mother, and she just looks at them, "Oh, yeah." And if I show my fa-
> ther he'd be like, "Oh, that's good." He starts encouraging me to do better
> and stuff.

It becomes more evident in this junior-year interview that Eva receives consistent support not only from friends, teachers, and coaches, but also from her father. Her resilience and self-confidence are clearly a result, at least in part, of this strong support network. People are drawn to her and *want* to encourage and support her because, perhaps, she is successful and determined. In turn, she is able to flourish.

Eva reports "okay" relationships with her siblings, particularly her older sister and her eleven-year-old sister. The only sibling with whom she actively struggles is her fourteen-year-old sister. Their difficulties stem from her sister's borrowing habits and her "lack of respect" for Eva's belongings. Eva tries to complain to her mother but to no avail; indeed, she says, she rarely feels supported by her mother when she is angry with her sisters.

Eva, once again, states that her friend Tamara is not only her best friend but also the person whom she most admires (along with Langston Hughes). She credits Tamara entirely for her self-confidence and improved school performance this year:

Is there anyone in your life that you're looking up to?

That I look up to? Yeah, my best friend, Tamara. I've always looked up to her and then, there's like I'm interested in poetry. I write a lot of poetry. And I like a lot of black poets, like Langston Hughes. Like in my freshman year, I used to be like an average student—a "C" student. And then I felt good about myself. I don't know, I think I got it from my friend Tamara. She encouraged me. And like this year I'm doing real good. And getting honors and stuff. I don't know, I think it was really her . . . [Tamara] would always compete with me like, you know, "Oh, I bet you can't do it." It wasn't in the negative stuff. Like she used be like, "I bet you can't get the honor roll before I do." And we used to be bad, okay, like in my freshman year, we used to get C's and D's and F's and always be missing school and all that. And all of a sudden, she's all like, "Yeah, forget that. We better start doing this instead of playing around."

The encouragement, competition, and inspiration from Tamara, whom she identifies along with another close friend, Caroline, as her most important relationships, makes Eva feel "good about [herself]" and motivates her to work hard in school. Discussions of *best friends*, or even same-aged peers, being role models and *most* important relationships were rare among the adolescents in the study. Role models were typically either unknown figures in the media or adult relatives, and *most* important relationships were typically mothers. The lack of support Eva experiences at home may be one reason why her friends fill such roles.

Eva believes that she and her best friend, Tamara, are both "very open and have high goals" for themselves. She appreciates that she and Tamara are so ambitious and very committed to school. (With clear pride in her voice, Eva tells Helena that she missed no more than two days out of the entire school year.) She also likes the fact that her friend is not "normal":

"If you really talk to her and understand her, she's just not normal. And I don't like to be normal either. I like to be different."

Eva sees herself as "more different," however, than her friend:

> The way we go about solving problems. Like if you see something here. Let's say a glass was broken on this table: she would look at it and she'd be like, "Oh, so what. A glass is broken." Whereas, as I would look at it and I'd be like, "Why is it broken? What happened to make this glass break." Or you know the reasons for that. She's like, "It's just a broken glass. Dag, leave it alone. Sweep it up. Throw it away." And I would look into why it got broken, who broke it, and why they touched it. Oh, like that.

In another intriguing description about her approach to life, Eva uses a metaphor of a broken glass to describe her active curiosity. Like a detective or a scientist, Eva is not satisfied with simply seeing something and ignoring or removing it ("sweeping it up"). She wants to get to the source, to know the facts behind an event. As I come to know Eva from our interviews, I begin to share her appreciation of her "different" way of thinking and behaving.

Eva's friendship with Tamara, she says, has "matured" over the past few years. When she and her friend fought last year, they would retreat from each other and think "I don't need that. I don't need no friends." Presently, however, they work it out together, staying up late at night discussing the reasons for their fights. Like many of her female peers, Eva has come to believe that disagreements are not threatening to her friendships but a regular part of them. Further on in the interview, Eva has a similar discussion about arguing with her family members:

> You know, you always argue with your family but that don't mean you don't care about them. So, it's always, you gotta have disagreements in a relationship, happiness comes along with it. But in order to have happiness, you also have to have a quarrel.
>
> *Okay, why do you think that?*
>
> 'Cause just like good and bad. You couldn't have a good unless you started out with bad. You know what I'm saying? There has to be—sometimes I think, how can you say something is good if you don't have nothing to compare it with?

Eva is aware of the necessity for contrasting conditions that throw both light and shadow on her feelings. She suggests that she is constantly "looking at a piece of glass" and reflecting on why it's there in the first place ("you couldn't have a good unless you started out with bad"). She investigates the nature of interpersonal relationships in the same manner she uses to describe her inquiries about a pencil or a piece of glass.

Eva says she has no group of friends at her school because she does not like most of the students:

> *What about them do you not like?*
> They act stupid [laughs]. Well, that's my opinion. I just don't want to get around them. 'Cause they act fake.
> *What do you mean?*
> Like one minute they'll be like, "Oh, how are you doing?" and next with their friends they don't know you or anything. I don't like people like that.

Believing her peers will betray her, Eva chooses to stay away from them. Nevertheless, Eva has had close and supportive friendships with girls each year of her interviews. Similar to many of the girls discussed in chapter 5, Eva's wariness of other girls does not lead her to avoid intimacy with all of her female peers.

Eva has no boyfriend this year. The boy she was interested in last year, Deshawn, distanced himself from her and she seems hurt by his behavior. Being hurt, however, is not a factor in Eva's explanation of why she does not have a boyfriend:

> I'm not looking for no relationship. That's just a pain in the neck.
> *What makes it a pain in the neck, do you think?*
> [Sighs.] Having to worry about, "Oh, I'm going to be all lost and caught up." And sometimes they may try to say that, you know, they're helping you or whatever. But I think they just keep you from doing what you really want to do cause you're young and you should keep your mind straight on what you really have to do. It's like, you know, okay, let's say . . . I'm on a diet, right, and my mother . . . makes a salad. With all these, you know, so I can eat because I'm on a diet. And then a boyfriend is like an ice cream sundae right there, you know. It's just tempting you to mess up your diet

process so I'd just be like no, if you have the willpower to say no, it's better.

Echoing a theme heard among several of the girls about the risks of marriage and of men, Eva likens having a boyfriend to cheating on a diet. Eva's pursuit is not for a relationship with a boy, but for discipline and the achievement of her ambitions. Her lack of interest in having a boyfriend may also stem, however, from Deshawn's rejecting behavior.

Regarding sex, Eva says she does not believe anybody should have sex until the relationship has lasted longer than a year:

> 'Cause when a person really really knows how you feel, it's hard for them to hurt you 'cause they know your mother. It's like if you had a boyfriend, and he was always coming over meeting your mother, eating dinner with your mother, with your parents or going over to his parents, it's hard for him to hurt you 'cause he knows a part of you that nobody else really knows. . . . But if it's just oh leave school, go over his house, have sex and all that. He don't really know nothing about you. He can just do anything to you and he don't care 'cause he don't know you.

In response to a question about sex, Eva speaks about her strategies for preventing boys from hurting her. Last year, Helena's question about sex provoked a discussion of the dangers of disease and pregnancy. This year sexual intimacy involves the possibility of hurt and abandonment. As she describes boyfriends' "keep[ing] you from doing what you want" and boyfriends' hurting "you," Eva sounds more vulnerable this year.

When asked about her desire to have children, Eva says that she wants to be financially stable before she has a child so that she could take care of her child by herself or help her husband take care of their child. She is determined not to have to depend financially on anyone in the future. Like several of the girls who valued their mothers' independence, Eva greatly values her own autonomy and wants to retain it when she has a child. Eva and her female peers commonly told us that they have learned from their mothers, aunts, sisters, *and* fathers not to wait for a man to take care of them, and they are uniformly determined to follow such advice.

When asked to describe herself, Eva says she is "goofy, goofy, goofy, very goofy . . . I like to laugh a lot. *Anything else?* No, just goofy." Eva's self-description has changed from last year when she said she was smart, trusting, loyal, and full of "potential." This year she describes herself as "goofy." There is a self-consciousness about Eva this year that was not evident in her previous interview:

What do you like about yourself?
Uh, I don't know. I don't know. Hmmm. I don't know. [Pause.] I don't know. There's something but I can't think about it. Oh, what do I like about myself? That I can cook. Yeah.
What don't you like about yourself?
Uh, I eat too much. I don't know. I haven't thought about that. I don't think about myself that much.

In a dramatic shift from last year, Eva is not only reluctant to talk about herself but in fact is hard pressed to remember what she appreciates about herself. When asked what she does not like, Eva responds impulsively that she eats too much, effectively undermining what she has just said she likes about herself. In an unusual wave of awkwardness, Eva claims not to think about herself very often.

At another point in her interview, however, Eva sounds more confident:

Somehow, I just learn real fast. I don't know how. But it's like anything I do, I learn it real fast. Like, I didn't know nothing about softball. I didn't know nothing about basketball or volleyball. Somehow I just learned it. I didn't go to, you know how they have the camp in eighth grade? I didn't go to none of them. And I became good. I'm not trying to brag or nothing
No, that's okay.
I became good. And I don't even practice [over the summer] and I'm really good.

Expressing pride in her intellectual and athletic abilities, Eva adds that she enjoys and is good at writing poetry. She writes poetry about "love," "the environment," and about "things that go wrong" and has successfully encouraged her friends to begin writing poetry. Unlike last year, however, Eva's responses betray a self-conscious note ("I'm not trying to brag or anything").

During the drug-and-alcohol-use section of the interview protocol, Eva admits to smoking cigarettes occasionally but not too often because of her involvement in sports. She says she no longer drinks unless there is a celebration, and she has not tried any illegal drugs because she is afraid they would "mess up her system." She has not and does not anticipate getting involved in any other risky activities such as stealing or selling drugs because she feels "too good" about herself to allow it:

> I don't like stealing 'cause I see where, it don't pay to steal. . . . I can't stand stealing. I think it was like three weeks ago, me and Tamara went to the store and she met this boy that she knew, I think, like a long, long time ago. I was with Tamara just walking around in town, and he was all like, "Yeah, let's go to this place." We thought he was going shopping or whatever. And he goes in the store and steals a hat and I was like, "Tamara, why is he stealing a hat?" And she was like, "I don't know, I don't know." And we left, we didn't leave him, but we went outside the door 'cause we didn't want nothing to do with this. And when he got out, he was all braggin', "Yeah, I got one of these, and another one." He had stole a whole bunch of them. I was like [thinking], "Oh man, that's foul. . . . He was just using us as a cover."
>
> *Did you tell him that when he was there?*
> I just rolled my eyes at him. I wouldn't disrespect him 'cause I don't know him, but he got the sign that, you know.
>
> *You didn't like that?*
> Yeah, that I didn't like that.

Angry at this boy's behavior, Eva chooses to convey her disapproval nonverbally. A certain ambivalence is suggested, however, when Eva chooses to leave the store but wait for the boy outside. Given her pride in having an independent mind and being outspoken, her reaction to this boy is not what I would have anticipated. Eva indicates that her lack of "knowing" him caused her to silence herself ("I wouldn't disrespect him"). However, Eva's silence, like that of many of her female peers, may stem from the fact that the person who angered her was male. While Eva suggests that she is forthright in many of her relationships, she does not seem outspoken with boys until her senior year.

Eva is on the honor roll throughout her entire junior year and says that she does well because she "cares" about her grades:

What do you think changed it for you? Why did it become important?
I don't know. It's just like you wake up one day and find that you're alive. Like you really know what you're alive for. Waking—waking up in the morning, like, "Huh," all happy. I don't know. I just woke up and started doing work. Seeing how hard it is out there.

Eva explains that even though she is doing well now, she understands that there is always a risk of a downturn:

You can change like that. If you really want to do it, it's just like that. If you want to be good, bad. But it's easier to be bad than to be good.
What do you mean by that?
'Cause bad stuff has always surrounded you. And you have to really be strong.

Although she is immersed in a world of "bad stuff," Eva seems to have navigated around many of these obstacles. She recognizes the ease with which one can turn from good to bad but ultimately considers such a change under her control ("You can change like that. If you really want to do it").

Eva wants to go to college, but is particularly anxious this year about her chances of getting in:

Why is it you feel that you wouldn't get in?
I don't know. It's just hard, people nowadays, like you see people all, um, like me, I see all the kids. Like when I was a freshman and they was a senior here, they used to be like, "Yeah, college, college. This and that." As soon as they got out, they didn't go nowhere. I see them right on the streets. I'd be like, "You ain't started college yet?" "No, not yet. Not yet." So it's like I feel the same way. I'm probably just saying that now. Like, "Yeah, college this and that," and when the time come, I'll be all, "I don't know, I won't go to college." . . . I don't know.
You seem so motivated in so many ways. But you feel like it'll be hard to follow through with it?

Like doing the work, no, I could do the work. I could do anything, any work.
I mean I like things that challenge me.
So what will you do if you don't go to college?
Go to college. There's no way I'm not going to college. I'm just scared.
There's no possible way that I would not go to college.

The opening of this passage contains one of the few moments in Eva's interview in which she voices insecurity about her ability to do what she wants in her future. Eva's reflections on what has happened to her peers throws her future plans into question. Yet, when Helena pushes her to contemplate the consequence of not following her plans, she resists and regains her earlier confidence ("there's no possible way . . ."). Her confidence, however, does not seem as stable as it was in her earlier interview.

Later in the interview, Eva suggests once again an insecure stance:

How does it make you feel when you think about the future?
Nauseous [laughs]. I don't know. You could say I'm scared.
What makes you scared?
And you know, I'm scared, but I'm excited. . . .
What do you see happening in your future?
All I see is education. I like to write, but I don't think I'm gonna make it as a
 writer. I think my profession would be teaching. And also as a second pro-
 fession, maybe nursing. But then I think about it, why be a nurse when
 you could be a doctor? But I don't want to work that hard.
Do you have any particular hopes for the future?
Yeah, I hope—I hope I live to see the future. That's one.
Do you have doubts about that?
I don't know, I'm not in any danger, but you know how things happen.
 You're never too sure of anything.

Eva repeats the hopes that she has mentioned before, but also, for the first time, hopes to "see the future." This response offers a new angle in her discussions of the future. Although Eva mentioned earlier that she does not feel threatened as long as she stays in her own neighborhood, she suggests here that her life is always at risk, regardless of her precautions. She feels hopeful about her future but is also acutely mindful of the unpredictability and possibility of death.

When Eva is asked what makes her life worth living this year, she says:

> Life itself [laughs]. I'm just thankful for living. You're living and you get to see another day. You get one more day to be with the people you love and care about. Living isn't as bad as they make it, if you have morals. If you don't, like some kids just get up, get dressed with an Uzi in their pocket, and go to school. Other people get up, look at the flowers, look at the trees, look at the birds, you know, and be thankful for what they have.

While her reference to "flowers," "trees," and "birds" seems a bit pat, Eva appears genuine in her response. Her statements about Uzis and "living isn't as bad as they make it" suggest that she is aware of the violence and hopelessness around her, but she resists this hopelessness, as do most of her peers in the study, with optimism and enduring beliefs and "morals."

Overall, Eva seems less self-confident this year than last. She questions her ability to get into college, struggles to tell Helena what she likes about herself, and answers with less elaboration than in the previous year. Even though her grades have improved and she remains a confident athlete and poet, these achievements no longer translate into the complete self-assurance and verve she displayed in her sophomore year. Her lack of self-confidence may lie, at least in part, with Deshawn's recent rejection of her. It may also lie with her growing understanding of potential obstacles and the unpredictability of her future. Her confidence, however, all but fully reemerges in her senior-year interview.

Eva's Senior Year

In Eva's senior year I am her interviewer. Like Malcolm, Eva seems comfortable with the change. I meet with Eva in the small interviewing room used in all three years of the study. Wearing baggy pants, a long-sleeved blouse, gold hoops in her ears, and with her hair pulled back in a ponytail, Eva sits and looks directly at me waiting for my first question. She exudes energy and self-confidence and appears comfortable, even excited, about being interviewed. Having heard about her repeatedly from many of the teachers and students, I am already well aware that she is popular in this school. As I watch her, I realize that I am feeling awkward and nervous. Her confidence and energy remind me of how little confidence I had at her age. I want this interview to go well. I look down at my list of questions and begin.

We start the interview by discussing the changes in her life over the past year. In the spring of her senior year, Eva was accepted and received a scholarship to the college of her choice. She will start college in the fall, and at the time of the interview she is preparing to move into the dorms. She is happy but believes that she will miss the "huge" bedroom in her mother's house. With a sigh of relief, she remarks that her dorm is only a short train ride from home.

Eva tells me that her relationship with her mother has not changed: "We don't get along at all."

> There's no communication whatsoever. . . . I was happy and really thrilled
> 'cause I got accepted [into college]. And I wanted to share that with her.
> And she was like, "I don't care." You know, she's not really motivated
> about me going to school, but it's what I want to do so.
> *Why do you think she's not motivated?*
> I don't know. Maybe 'cause—all right, first of all, a mother doesn't want her
> daughter leaving home at a young age. Well, you know, I'm young and
> everything. But I don't think that's it. I think that, I don't know, with my
> brother, it's like, she brags to her friends about him, but with me, she just
> thinks the worst of me. . . . Now, I'm the one bringing home trophies, re-
> port cards, good report cards. Accepting scholarships, I got scholarships to
> college. And we have our miscommunications, but mainly I just stay in my
> room or whatever. When I'm going out, I knock on her door and say I'm
> going out. I go out and come back, like that.

Feeling unappreciated and unable to communicate with her mother, Eva is not only frustrated but also hurt by her mother's behavior, which she struggles to understand:

> [My mother] is from the islands, and I don't think that she has much respect
> for education. Well, you know, she encourages kids to go to school and
> everything, but—it's like back there, it's really like a whole different thing. I
> think she would prefer me—much rather me to get married, have kids, and

stay in the house, and be a mother figure, which is good, you know. I just want something more than just staying in the house. Or maybe she might even envy me. But I don't know.

Voicing a desire that is shared by many poor immigrant adolescents, Eva tells me that she wants "more" for herself than what her mother had (and what her mother wants for her) and this "more" means an education and working outside the home. In acknowledging that her mother's desires may stem as much from envy as from tradition, Eva recognizes, almost in spite of herself, the complexities of both her own and her mother's feelings.

Eva says her relationship with her mother has gotten worse over the years because she has refused to "open up" and reveal her personal life to her. Had she been more forthcoming, she thinks, her mother might not have been so frustrated with her. Although Eva briefly seems to assume sole blame for the state of their relationship, when I ask her directly her response reveals a more balanced perspective:

> *So you really see it as more, sort of, I don't want to say your fault, but your problem, in a way, why you guys haven't gotten along?*
> It's equal. I'm not a—I'm not an angel. But neither is she. I mean, she goes to church and everything. And preaches righteousness. And she turns around and does stuff that you would not expect someone who—I mean, every night she goes to church. And she's supposed to be so religious or whatever. And then, I like that in her, but—
> *You like what in her?*
> Going to church and everything like that. But what I don't like is how she contradicts it. Like when she comes home sometimes she'll say something that you would not [expect]. I'm like, "Well, you go to church, and you believe in this, and yet you're saying that." But I don't say that to her, but I'm thinking that. 'Cause everyone's human. Nobody is perfect. But she does it too much. Like for [example] my sister was going to church with her. And my sister is, she—she's like me really. And she's like wearing baggy jeans and sneakers. My mother's like, "No, you're not going to church like that. You gotta go put on [other clothes]." And my sister's like, "Why? Why?" You know. It's supposed to be God takes you as you are or whatever. [My mother] starts preaching like that. . . . Like she's

more into what people think of her. "Well, I don't want you to go like that. [Get] clean, nice and dressed and everything." But I mean, why? The reason I say that is because for a person who believes, okay, she is always, you know, she's poor and everything. . . . [She says:] "Well, people think 'cause I'm poor this and that. I don't care. God'll take me," or whatever. And then yet [she] says, you know, "Well, you have to dress nicely."

Angry with what she perceives to be her mother's hypocrisy, Eva finds it particularly frustrating that her mother is not as consistent in her beliefs and actions as Eva perceives herself to be. Eva, however, rarely chooses to speak directly with her mother about her anger or frustration ("You believe in this, and yet you're saying that. But I don't say that to her, but I'm thinking that"). When she is angry with her mother, Eva retreats to her room. Given Eva's general outspokenness with her friends, teachers, and her interviewer, I am surprised that she is not more confrontational with her mother.

Further in her interview Eva says that she is not outspoken with her mother because she has "too much respect" for her. Eva does not, however, believe that her mother respects her:

I was in the papers a lot this year for basketball and volleyball. And it's like, my uncle came by and the first thing he says: "Oh, you seen your picture in the paper?"
Your picture was in the paper?
Yeah, we cut it out and everything. [My mother] goes, "Yeah, whatever" [laughs]. She doesn't really care. He showed it to her, "You seen Eva?" She's like, "Oh," and that's it.

With her voice rising and her eyes looking both angry and hurt, Eva tells me about her mother's lack of interest in her accomplishments. She wants her mother to be proud of her and seems deeply pained by her mother's lack of overt response and encouragement.

Eva still feels good about her relationship with her father. She thinks he "understands" her and they talk "like sisters and brothers. You know friends, good friends." She finds him easy to talk with because he listens to her in ways her mother can or will not. Eva believes that she and her father are, in fact, very similar to each other:

Like, how do you see yourself similar to your dad?
Oh, he's really funny. I like to joke around too. . . . There was a time where it
was me and my mother and . . . she was like, "Why don't you go cook the
food?" Like that. I'm like, "I'm doing my homework. I gotta do this."
And she was like, "What are you gonna do when you get married to your
husband?" And I was like, "First of all, I'm gonna come home and he's
gonna have the food ready for me." And she was like, "Yeah, right." She
got mad. She thought I was being smart. And my father said, "No, that's
right. That's good, don't sit around waiting for a man to take care of you."
And me and him, we think the same way.

Eva identifies with her father not only because of his humor, but also, strikingly, because of his similar views concerning how she should behave with
men. She resists her mother's more traditional expectations and seeks to
be the modern woman whom her father encourages her to be.

She does not, however, approve of her father's behavior with her
mother:

What are things that you can think about with your father that you don't like?
I don't like the fact that, um, I don't know, like he dates—goes out on dates
and stuff. . . . I think he just be messing with my mother when he talks,
when he be like, "Yeah, I went on a date." . . . And he'd just say that just
to make her [jealous]. I don't like that. I don't like the way she lets him do
that to her. But you know, if I say anything, it ain't my business. It's like,
"Dag, man, you know, you cook for him, you clean for him, you do all
that for him." If that was me and my boyfriend was acting like that, I
would be like, "See ya," you know. I wouldn't be doing. . . . Well, that's
because she's been married to him almost all her life probably. She has like
six kids by him. You know I can understand a little bit. But some of the
stuff he says—he'd be joking around, but I wouldn't let jokes like that go
by. If I were her, I'd get on him.

Although upset with her mother for not standing up for herself with her
father, Eva is nevertheless protective of her and wants her father to stop
making her mother's life so difficult. In a rare moment of sympathy for her
mother, Eva justifies her mother's behavior based on the context of her
parents' long-term relationship. While Eva presents a fairly one-sided

image of her relationships with her parents in the first two years of her interviews, her representations this year seem more three-dimensional and include feelings of anger, frustration, compassion, and understanding. Her descriptions seem more mature.

When I ask Eva about her friendships, she tells me about her three best friends this year: one is her boyfriend and the other two are the same two girls she spoke about in previous years. What she likes about her girlfriends is that they are "real, not fake." "Fake" people, she explains, are people who "say one thing and do the other . . . hypocrites, like." Eva disapproves of hypocrisy, dishonesty, and inconsistency in her peers' behaviors just as she did in her mother's. In contrast to her mother, she considers herself and her best friends to be consistent in their beliefs and their actions.

Eva says she is drawn to her best friends because of their different perspectives:

> The reason that we really got close is that they like me for my differences and I like them for their differences. . . . 'Cause I don't know, it's just that [Tamara] would respond in a way that would make me understand a little more better whereas Caroline she'll flip it around and try to make me conclude to my own decision instead of really [giving her own opinion]. You know, try the little trick hints to try to make me understand things, whereas Tamara would just come and express herself and, you know, tell me what she would do or whatever. Caroline doesn't like to do that 'cause she doesn't like to get really involved because she feels as though if something goes wrong, she doesn't want to be blamed. Caroline's way of doing things make me think more. But Tamara is like different, which is good, you need both sides of it.

Eva's remarkable ability to appreciate the shades of relationships and empathy is vividly expressed in this passage. While she identifies more with Tamara's technique of giving advice or expressing herself, she appreciates Caroline's more dialectical approach.

Both of Eva's best friends are mothers, and the three of them spend a lot of time with the children. Watching her friends with their children, Eva says, has decreased her desire to have children at this point in her life. She says she will not be ready to have children for a long time: "I want to be able to educate my children. . . . If you don't teach them, that's why they

turn to the streets. You have to have good morals." Eva's strong commitment to education is once again evident and may explain, at least in part,
why she has not become a mother like her best friends.

Eva's boyfriend is (finally) Deshawn, the same boy of whom she spoke
so fondly in her sophomore year. She tells me that when she was a sophomore, Deshawn did not want to be in a committed relationship (as I had
suspected in listening to her sophomore-year interview), so they went their
separate ways during their junior year. Recently, however, they became romantically involved, and Eva is happy about this decision:

> *What do you like about the relationship?*
> Uh, respect. That's the most important. Respect. Trust. He trusts me a lot
> and I trust him and what else? There's a lot of love. We talk about any-
> thing. AIDS, anything. Pregnancy, everything.

Eva adds that she also feels good about the relationship because she
feels free to speak her mind with him:

> Yep. I challenge any, it's like he's really intelligent. Smart. I mean really
> smart, he's just really educated. Just because I know that, doesn't mean I lis-
> ten to every word. I challenge him. And he goes, "Well, yeah. That could be
> true." And he likes that. 'Cause we challenge one another mentally, you
> know, like intellectually.

Unlike many of her peers and her mother, Eva appears neither timid nor
nervous about speaking her mind with her male peers this year. This is also
the first year she describes herself as an outspoken person. Her sense of
confidence seems to be back in full force.

Eva says her sexual relationship with her boyfriend is also "really good."
"He don't pressure me. I don't pressure him. It just happens. It falls into
place." They always use protection because she explains that both of them
have "high expectations" of themselves and do not want to be forced to
alter their plans because of an unwanted pregnancy.

The people Eva says she looks up to this year are the poet Nikki Giovanni and Dr. Martin Luther King Jr. She finds Giovanni's poetry inspirational and believes in Dr. King Jr.'s messages concerning the importance
of education. But in addition to these public figures, Eva still looks up to
her best friends because they motivate her to try her hardest in school. Her

friends, along with Giovanni and King, inspire and encourage her to overcome the obstacles she confronts, whether in writing poetry or in doing
her schoolwork.

When asked to describe herself, Eva says:

> Funny, goofy, funny, smart at times . . . I have a voice. I mean I like to be
> heard.
>
> *Are you heard?*
>
> In most of my classes, yeah. They look to me for answers. 'Cause, you know,
> I'm always trying to make a point or a statement.
>
> *Do you think that you've ever had a time in your life where you haven't felt
> heard? Or do you feel like you have felt heard most of your life?*
>
> . . . I've always made a strong statement.
>
> *You always have?*
>
> Always. Yep, always . . . I've always been heard.

Eva offers a perceptive and moving statement about herself. She is clearly
proud of her sense of humor, outspokenness, her unpredictability, and her
nonconformist stance. While she is one of many girls who discussed being
outspoken in and out of school, she is the only one who states that she has
always been heard by others. It is precisely this certitude that drew me to
her story.

> *You know, I think a lot of girls have a hard time [with being so outspoken].*
>
> That girl stuff gots to go.
>
> *What do you mean?*
>
> I don't think of myself as a girl. I mean, it's good being feminine, but a girl?
> Nope.
>
> *What do you mean? What don't you like about it?*
>
> 'Cause when one hears the word "woman" or "girl" automatically, you know,
> you feel inferior to a man or whatever. I'm just a human being just like an-
> other.

Considering Eva's apparent pride in who she is, I am surprised by her resistance to identifying herself as a girl or a woman. Her exasperation with
"that girl stuff" seems to extend to my question as well, as if I, simply by
asking about girls, am participating in the rhetoric and belief system that

Eva refuses to accept. She does not want to be boxed or categorized, and her opposition to my question demonstrates this refusal.

Following up on this, I ask:

How would you identify yourself? Like, who is Eva?
I don't know. That's a hard question. I don't know. But it's like most of the guys in this school they really, you know, they don't play none of that stuff with me that they play with other girls. 'Cause they know I get on 'em. They do not like me lecturing 'em. I'll be like, "What blah blah." They would rather not ask the question if they knew what the response is gonna be. So you know, I was talking to a guy on the phone. . . . He [said], "Yeah, I really liked you and I asked my friend, 'Who's that girl?' and he immediately said, 'No, you don't want to mess with her.'" [Laughs.] I was like, "What do you mean by that?" Thinking, you know, that maybe something was wrong with me. He was all, "He was just saying that you were strong and independent. And he wasn't going for none of that."

In response to my question, Eva initially hesitates but then moves swiftly into a description of how boys think of her and how she thinks of herself— strong, capable, and independent. Her resistance to the category "girl" was a reluctance to being equated with "the other girls" who permit boys to "play games" and who, by implication, do not share her qualities. In order for Eva to maintain her sense of who she is, she distances herself from the collective "girl."

When I ask her about the source of her strength, she says:

It's basically self-motivation. Because, I want to succeed. I don't mean just like, "Oh yeah, make crazy dough." You know, and jet or leave out of here. I want to contribute to my community. Like, you hear a lot of people say that. But they just say that 'cause people want to hear it. I mean, I really feel that and I want to do that. Around my neighborhood I see a lot of baseheads and junk and everything. And I have little sisters which, you know, they do well in school except for the older one. She's really like boy-crazy or whatever. But, I just want to have a good life and not have to worry about this. But yet I want to make a difference in the black community. Like I live around [a neighborhood with a predominantly black population]. I want to get through to other people, other kids, like minorities like myself and stuff like that.

In a voice brimming with passion, Eva reveals her individual and communal spirit. She strives for individual success but also wants to give back to
her community: "*What do you think of when you think of your future?* Well,
school and education, just school and education. And bringing something
back [to my community]." Her individual and collective values are evident
throughout her interviews. She is proud of being a "black woman" yet she
refuses to identify with the collective "girl" or "woman" because, she
claims, it erases her individuality. She attributes her strength to "self-motivation" yet this motivation leads her back to her community. The way
Eva braids her values together is unique among the adolescents in this
study.

Feeling nervous about college, Eva says that she has decided not to play
sports during her freshman year in college so she can focus on her schoolwork. What may be "strange" about her new school, she tells me, is that
she may be one of only a handful of minority students. This does not "really" bother her, she says, because she will be close to the city where all her
friends live.

Are you nervous about how well you'll do?
Yeah, definitely. No, I know. . . . Nothing is really hard, a challenge, like
working with computers or whatever. I mean, if you first go into a corpo-
rate office or something, and you applied for a job and it's your first day,
and you really don't have any training. Once someone takes you and trains
you it becomes easy for you. So I believe that, you know, nothing is really
hard as long as you really try to do it or you want to do it. But if I'm being
lazy, and I'm like, oh, I don't want to do this. Then I won't do it.

Tentative but self-assured, Eva believes she will learn what is expected of
her when she gets to college. In fact, she says, "Truthfully, all I want is to
learn in life. Profession-wise I did say I want to be a teacher. What with becoming a teacher you also learn. So it's an education all the way."

When I ask Eva what she fears most about the future, she answers,

I fear becoming someone that is not heard.
Why?
'Cause I believe too many people, black people mainly, are not being heard.
You know, they're turning the "well nobody's listening to me" into "I must

be a nobody," you know, turning to crack, drugs, or whatever. I don't want to be like that. I can't stand baseheads. . . . When I see them in the streets, man— and when my little sister's walking with me—I hate that.

Perceptive to the injustices in the world, Eva draws a disturbing and undoubtedly real connection between society's indifference toward black people and black people's responses to this apathy. When I press her to tell me whether she really thinks that she will not be heard, she says, with a laugh, "I doubt it":

Truthfully, I'm the type of person they need in the presidency.
Why do you say that?
Because I would not try to put a lot of pressure on myself just because I'm the president. I would look towards the people to help me become a good person as well as helping the country become a good country. Instead of just, "Oh, yeah, I'm the president. I'll make all the big moves." I would want more people to be heard.

The importance of community, of listening, and of being heard is once again underscored by Eva in this insightful spin on being president. When asked about society, Eva says:

Like, I believe not all people but some people that are in high positions really don't want kids like us to succeed. 'Cause if they did, look at this school, look at our facilities. You know what I'm saying? The corporations . . . the people who work there are like forty, fifty, ready for retirement. And who's gonna take care of your business when you're gone? You should really be thinking, you know.
Why do you think the corporations don't hire the kids?
Well, first of all, I think like minorities have it bad. Blacks and Hispanics and all that. . . .
Do you think it's sort of another sign of racism in the society?
Oh, crazy racism. I mean, you have people that don't even know they're racist that are racist.

Looking directly at me, Eva tells me—potentially one of the people who work in the "corporations" ("who's gonna take care of *your* business when you're gone?")—about the state of the work world. As she has done throughout her senior-year interview, Eva reveals her outspoken and honest voice.

At the end of her interview, Eva says that she is passionate about poetry:

> Through reading their books—like Langston Hughes—they had motivation which I find in myself. You know, motivation sometimes directs you to write or do something constructive. I feel the poetry. I feel some of the motivation that they have when they write. It's like I can feel what they felt.
>
> *Do you feel there's a certain kind of experience that you can relate to?*
> It's an experience. . . . I mean black people have, I mean, although they don't know it they have the same feelings inside of 'em. Sometimes they hide it, but like you can read a book maybe Alex Haley wrote and he expressed some type of feeling of aggression or something . . . and then, you know, you're like: "Well, that was in 1960, 1950, or slavery time whatever, I don't know. I'm here now. You know I don't feel that." But it's in you. It's in you.
>
> *So you feel like there's a connection in the black community?*
> Yeah, a connection.

Through her poetry, Eva experiences a bond with her black community. However, as she suggested in earlier parts of her interview, Eva also describes how her experiences and feelings are different from others in her community:

> I'm proud to be black and everything. But, um, I'm aware of you know, racist acts and racist things that are happening in the world, but I use that as no excuse, you know. I feel as though I can succeed. . . . I just know that I'm not gonna let [racism] stop me. . . . Being black is good. I'm proud to be black but you also gotta face reality. And what's going on, you know, black people are not really getting anywhere in life, but I know I will and I don't know—I just know I will. Well, I'm determined to . . . and with God's help, you can't go wrong.

Eva's determination, frustration, and outspokenness tumble together in this passage as she emphasizes that she is a proud member of the black community but also an outspoken individual who will not let the state of

her community (her perception of it) obstruct her desire to make a difference.

Eva ends the interview by quoting from one of the poems on which she
is currently working. It is entitled "Black Child" and she says that it is a
poem about herself. In the poem, a child says: "Some may say where did I
get this strength from? Because I've been so brutally bruised, you know,
raped of my history. Can't you see the courage, the strength that I have?
For today I am born, for I am a black child."

I am moved by Eva's story, her strength, her determination. Listening
to over six hours of her interviews, I have grown to admire her creativity,
her curious mind, and her complex understanding of her relationships. I
am struck by her passion and her intelligence. I wonder how she is doing
now, four years after she was last interviewed. As with Malcolm, I plan to
recontact her in the next few years to find out.

Reflections on Malcolm and Eva

In reviewing Eva's and Malcolm's interviews, it became clear to me that
Eva benefited from an extended support network that included female and
male friends, teachers and coaches, uncles, and her father. Malcolm, in
contrast, was primarily supported by his mother and a few of his teachers
and had great difficulties finding supportive friends. Malcolm seemed
more alone and depressed than Eva. Both of them, however, were "fight-
ers." Although Malcolm received little emotional support from his peers,
became a teen parent, and was coping with a terminally ill sister, he eventually graduated from high school on the honor roll, attended college, and
continued to be an involved father. Eva, who did not receive emotional
support from her mother and continually rejected all the "bad that sur-
rounds" her, also finished high school on the honor roll, and enrolled in
the college of her choice. Malcolm and Eva both finished high school with
confidence and hope.

In presenting Malcolm's and Eva's stories, I set out to remind the
reader of the individuality of the adolescents with whom we spoke. Although occasionally I provide interpretations, my goal was not to provide
analyses of their stories, but to present a detailed description of what they
said to us when we sat and asked them about their lives. Like a conversation, these case studies cover a lot of ground, ramble and pause, fire up and

dwindle out. But in the half-finished sentences, the turn of a seemingly minor phrase, the repeated effort to articulate a feeling or perception accurately, the authenticity of the speaker can be felt. I wanted the reader to experience the complexity of the adolescents' perceptions, the pulse of a life in progress, and the texture and nature of the relationship between the interviewers and the interviewees. The patterns that I describe in this book only begin to scratch the surface of the adolescents' stories. The case studies were intended to enrich and promote our ability to see and experience the nuances of a life as well as reveal the relational nature of research.

Epilogue

So what have we learned by listening to urban teenagers speak about their worlds over time? Their stories challenge not only our understanding of urban adolescents, but also of adolescence itself. Using qualitative research methods with a population that has been excluded from developmental research, we have learned that the popular story of urban poor or working-class youth—the story of hopelessness, pathology, and high-risk behavior or of superheroes and invincibility—is not accurate. The teens in this study never suggested such stark and flat imagery. They spoke about being hopeful while sounding pessimistic; they discussed being present- and future-oriented; they told stories of engaging in "risky" behavior and holding two jobs at one time; they distrusted their peers but the girls, at least, still had close friendships. They told stories of becoming parents and being more determined to go to college as a consequence; of dropping out of school and finding their voice *because* they dropped out. These urban poor or working-class adolescents also told stories of going to the prom and the movies, of hanging out with their friends, watching videos, and going to school. Their stories were quite ordinary and everyday and also courageous.

We have also learned that the two most widely accepted stories of adolescent development—the story of independence and autonomy told about adolescent boys and the story of relationships and voice told about adolescents girls—are not universal stories. While the issues of independence, autonomy, relationships, and voice indeed infused the interviews, the ways in which these issues or goals were understood or sought were different from what we have heard before. The adolescents in this study sought independence and autonomy, but it was primarily the girls who pursued such goals, and it was not from their parents that they sought refuge but from boys and men. Both boys and girls typically told stories of growing closer and more emotionally dependent on their parents, particularly their mothers, over time. They struggled more with how to have and maintain satisfying peer relationships than with becoming autonomous and independent from their parents. Furthermore, they commonly sought *intimate* friendships with their same-sex peers. Remarkably, the girls were no more likely than the boys to desire intimate friendships even though they were more likely to have them. "Having a voice" was critical for most of the adolescents; yet the girls seemed more outspoken than the boys. Both the girls and boys, however, felt silenced by or were silent with other boys. Occasionally, these adolescents expressed feelings of invulnerability, but unlike "typical adolescents" who perceive themselves to be invincible, they also communicated their own sense of vulnerability, pain, hurt, and risk. In several decisive areas, these adolescents told a different story of adolescence from those told about predominantly white, middle-class adolescents.

Relational Themes

The first set of themes focused on "having a voice" in relationships. In contrast to the numerous reports on the silences of girls, the girls in the present study were willing to be outspoken in many of their relationships, particularly by their junior and senior years. They typically spoke of a time in which they found it difficult to speak their minds, and then of overcoming their fears and becoming outspoken. Furthermore, they suggested that being outspoken about anger and affection enhanced rather than threatened their relationships, particularly with their female peers. In contrast, the boys expressed having more difficulties than the girls communicating their thoughts and feelings to others throughout all three years of their interviews. The boys told numerous stories of retreating from conflict or disagreement, and thereby silencing their anger and frustration—particularly with their male peers. Remarkably, *both* the boys and girls struggled to be outspoken with other boys. They feared endangering these relationships or themselves if they spoke openly about their anger with them. Some of the boys also spoke about distancing themselves from or becoming violent with male and female peers who chose to freely express their thoughts and feelings. These particular boys suggested that their peers' fears about speaking out are based on reality: speaking out with boys may, in fact, endanger relationships and, occasionally, personal safety. Being outspoken for girls and boys was clearly not unequivocally good or bad. The value and effectiveness depended on, as the girls and boys suggested, to whom, when, how, and in what context one is speaking.

These concerns about endangering or strengthening relationships were continued in the second set of themes, which centered around distrust and betrayal in friendships. Boys and girls spoke at length about both distrusting same-sex peers and desiring same-sex friendships. Like the theme of outspokenness among the girls, themes of mistrust were more prevalent in the teens' junior- and senior-year interviews than in their freshman- and sophomore-year interviews. The boys found it not only difficult to trust their male peers but frequently concluded, as a result, that they could not have close or best male friends. The girls, in contrast, typically had exceptions to this anticipated pattern of betrayal and distrust throughout all three years of their interviews. Although they worried that their friends may betray them, the girls were willing to confront one another with their anger and frustration. It was precisely this approach that seemed to preserve their friendships. In contrast, the boys sought ways to maintain their relationships with their peers (e.g., *not* speaking out), but these strategies appeared to lead to loneliness rather than close relationships. The boys appeared caught in a relational dilemma. They did not speak their minds in their friendships because they worried they would lose their friends but, at the same time, they kept their distance in these relationships because they did not trust their peers. A lack of trust prevented the boys from risking outspoken strategies—strategies employed by girls to *maintain* their friendships. Both the boys and girls, however, actively sought friends with whom they could share their secrets and tell everything. Surprisingly, there appeared to be no gender differences in the desire for close, intimate friendships with same-sex peers.

When one considers the third set of themes, the relational picture becomes even more complex. The adolescents repeatedly spoke about the closeness and importance of their relationship with their mothers. Although a number of gender differences were suggested when they described their peer relationships, I only detected a few in the teens' discussions of their mothers. For many of them, their relationships with their mothers seemed to provide the trusting companionship for which they yearned. It did not seem simply coincidental that as they grew older they became more distrustful of their friends and felt closer to their mothers. Yet the boys' relationships with their mothers were also different from what they yearned for with their peers. Mothers did not seem to be simply substitutes for friends. The boys spoke about their *wish* to share their "secrets" with a male peer while they typically chose not to share such personal information with their trusted mothers. The girls, on the other hand, had relationships with their mothers that resembled those with their close female friends. The girls stated that they expressed their "real" thoughts and feelings in both relationships. Their close relationships with their mothers did not seem to fill an absence or gap. Instead, they seemed to be an extension of their intimate friendships with girls (or vice versa).

In dramatic distinction to our mainstream theories of adolescence, the teenagers in the present study indicated that their primary struggles lay with maintaining satisfying and intimate peer relationships rather than in gaining autonomy from their families. When the adolescents discussed their relationships with their parents, none seemed preoccupied with or focused on issues of separation. In fact, they spoke repeatedly about growing closer to their mothers as they went through adolescence. Their struggles, concerns, and questions were *explicitly* about connection and about how to maintain connections, and these concerns only grew stronger over time.

The topic of autonomy and independence, however, did arise when the girls spoke about relationships with boys and future male partners. The girls typically did not want to "depend on a man" for financial or material needs. They often spoke of being warned by their mothers, aunts, sisters, cousins, and fathers that they needed to "provide for themselves" and not "wait for a man." Some of these girls spoke about learning to be independent by watching their mothers while others wished that their mothers were more independent. Notably, the girls' discussions of existing or future male partners (their mothers' and their own) were the only ones in which issues of independence were a central focus.

These findings raise the question of why these relational findings are different from those of studies of primarily white and middle-class adolescents.[1] Such studies have repeatedly indicated that gaining independence is a central struggle for adolescents. Perhaps the boys and girls in this study were more concerned with maintaining connections than with gaining independence because of their social status. Lacking perceived and real power in the world may increase the importance of relationships.[2] Without such power it is clearly more difficult to reap the benefits of being independent and autonomous. Furthermore, gaining autonomy may not be a primary concern or desire when survival depends primarily on relationships. Urban poor and working-class boys may learn quite early, as do girls from different socioeconomic communities, that relationships can provide an effective means for coping with the world. White adolescent boys from more middle- and upper-class backgrounds may not feel the same urgency about maintaining close male friendships, for example, because they are supported by the larger society in their visions of autonomy and in their attempts to be independent.

In addition, African American and Latino communities may not value independence and autonomy as much as other ethnic communities.[3] According to Tracy Robinson and Janie Ward,[4] the sense of self among African Americans may be an "extended self" that includes the self as "we." "Embedded in this 'extended self' is an individual's connectedness with others."[5] Gloria Anzaldua states that in Latino communities, "the welfare of the family, the community . . . is more important than the welfare of the individual."[6] Latino and African American communities may place more value on establishing and maintaining human connections and, therefore, the children—both boys and girls—raised in these communities may be more relationship-oriented than those raised in European American, middle class communities.[7] However, this distinction fails to address the fact that the African American and Latino adolescents in the present study were not only relationship oriented, but also fiercely committed to individualistic values. While these adolescents did not appear to be struggling, in particular, with issues of autonomy and independence; they were strong individualists who were seeking authentic connections. Cultural distinctions, therefore, do not fully address the question regarding why the patterns detected in the present study are different from those found among white, middle-class teens.

The methods used to assess development may also be responsible for the fact that the relational findings in this study, particularly regarding the boys, are different from the findings in the mainstream social science research literature. If the "listening" methods used in this study had been used with white, middle-class boys, it is quite possible that similar themes may have emerged. Since research findings are to a large degree a reflection of the methods we use,[8] it is difficult to compare earlier research findings with the present ones because the methods of investigation have been quite different. The majority of research on adolescent friendships, for example, has been survey-based. Consequently, if researchers did not begin their research making a distinction between having and desiring same-sex intimate friendships, they are not going to detect such distinctions in their forced-choice measures. By listening closely to the variations in the stories told by adolescents, as feminist researchers have been doing with girls over the past two decades, we can see new themes and have new insights into the worlds of adolescents. The differences detected between the present and earlier studies may be a difference of method rather than of population.

As developmental psychologists, we may need to listen more carefully to what these adolescents from different social-class, racial, and ethnic communities are telling us about their own development. In order to hear their concerns, we may have to use new methods, ones that pay close attention to how adolescents perceive their worlds on their own terms. Subsequent to such a shift in method, we may find ourselves needing to create new developmental theories that directly respond to these concerns. If searching for and struggling to maintain connected relationships is a concern for teenage boys and girls, as it is for my participants, then parents and professionals (e.g., teachers, principals, counselors) need to help them develop ways of finding and maintaining relationships that are truly satisfying. Rather than focusing on what adolescents *should* be struggling with (e.g., to separate from their parents), perhaps we should listen to what they are *actually* struggling with.

Futures, Schools, and Discrimination

The adolescents' discussions of their futures and their school highlight similar struggles, expectations, and desires. When they spoke about their lives, they spoke about their optimistic expectations as well as their daily fears of failure, violence, and death. While a few of the students seemed thoroughly optimistic and others seemed consistently worried, the majority maintained a "split consciousness" about their futures. They were acutely aware of the many and very real possibilities of dying "early" while, at the same time, felt optimistic that they would accomplish their goals if they worked hard enough. They maintained a "positive attitude" in the midst of their lived realities. In fact, as Marie and Malcolm pointed out, their lived realities enhanced their positive attitude and motivation to accomplish what they set out to achieve.

These beliefs in individual effort, motivation, and positive attitude were repeated in their discussions of their school performances, and in their experiences of discrimination. Most of the adolescents in the study stated that through their own effort and the "right attitude" they could reach their goals in school and break down the barriers of discrimination. They blamed their level of effort for their past, present, or anticipated academic struggles and staunchly asserted that effort and accomplishment, and failure and individual responsibility are intrinsically connected. Believing otherwise may, in fact, feel too risky. To lose their faith in the power of individual effort and hard work may lead to hopelessness and frustration in a system where the collectives that represents their interests—their families, peers, and communities—are not, as Eva tells us, "being heard." Believing that individual effort and determination will allow them to achieve the "American Dream," even when they are surrounded by lives that prove otherwise, may feel essential for survival.

Within each of their responses about the future, school, and discrimination, however, there were complications; nothing was as straightforward as it initially appeared. Their high hopes for their futures were direct responses to the keen awareness that their lives were constantly at risk. Their optimism was not a denial or a contradiction of their reality but a direct response to it. Their perceived laziness was variable, and their reasons for "being lazy" were not consistently self-blaming. They focused on individual effort and responsibility, but they also discussed, at times, a collective "we" as they spoke with a communal rather than an individual voice. Like Malcolm and Eva, the adolescents were not consistently hopeless or hopeful, consistently fearful or cavalier, self-blaming or other-blaming. Their stories reminded me that when social scientists, including myself, place their thinking into categories such as "self-blaming," "individually oriented," or even holding a "split consciousness," they risk oversimplifying the teens' desires, thoughts, beliefs, and values. The difficulty of complicating a story—of making it more authentic and real—while also revealing patterns, drawing broad strokes, and "having a point" is an ongoing difficulty. I attempted to resolve this dilemma, at least in part, by presenting case studies along with thematic chapters. The task for future researchers is to determine what I have overlooked or oversimplified in my attempt to add complexity to our understanding of urban adolescents.

The findings with respect to the adolescents' perceptions of their school performance and their perceptions of race/ethnicity, racism, and sexism challenged me in ways in which the other findings did not. While some of their responses were expected (the boys' angry stories of racism), many of them directly contradicted my own knowledge. Given what I know about their school, I did not expect to hear such rampant stories of self-blame when they spoke about their school performance. I did not expect the girls to tell me that they had not experienced racism "yet" or that sexism will not affect them. Furthermore, I did not expect them to tell me that my race did not influence what they chose to tell or not tell me, or that my gender, age, personal warmth, and familiarity were more important than my race or ethnicity. Their *spoken* outlook on issues of race and gender, similar to their spoken outlook about their school performance, differed from mine (what was left unspoken, of course, is not known). I struggled, at times, to write down their perspectives without overwhelming these discussions with my own notions of what I thought their perspectives should be. I sought "great stories" or stories that affirm what I believe about their school and their lives.[9] Mun Wong writes in his study of poor women on welfare that he wanted his participants "to furnish good data, arm[ing] us with an arsenal of voices to write against the social injustices."[10] In his study, however, the women rarely provided such stories. I, too, found myself wanting the adolescents to tell me that they were going to take to the streets to protest the poor quality of their school, or collectively fight against discrimination. Yet I heard them say that the reason they were doing poorly was because they were "lazy" and that they were not going to use race or gender "as an excuse" for not pursuing their goals. My belief about the importance of being receptive to "the unexpected" or "listening with both ears" was pushed into practice during these conversations. Their responses showed me that what I thought I knew about their perspectives, I did not know; and what I wanted to hear, I could not hear. Given that the purpose of my project was to listen and understand *their* views, I found myself with only one option: to represent their thoughts and feelings as they represented them to us.

Concluding Reflections

In my study, I entered into relationships with urban youth and listened to them speak about their worlds. I learned from them what they see, what they know, and what, perhaps, they do not know. The moments when Eva, for example, felt that she had to make me understand her more fully by reading one of her poems to me suggested that the teens wanted to be known as much as I wanted to know them. As a result of listening to different parts of their worlds, I was challenged, soothed, impassioned, and most of all emotionally and physically absorbed. When I asked them how they felt about being interviewed, they commonly stated that they enjoyed being given a chance to think about issues on which they rarely reflect in their daily lives. A few expressed enthusiasm about the opportunity to speak about themselves to someone who thought their perspectives were important. Their experiences of being interviewed seemed to affect some of them as deeply as I was affected by sitting with them and listening to their stories.

I leave this project with a sense that although I learned only about relatively small segments of their lives, these fragments challenge some of the most basic assumptions about urban youth specifically and adolescence in general. The next step is to conduct qualitative research with other samples of urban poor and working-class adolescents to see if the patterns detected here will be detected once again. My research and my clinical work with urban teens from Boston and New York City over the past eleven years, and my ongoing discussions with professionals and researchers who work with or study this population, suggest that they will. The stories told by the adolescents in this study need to be heard not only by students and teachers of adolescent development, but also by parents, teachers, and pol-icymakers who are trying to help teens thrive. We must move forward in our understanding of urban youth and of adolescent development and stop relying on negative stereotypes of the former and outdated, "univer-sal" models of the latter. According to my research and other recent re-search studies,[11] such stereotypes and models do not accurately reflect the lives of poor, working-class, or ethnic-minority adolescents (and perhaps not even those who are white and middle-class). Listening to urban poor and working-class youth will not only help us to better understand adoles-cence as a developmental period, it will also help us create policies and in-terventions that better suit adolescents' needs, and consequently, of course, our own needs. We also need to show these youths alternative models of change that do not rely exclusively on individual responsibility, motivation, and "positive attitude." Given that we, as parents, profession-als, and students, know that change will come only in response to both col-lective and individual responsibility and action, we need to help these urban youth find the "we" that they are seeking.

Appendix A

Research Interview Protocol

1. Family Information

    Whom do you live with? [If the teen lives with neither parents or with only one parent, inquire as to the whereabouts of their parents and ask why she or he doesn't live with both or lives with only one parent. Whether parents are separated, divorced, or still together, ask how long the teens have been in this current situation.]

    How long have you been living in your current situation?

    How many brothers and sisters do you have? Which brothers and sisters live with you?

    Does your mother (or the person they consider to be their mother) have a job? What does she do?

    Does your father (or the person they consider to be their father) have a job? What does he do?

2. Relationship with Mother

    [If they don't live with their mother, ask how often they see her.]

    Can you describe for me your relationship with your mother?

    [Whatever description the teen gives you, such as "we are close" or "we don't get along," ask what they mean by close or what

makes them feel that they don't get along, and then ask them to give you an example of being close or not getting along with their mother. Try to get examples from their descriptions.]
What do you like/dislike about your mother?
What do you think your mother likes/dislikes about you?
What do you like/dislike about the relationship with your mother? Explain.
Do you think your relationship with your mother has changed since last year?
How do think it has changed, or why do you think it hasn't changed? Give me examples of how it has changed or not changed? Why do you think it has or hasn't changed?

3. Relationship with Father
[If they don't live with their father, ask how often they see him.]
Can you describe for me your relationship with your father? [Follow same probing procedure as with the description regarding relationship with the mother.]
What do you like/dislike about your father?
What do you think your father likes/dislikes about you?
What do you like/dislike about the relationship with your father? Explain.
Do you think your relationship with your father has changed since last year?
How do you think it has changed or why do you think it hasn't changed? Give me examples of how it has changed or not changed?
Why do you think the relationship has or hasn't changed? [Try to encourage the teenager to be as specific as possible.]

4. Relationship with Primary Caretakers
Ask the same questions above for the people who are the primary caretakers for the child, if they are not the natural parents.

5. Sibling Relationships
How would you describe your relationships with your brothers and sisters? [Probe whatever description is given for each brother and sister. Probe in similar fashion as directed above.]
Do you feel that you are closer to one brother or sister more than the others? Which one? Why do you feel this way? Why

do or don't you feel that way with your other sisters and
brothers?
Do you think any of your relationships with your brothers and sisters have changed since last year?
How have they (the relationships) changed? Why do you think they
have changed? [Try to encourage the teenager to be as specific
as possible.]
6. Relationship with Best or Closest Friends
Is there one person (or more) whom you would consider your clos-
est or best friend? [If no, are there any reasons why? If the teen
has chosen a group of friends as the closest then adapt the ques-
tions to include many people.]
Who? How long have you been closest or best friends?
What makes this person your closest friend?
Describe your friendship with this person. What is it like?
What do you like/dislike about your friend? Explain.
What do you think your friend likes/dislikes about you?
What do you like/dislike about the relationship?
Is there anything you would like to change about the relationship?
Are you similar/dissimilar to your friend in any way? Explain.
Do you think your friendship has changed over the past year? [If
the friendship has not lasted a year yet, ask if they think this
friendship is any different than the close friendships they had last
year or in the past.]
In what ways has it or your friendships changed over the past year?
Why has or hasn't it changed?
7. Romantic Relationships
Do you have a boy/girlfriend right now?
If yes:
Describe your relationship with him/her.
How long have you been seeing him/her?
What do you like/dislike about him/her? Explain.
How do you feel about him/her? Explain.
How do you think s/he feels about you? Explain.
Would you say you're in love? What does that mean for you?
What do you like/dislike about the relationship? Explain.
Is there anything you would like to change about the relationship?

Are you sexually involved with him/her?

If yes:

How long have you been sexually involved?

What made you decide to become sexually involved?

What is that like for you to be (or not to be) sexually involved with this person? [If they have difficulty answering you can give them options such as, "Is it fun? Scary? Boring?" And then probe whatever answer they give you.]

Do you use protection? Why or why not?

Do you think your relationship has changed over the past year? [If the relationship hasn't lasted a year: Do you think your relationship with this person is any different than your previous relationship?] How has or hasn't it changed and why?

If the teen does not have a boy/girlfriend right now:

How do you feel about not going out with somebody at this point?

Why do you think you don't go out with anybody right now? Have you ever had a boyfriend or girlfriend? Do you want to in the future?

8. Role Models

Which relationships or relationship is particularly important or most important for you right now? Why?

Whom do you look up to? Who is a role model for you? Who would you like to be like? Why?

9. Self-Description

How would you describe yourself? [If they have difficulty, ask them how someone else (someone they are close to) would describe them. Whatever adjectives they give to describe themselves, ask the teen to give an example of that adjective, e.g.: How are you nice; can you give me an example?]

What do you like/dislike about yourself? [Probe for examples.]

What would you like to change/keep the same about yourself? [Probe for examples. Teenager should be encouraged to be as specific as possible.]

Do you think you have changed over the past year? How have you
changed or in what ways have you not changed? What has
caused the changes?

10. Drug and Alcohol Use

Do you use drugs/alcohol? [Ask about each separately.]

Why or why not? Why don't you use more than you do? [*If yes:*
What kind of substance? In what situations do you use them?]

Has your use changed since last year?

Do you think you will use drugs/alcohol in the future?

Why or why not?

11. Values and Beliefs

What values or beliefs are really important for you? Why? What
makes them important?

Do you consider yourself religious? In what ways? Is it important to
you? Why? If not religious, why not?

What makes your life worth living? Why?

12. Views of the Future

When you think of the future, what do you think of? How do you
feel when you think about your future?

What do you see happening in your future?

How do you see yourself getting there?

What are your hopes/fears about the future? Why do you
hope/fear these things?

Has the way you think about the future changed over the past year?
How and why has it changed or not changed?

13. School Questions

How do you feel about school? Why?

What do you like/dislike about school? Why? Give examples. How
long have you felt this way?

What kind of grades do you get typically? Are you satisfied with
how you do in school? Why or why not?

Why do you think you do so well or why do you think you don't
do as well as you would like?

Do you think how you do as a student will have any effect on you
later in life?

Do you think your thoughts about school have changed over the
past year? How have they changed? What's changed? Why have
they changed or not changed?

14. Perspectives on Larger Society

How do you see the larger society in which you live? What kind of
world do we live in? How would you describe the society we live
in? [Encourage specificity.]

Do you think there is discrimination in this society? What kind?
Have you ever experienced any kind of racism/sexism? Describe
the situation. What was that like? Explain. [If they say they
haven't, ask if they think they will in the future, and then on
what grounds?]

15. Concluding Questions

We have now finished the interview, are there any comments about
yourself that you want to add? Explain.

Do you have any questions for me?

Thank you for participating in the project.

■ ■ ■ ■ ■ ■ ■ ■

Appendix B

Conceptually Clustered Matrix for Relationships with Peers

Adolescent	Relationships with Friends	Relationships with Romantic Partner
Marie	*Year 1*	
	Her best friend is her cousin. Speaks about friends' being "two faced," but not her cousin. "Really trusts her," never had an argument. Mother warns against trusting friends and implies that she is also wary of trusting peers. Says friend is "understanding, nice, honest." Evidence of mutual caring. Says they are both "ambitious" but have "different attitude."	She has a boyfriend whom she rarely sees. Doesn't want to "get serious" and risk getting hurt by him. She "thinks" he cares about her and she "knows" she loves him. She has not had sex and wants to marry as a virgin. Having sex may result in being hurt so wants assurance of marriage.
	Year 2	
	Best friend is the same as last year because she's honest. Never had a big argument. They tell each	Seeing the same boy. She thinks he likes her more than she likes him. She loves him but sounds

other their problems. Mutuality to the friendship. Says they are both honest but her friend can control her feelings more. Doesn't trust her peers.

ambivalent. She says she doesn't want to have "too many" feelings for him because she might get hurt. Still is virgin because she doesn't want to "insult" her mother.

Year 3

Still states that best friend is same as last year but doesn't see her as much. She says she never really had a "real" best friend whom she sees every day. When she has a problem, she calls her friend. She doesn't "tell everything to anybody" because of her reservations regarding trusting others.

New boyfriend with whom she doesn't want to "get serious." She likes that he is very ambitious unlike her other boyfriend. Feels "proud to bring him home." Hasn't had sex. She describes their relationship as understanding.

Notes

Notes to the Introduction

1. Throughout this book, "urban adolescents" will refer to those who live in urban areas and who are from poor or working-class families. While the study presented in this book focuses primarily on ethnic-minority urban youth, it is critical to remember that urban youth are ethnically diverse and include white teenagers. My focus on ethnic minorities reflects the student body of the particular school in which I collected my data.

2. See also Dash, 1989.
3. Massing, 1995.
4. Gilligan, 1982.
5. Alan Guttmacher Institute, 1994.
6. Sum & Fogg, 1991.
7. Jessor, 1993, p. 118.
8. Feldman & Elliot, 1990, p. 488.
9. Burton, Allison, & Obeidallah, 1995, p. 119.
10. See Bell-Scott, 1987; McKenry et al., 1989.
11. Gibbs, 1985, p. 28.
12. Reid, 1993.
13. Bell-Scott & Taylor, 1989; Garcia Coll et al., 1996.
14. Leadbeater & Way, 1996.
15. Bell-Scott & Taylor, 1989, p. 122.
16. Children's Defense Fund, 1991.
17. Ibid.

18. While these numbers refer to ethnic/racial groups rather than to urban poor or working-class youth, they are relevant for understanding urban adolescents since the majority of urban youth are black, Latino, or white. It is difficult to find statistics about urban adolescents specifically. The social science literature usually classifies studies of urban adolescents as studies of particular ethnic groups. Only recently have social scientists begun to identify adolescents by the geographic location in which they reside (Fine, 1991; Leadbeater & Way, 1996; Seidman, 1991).

19. Children's Defense Fund, 1991.

20. Alan Guttmacher Institute, 1994.

21. Jessor, 1992.

22. In a study of 234 seventh-grade students from an inner-city school, Price & Clarke-McLean (1997) found that only 14 percent of their participants fit into their high-risk subgroup (based on school grades and conduct).

23. Earls, 1993; Feldman & Elliot, 1990; Garcia Coll et al., 1996; Gibbs, 1985; Jessor, 1993; Leadbeater & Way, 1996; Spencer & Dornbusch, 1990; Way, 1995.

24. Bronfenbrenner, 1979; Lewin, 1951.

25. Campbell, 1984; Fine, 1991; Taylor, Gilligan, & Sullivan, 1995; Ladner, 1971; MacLeod, 1987/1995; Riley, 1985; Steinitz & Solomon, 1986; Willis, 1977.

26. Key exceptions to this general pattern include Ladner's study and Hauser and Kasendorf's study, both conducted in the 1970s. Ladner (1971) conducted an ethnographic study of thirty urban black girls of different ages to find out how "low income black girls go about the actual task of becoming women" (p. 235). Ladner's study is one of the few in-depth developmental studies of urban black girls. Her study, however was cross-sectional rather than longitudinal, which many researchers recommend when studying change over time (Damon, 1979; Hauser & Kasendorf, 1983). Hauser and Kasendorf (1983) examined the identity development of twenty-two low-income black and white adolescents. They followed the adolescents over a three-year time span to examine how their perceptions of themselves changed over this period. Their study is unique in its approach to the study of low-income adolescents; the population under consideration, however, was restricted to boys.

27. Campbell, 1984; MacLeod, 1987/1995.

28. Bronfenbrenner, 1977, p. 515.

29. Harries, 1987, p. 140.

30. Although there are certainly a multitude of additional aspects of one's world (perhaps even infinite), I have chosen these areas because they seemed to me, as a psychologist who has worked with adolescents for over eleven years, the most obvious components of an adolescent's world.

31. This expression was taken from a talk given by Toni Morrison at the Massachusetts Institute of Technology in April 1992.

32. This expression was also taken from a talk given by Toni Morrison concerning the reasons she wrote her novel *Beloved* (1987).

33. Jones, 1989; Leadbeater & Way, 1996; Spencer, Brookins, & Allen, 1985; Taylor, 1995.

34. By "ethnography" I mean a study that typically involves a participant observer collecting data from multiple sources (parents, teachers, students, administrators, neighbors, etc.) using multiple methods (e.g., interviewing, observing) over a period of time. A common aim of such studies is to understand the ways in which a particular community thinks and acts. Classic ethnographic studies include Stack's (1974) study of African American families or Liebow's (1967) study of black men from an urban community. In contrast, my study involved analyzing the interviews of a small group of adolescents over time. I was not interested in how the adolescents acted, but rather how they *perceived* their actions and, more generally, their worlds.

Notes to Chapter 1

1. Rabinow & Sullivan, 1979.
2. Ibid., p. 6.
3. Brown & Gilligan, 1992; Flax, 1990; Gadamer, 1984; Gergen, 1985; Hare-Mustin & Marecek, 1988; Rorty, 1979; Segal, 1986.
4. Messer, Sass, & Woolfolk, 1984, p. 4.
5. Gilligan, Brown, & Rogers, 1990, p. 88.
6. Many researchers have noted the problems with a deficit model of development (see Garcia Coll et al., 1996; Gibbs, 1985; Hauser & Kassendorf, 1983; McKenry et al., 1989)
7. Garcia Coll and her colleagues (1996) discuss this particular problem and provide numerous references for studies that have made such a claim (e.g., Bloom, Davis, & Hess, 1965; Dunn, 1987; Passow, 1963).
8. Gadamer, 1984.
9. Sass, 1988, p. 253.
10. Lather, 1988, 1991; Stacey, 1988.
11. While it is clearly not possible to reflect on all of one's own prejudices, it is possible to engage with and constantly reflect on the prejudices of which we are aware.
12. Gadamer, 1979, p. 150.
13. Ibid., p. 151–157.
14. Hoshmand & Polkinghorne, 1992, p. 61.
15. I define "developmental theory" as a theory that attempts to explain what happens (cognitively, emotionally, and behaviorally) during or across certain periods (infancy, childhood, adolescence, or adulthood) in the lifespan. I distinguish these formal theories from the day-to-day explanatory models of thought that we carry around with us to make sense of our worlds.

16. I am focusing here on where one begins one's research project conceptually. I am not critiquing the use of developmental theories to explain one's findings in exploratory research, but rather using a developmental theory as a frame for one's research.

17. Hirschman, 1979, p. 19.

18. Heidegger, 1927/1962, p. 153.

19. Lyotard, 1984.

20. Ibid., p. xxv.

21. Ibid.

22. Harding, 1986, p. 15.

23. Blos, 1941, 1979; Erikson, 1963, 1968.

24. Erikson, 1968.

25. Blos, 1979; Erikson, 1963, 1968; Kohlberg, 1981; Selman, 1980.

26. Erikson, 1958, p. 114.

27. For overviews of this perspective, see Feldman & Elliot (1990) or Balk (1995).

28. Gilligan, 1982; Miller, 1976; Steinitz & Solomon, 1986.

29. Gilligan, Brown, & Rogers, 1990; Brown & Gilligan, 1992; Rogers, 1993.

30. Douvan & Adelson, 1966; Marcia, 1980; Miller, 1991; Thomas, 1996.

31. Belle, 1989; Buhrmester & Furman, 1987; Caldwell & Peplau, 1982; Epstein & Karweit, 1983; Miller, 1991.

32. Way, in press.

33. Flax, 1990, p. 57.

34. Bordo, 1990.

35. Rorty, 1979, p. 364.

36. Brown & Gilligan, 1992; Campbell, 1984; Fine, 1991; Gilligan, 1982; Ladner, 1971; MacLeod, 1987/1995; Steinitz & Solomon, 1986.

37. White, 1952.

38. Since Robert White, many other researchers from diverse fields, including sociology, anthropology, and psychology, have conducted similar studies of human lives in various contexts (e.g., Campbell, 1984; Fine, 1991; Gilligan, 1982; Ladner, 1971; Lewis, 1961; Liebow, 1967; MacLeod, 1987/1995; Stack, 1974). Although these researchers have chosen different methodologies (participant observation or semistructured research interviewing), all agree that the depth and richness of human lives can be revealed only by carefully observing and listening closely to each person's story. In their studies, the lives of the research participants are drawn out in vivid detail, frequently revealing an intimate understanding on the researchers' part of the environment in which the research participants are immersed.

39. Brown & Gilligan, 1990, p. 3.

40. Gilligan, Brown, & Rogers, 1990, p. 89.

41. Ibid.

42. Ibid., p. 107.

43. Gilligan, 1991.

44. "No one, not even the least privileged among us, is ever entirely powerless over the messages that traverse and position him at the post of sender, addressee, or referent" (Lyotard, 1984, p. 15).

45. Rogers, 1990, p. 3.

Notes to Chapter 2

1. The project initially began as a cross-sectional study funded by the National Institute of Drug Abuse (Perry London, principal investigator) to examine the socio-emotional correlates of high-risk behavior among urban and suburban adolescents (see Way et al., 1994).

2. From a cross-sectional NIDA study of urban adolescents (see previous note), ninety adolescents were individually interviewed (all those who agreed to be interviewed). From this subsample of adolescents, I asked all the ninth and tenth graders (N = 30) to participate in my study. Twenty-eight were willing to participate. However, four of these students left the school after the first year, and one left after two years. The remaining twenty-three students were interviewed over three years and one was interviewed over two years.

3. The school from which I have drawn my sample has fifty-six ethnic groups represented in the student body, with African Americans and Puerto Ricans comprising the majority. The school's ethnic diversity is typical of many urban schools.

4. Social class was determined by the resident parents' occupation and level of education completed. Those parents who depended on public assistance for their daily livelihood (N = 10) were considered poor.

5. All but one of the interviewers were doctoral students in psychology at the time of the interviews; the fifth was a master's student in psychology. Two of the interviewers were white males from working-class families, two were white females from middle-class families, and one interviewer was African American from a middle-class family. Throughout my data analyses, I will refer to the interviewers by their first names.

6. Brown et al., 1988; Brown & Gilligan, 1990.

7. Miller, 1988.

8. Miles & Huberman, 1984.

9. Brown et al., 1988.

10. Brown & Gilligan, 1990, p. 5.

11. Ibid., p. 6.

12. Miller, 1991.

13. Ibid., p. 42.

14. Miles & Huberman, 1984.

15. Gilligan, Brown, & Rogers, 1990, p. 96.

Notes to the Introduction to Chapter 3
1. Fine & Weis, 1996, p. 260.

Notes to Chapter 3
1. The descriptions of Malcolm are drawn from Mike's notes at the end of his interview with Malcolm.

2. Kneia DaCosta (1996) found, in her study of urban black adolescents, that they often distinguished between "trustworthy, real friends, who come in short supply, and mere 'associates,' who are the ubiquitous defaults" (p. 21).

3. What seems like a term of affection used to describe Paul may indicate that Paul is not an associate, but rather a friend. Malcolm, however, does not discuss this relationship. The term, however, may merely refer to the boys with whom he associates.

4. While listening to the adolescents in this study, I was often struck by their disclosures of their private thoughts and feelings while at the same time discussing their distrust of others. Eva says in her junior-year interview: "I won't talk to people like I'm talking to you now, you don't know me so it really don't matter to me what you know [now]. It's like crazy, you know, people that you see every day that knows things about you and you know they bring it up." Eva suggests a sense of vulnerability about others in her community knowing her stories, knowing her weaknesses, and using them against her (this fear is discussed at length in chapter 5). The interviewers will not do that precisely because they are not part of her community. In addition, the adolescents may have been encouraged to speak openly with their respective interviewers because the interviewers took their perspectives seriously—they sat with each adolescent and carefully listened to their stories.

5. Questions about potential discrimination based on race, ethnicity, or gender were only asked during the second- and third-year interviews.

Notes to Chapter 4

Parts of this chapter have been previously published in *The Psychology of Women Quarterly, 19*, 107–128

1. The concept of "ordinary courage" is drawn from Annie Rogers's (1993) work with adolescent girls. Her definition of this concept is drawn from a fourteenth-century definition of courage "to speak one's mind by telling all one's heart" (Simpson & Weiner, 1989, p. 1051).

2. Of the ten adolescent girls who suggested this outspoken theme, seven did so in their junior or senior year. While many qualitative researchers avoid presenting numbers or frequencies, I provide such data because I believe it is critical to provide as much thematic information to the reader as possible. Themes are often evident among only a subset of participants and I do not want to imply otherwise.

Furthermore, I do not want to leave my reader wondering what I meant by "many" or "some" or "a few" and I also do not want to simply say "the girls stated . . . ," leaving the reader incorrectly to assume that all the girls suggested a particular theme. Numbers are presented to underscore the diversity within the sample. Rarely did all the adolescents indicate any of the themes I discuss. To avoid disrupting the flow of the narrative, however, these numbers are presented in the endnotes.

3. I frequently note the ethnicity of the adolescent I am describing in order to remind the reader that the themes discussed in this book were suggested by adolescents from different ethnic groups. None of the themes were more prevalent among one ethnic group than another.

4. Pastor, McCormick, & Fine (1996) discuss the safe spaces for girls as "homes."

5. Brown & Gilligan, 1992, p. 112.

6. Fordham, 1993.

7. Ibid.

8. Nine out of the twelve girls suggested this theme.

9. A year after this interview took place, I was told by a guidance counselor that Tyiesha was on antidepressants when I interviewed her.

10. Only one boy told us he was "outspoken" in his relationships. Four boys suggested that they were direct and honest in some of their relationships but did not refer to themselves as "outspoken." Nine boys suggested that they were silenced by or silent in some of their relationships, and five boys indicated that they were silenced by or silent in most of their relationships.

11. A similar strategy has been observed in other studies of friendships among white, primarily middle-class adolescents. Shulman (1993) found, in his study of close friendship pairs among tenth-graders, that those who had "disengaged friendships" reported that disagreements could terminate their close friendships. They therefore sought to avoid conflict in their friendships: "they kept a certain distance to avoid differences of opinion or conflicts. Paradoxically, disengaged close friends preferred to be 'distant' in order to preserve the closeness of their friendships" (p. 68). The present study suggests similar findings among the boys.

12. Brown & Gilligan, 1992, p. 3.

13. Pipher, 1994; Mann, 1994.

14. Brown & Gilligan, 1992; Gilligan, Brown, & Rogers, 1990; Rogers, 1993.

15. Eichenbaum & Orbach, 1988, p. 147.

16. Ibid., p. 148.

17. Numerous social science research studies, in addition to the ones already cited, have discussed the "silences" among women (Belenky et al., 1986; Lakoff, 1975). The majority, however, with a few exceptions (Belenky et al., 1986), have focused on middle- and upper-class girls and women.

18. Simpson & Weiner, 1989, p. 1051.

19. In contrast to the present findings, Fordham's (1993) study of adolescent girls from Washington, D.C., indicated that the girls who were doing poorly in school were more likely to be the "loud girls" than the girls who excelled in school. No such differences were found in the present study.

20. Taylor, Gilligan, and Sullivan have recently (1995) completed a study of "high risk" urban adolescent girls. They note, in accordance with the present study, that many black adolescent girls in their study appear to "speak their minds" in many of their relationships.

21. Wade-Gayles, 1984, p. 12.

22. Ladner, 1979, p. 3.

23. Torres, 1992.

24. It is important to note that while adolescent girls may not feel heard by their fathers or mothers, parents may still encourage their daughters' outspokenness.

25. Pastor, McCormick, & Fine, 1996, p. 16.

26. Brown & Gilligan, 1992.

27. Eichenbaum & Orbach, 1988.

28. The adolescents are part of a constellation of cultures which include cultures based on race, ethnicity, gender, social class, as well as family, school, and geographic location. In the present discussion, however, I am referring to an American culture that encompasses all of these.

29. Joseph, 1984, p. 18.

30. Debold, 1991.

31. Raymond, 1994.

32. Turner et al., 1994.

33. Fine & Weis, 1996, p. 261.

34. hooks, 1989, p. 6.

Notes to Chapter 5

Portions of this chapter were previously published in B. Leadbeater & N. Way, eds., *Urban girls: Resisting stereotypes, creating identities* (New York: New York University Press, 1996).

1. Guillermo is the only participant in the study who is interviewed for two years.

2. Sullivan, 1953.

3. Considering a girlfriend to be a romantic partner and a close friend was not typical among the boys; only two boys in the study expressed such feelings.

4. All but one of the twelve boys claimed *not* to trust other boys by their third interviews (four boys voiced complete distrust of all of their male peers during all three of their interviews), and nine boys reported that this lack of trust prevented them from having close or best friends. Similarly, all but two of the twelve girls

spoke about not trusting other girls by their third-year interviews (none of the girls voiced complete distrust of all of their female peers during all three interviews). Only four girls reported that their lack of trust in their female peers kept them from having close or best friends.

5. Although the adolescents were never specifically asked to respond about *same-sex* peers, all of the adolescents spoke about same-sex peers when asked about close or best friends. Only three adolescents explicitly included opposite-sex friends in their network of close or best friends.

6. Three of the boys, and none of the girls, discussed concerns about their peers stealing from them.

7. Caldwell & Peplau, 1982; Belle, 1989.

8. Raymond, 1994; Lehne, 1989.

9. Although many of the boys spoke about knowing peers who had died, Tyrone was the only boy who spoke about the death of close friends.

10. Wortham (1997) notes in his ethnographic study of immigrant Latinos from a small town that "the transience of Latino families also takes a toll both on adolescents and other Latinos. . . . Even children from families resident for several years often speculate that they will be leaving soon, and this expectation disrupts their commitments to school and friends. As a result of all of this transience, children seem particularly sensitive to loss and suspicious of others' commitment to them" (p. 6). While it is unknown how transient the population that participated in the present study was, this type of sensitivity to loss is suggested.

11. These two qualities of friendship are considered the most important ones by adolescents from many different ethnic and social-class backgrounds (Savin-Williams & Berndt, 1990).

12. Nine boys in the study indicated that they experience a shift from trusting to not trusting their male peers. Two boys in the study consistently stated that they had close or best friends, but they wanted to maintain caution in these relationships because of the potential for betrayal. For these two boys, being cautious or wary of their peers did not exclude the possibility of having a close or best friend. One adolescent boy in the study had a best friend each year of the study and never mentioned having difficulties trusting his peers or wanting to have more intimate friends.

13. Mac an Ghaill (1994), in his astute and powerful study of working-class boys' friendships (from England), notes that many of the adolescent boys describe feeling lonely with their "mates." "During the research, they reflected on their difficulty in expressing personal feelings with each other, resulting from their learning to hide from others and themselves what they felt" (p. 97). Furthermore, the boys in his study often discussed not being able to trust other boys with their personal issues and concerns.

14. Eight out of twelve of the adolescent girls stated that while they struggled with trusting their female peers, they had one or more close or best friends.

15. It is important to note that these adolescents were not having close relationships with those who were betraying them, but rather with those who were not betraying them.

16. It remains unclear in listening to Felicia's interview if, when she uses the word "nowadays," she believes that as she has grown older it has become more difficult for her to trust others or whether a specific incident or experience during the past year led her to no longer trust her peers.

17. Unfortunately the interviewers never asked the students what they meant by "these days" or "nowadays." Since Tyiesha had a best friend in her freshman and sophomore year, however, it is likely that she means that she cannot trust people as much as she could in the past.

18. Previous studies of adolescent friendships have suggested that males are more likely to mistrust their same-sex friends than are females (Armsden & Greenberg, 1987; Sharabany, Gershoni, & Hofman, 1981; Youniss & Smollar, 1985).

19. Similar findings regarding boys having "avoidant attachments" to their same-sex peers have been reported elsewhere (Bartholomew & Horowitz, 1991).

20. See review by Savin-Williams & Berndt, 1990; Youniss & Smollar, 1985.

21. Belle, 1989; Buhrmester & Furman, 1987; Caldwell & Peplau, 1982; Epstein & Karweit, 1983; Miller, 1991.

22. While Sullivan (1953) has written about the intimacy that exists among early-adolescent boys, other researchers have suggested that these boys have less intimate friendships than early-adolescent girls (Berndt, 1982).

23. Caldwell & Peplau, 1982; Camarena, Sarigiani, & Petersen, 1990; Douvan & Adelson, 1966; Furman & Buhrmester, 1985; Reisman, 1990; Savin-Williams & Berndt, 1990.

24. Leadbeater, Batgos, & Lin, 1992.

25. Brown & Gilligan, 1992.

26. Raymond, 1994, p. 120.

27. The impact of socialization pressures on adolescent girls' and boys' friendships has been noted by numerous researchers (Clark & Reis, 1988; Eder & Hallinan, 1978; Leadbeater, Batgos, & Lin, 1992; Rose, 1985).

28. Brown & Gilligan, 1992; Savin-Williams & Berndt, 1992; Youniss & Smollar, 1985.

29. Youniss & Smollar (1985) found that approximately 30 percent of the white, middle-class adolescent boys in their studies did not have supportive and trusting relationships with their male peers.

30. DaCosta (1996) has also noted in her qualitative study of urban black adolescents the theme of distrust of peers and classmates.

31. Ibid.

32. Epstein & Karweit, 1983, p. 60.

33. Haynes & Emmons, 1994.

34. Gold & Yanof, 1985.

35. The typical assertion concerning the connections between parent and peer relationships has been that those adolescents who have close relationships with parents are more likely to have close relationships with friends (Greenberg, Siegel, & Leitch, 1983; Kerns & Barth, 1995). Others have noted, however, that it is also possible for adolescents who have poor relationships with their parents to have close relationships with their peers in order to compensate (East & Rook, 1992).

36. Salguero & McCusker, 1996; Stack, 1974.

37. Laursen, 1993; Shulman, 1993; Youniss & Smollar, 1985.

38. DuBois & Hirsch, 1990; Gallagher & Busch-Rossnagel, 1991; Jones, Costin, & Ricard, 1994.

39. Jones, Costin, & Ricard, 1994.

40. DuBois & Hirsch, 1990.

41. Gallagher & Busch-Rossnagel, 1991.

Notes to Chapter 6

1. Half of the adolescents (six girls and six boys) suggested the themes discussed in this chapter. The other half of the adolescents either did not have mothers who were alive (N = 3) or did not speak about their mothers in ways that suggested patterns across their stories. While one of these adolescents spoke warmly about her mother and the others seemed more ambivalent, they never suggested the passion and intensity that I heard among the adolescents I describe in this chapter.

2. Collins (1987) notes that one of the most common messages heard among African American women from their mothers was that they should be self-reliant and resourceful: they should not depend on a man to take care of them either emotionally or financially.

3. Anzaldua, 1987; Bell-Scott et al., 1991; Greene, 1990; Kandel, 1974; Joseph, 1991; Shade, 1983; Shorris, 1992.

4. Joseph, 1984, p. 17.

5. Mac an Ghaill (1994) also notes that among the working-class adolescent males in his ethnographic study, many spoke extensively of their emotional closeness to their mothers. He states that this contrasted with the middle-class boys who directed much hostility toward their mothers and fathers.

6. Other social science researchers have noted similar findings among ethnic-minority adolescents (Eccles, 1997; Mac an Ghaill, 1994; Wortham, 1997).

7. Way et al., 1994.

8. Ward, 1996.

9. Wade-Gayles, 1984, p. 8.

10. Shorris, 1992.

11. T. Morrison, 1992, talk given at the Massachusetts Institute of Technology.

Notes to Chapter 7

1. Lamm, Schmidt, & Trommsdorff, 1976.
2. The theme was evident in the interviews of seventeen of the adolescents.
3. They feared death not only as a result of the violence in their neighborhoods but also as a result of disease. There were many stories of parents having cancer, heart, lung, or kidney problems or other potentially life-threatening diseases.
4. Ward, 1990, p. 223.
5. Heidegger, 1927/1962.
6. Riley, 1985; Weininger, 1975; Way, 1990.
7. In her forthcoming book, Carol Stack also notes this pattern in her interviews with urban youth.
8. MacLeod, 1987/1995.
9. Steinitz & Solomon, 1986.
10. Harding, 1986.
11. There is an abundance of social science literature which discusses the "split," "dual," or "contradictory" consciousness evident among women, poor and working-class people, and people of color (Gramsci, 1971; Liebow, 1967; Stack, 1974; Strauss, 1990).
12. Pastor, McCormick, & Fine, 1996, p. 28.
13. Steinitz and Solomon (1986) write about "individual responsibility as a source of hope and self blame" (p. 233) in their book on the perspectives of working-class youth.
14. Fine & Macpherson, 1995.

Notes to Chapter 8

1. MacLeod (1987/1995) notes that the black, urban adolescent boys he interviewed repeatedly blamed themselves for their academic mediocrity (see also Fine & Zane, 1989; Steinitz & Solomon, 1986).
2. Theorists and researchers have noted that hopelessness is commonly associated with a sense of lacking control (Ames, 1985; Ames & Lau, 1982; Weiner, Russell, & Lerman, 1978). Those who believe that certain characteristics, such as being "lazy," are permanent characteristics will feel more hopeless about the possibilities of change than those who see such a characteristic as more fluid and variable.
3. While terms such as "internal" and "external" are problematic given their implication that an experience can be neatly divided, I will use these two terms as a way to distinguish those experiences which appear to involve only the adolescents themselves (e.g., being "lazy" or having an "attitude") and those which involve institutions or relationships with parents, teachers, and peers.
4. Fine & Zane, 1989.
5. Ibid.
6. MacLeod, 1987/1995, p. 262.

7. Pastor and her colleagues note: "Critical insights without opportunities for students to reconstruct a world rich in the wonders of race, culture, gender, and social justice may wound a sense of possibility" (Pastor, McCormick, and Fine, 1996, p. 29).

Notes to Chapter 9

1. Social class seemed less clearly defined than race, ethnicity, and gender and, therefore, more complicated (awkward, perhaps) to directly inquire about when discussing oppression.

2. Nine of the twelve boys suggested the theme discussed here.

3. Stacy Scott, the only black interviewer, was not a part of the interviewing team during the third-year interviews.

4. Wong (1997), in his study of women on welfare, noted that while women were quick to note acts of discrimination enacted on others, they often denied having been discriminated against themselves. Wortham (1997) and Weis & Fine (1996) note that boys are more "prone to see macro-level discriminatory patterns in society [than girls] . . . they are less willing than females to . . . ignore the discrimination" (Wortham, 1997, p. 12).

5. Our third-year interviews were conducted by a white man from a working-class family and myself.

6. This particular finding has been noted by Michelle Fine in her research with urban adolescents from Philadelphia and New Jersey as well as in my own research with adolescents from the Lower East Side of New York City. It has also been noted by Frankenberg (1994) in her study of white working- and middle-class women. For some of the women in her study, "seeing race differences at all made one a racist" (p. 138).

7. Frankenberg (1994) in her book *The Social Construction of Whiteness*, distinguishes between essentialist racism, color and power evasion, and race cognizance. Essentialist racism asserts that ethnic minorities are inherently inferior. Color and power evasion is the discourse heard in the present study and asserts that race doesn't make a difference. Race cognizance is the discourse that insists on recognizing differences but also on valuing the culture and aesthetics of different cultures.

8. Weis & Fine, 1996; Wortham, 1997.

9. Orenstein, 1994; Sadker & Sadker, 1994.

10. Sadker & Sadker, 1994.

11. See also MacLeod, 1987/1995.

12. Freire, 1970; Taylor, Gilligan, & Sullivan, 1995.

Notes to Chapter 10

1. This information was obtained from Helena's notes of this first-year interview.

Notes to the Epilogue

1. Belle, 1989; Deaux, 1977; Douvan & Adelson, 1966; Epstein & Karweit, 1983.

2. See Steinitz and Solomon (1986) for a more extensive discussion of this dynamic.

3. Anzaldua, 1987; Nobles, 1980; Robinson & Ward, 1991; Stack, 1974.

4. Robinson & Ward, 1991.

5. Ibid., p. 92.

6. Anzaldua, 1987, p. 19.

7. This distinction between African American and Latino and European American communities has been made repeatedly over the past ten years. The problem with this distinction, however, is not only does it not acknowledge that many Black and Latino youth are struggling to find the connections they seek, it also ignores the large body of research on white, European American girls that indicates that they are particularly desirous of connection (see Brown & Gilligan, 1992).

8. Way, in press.

9. Fine, 1991; Wong, 1997.

10. Wong, 1997, p. 26.

11. Burton, Allison, & Obeidallah, 1995; Fine, 1991; Fine & Zane, 1989; Fine & Macpherson, 1995; Leadbeater & Way, 1996; MacLeod, 1987/1995; Steinitz & Solomon, 1986; Taylor, Gilligan, & Sullivan, 1995; Winfield, 1995.

References

Alan Guttmacher Institute. (1994). *Sex and America's teenagers*. New York.

Ames, C. (1985). Attributions and cognition in motivation theory. In M. Alderman & M. Cohen, eds., *Motivation theory and practice for preservice teachers*. Washington, DC: Clearinghouse on Teacher Education.

Ames, R., & Lau, S. (1982). An attributional analysis of student help-seeking in academic settings. *Journal of Educational Psychology, 74.*

Anzaldua, G. (1987). *Borderlands la frontera*. San Francisco: Aunt Lute Books.

Armsden, G. C., & Greenberg, M. T. (1987). The inventory of parent and peer attachment: Individual differences and their relationship to psychological well-being in adolescence. *Journal of Youth and Adolescence, 16,* 427–454.

Balk, D. E. (1995). *Adolescent development: Early through late adolescence*. New York: Brooks/Cole Publishing Company.

Bartholomew, K., & Horowitz, L. M. (1991). Attachment styles among young adults: A test of a four-category model. *Journal of Personality and Social Psychology, 61,* 226–244.

Belenky, M. F., Clinchy, B. M., Goldberger, N. R., & Tarule, J. M. (1986). *Women's ways of knowing*. New York: Basic Books.

Bell-Scott, P. (1987). Introduction. In Consortium for research on black adolescence, *Black adolescence: Topical summaries and annotated bibliographies of research*. Storrs, CT: University of Connecticut, School of Family Studies, Author (ERIC Document Reproduction Service No. ED 285 924).

Bell-Scott, P., Guy-Sheftall, B., Royster, J., Sims-Wood., J., DeCosta-Willis, M., & Fultz, L. (1991). *Double stitch: Black women write about mothers and daughters*. Boston: Beacon Press.

Bell-Scott, P., & Taylor, R. L. (1989). Introduction: The multiple ecologies of black adolescent development. *Journal of Adolescent Research, 4*(2), 119–124.

Belle, D. (1989). *Children's social networks and social supports.* New York: Wiley.

Berndt, T. J. (1982). The features and effects of friendships in early adolescents. *Child Development, 53,* 1447–1460.

Bloom, B. S., Davis, A., & Hess, R. (1965). *Compensatory education for cultural deprivation.* New York: Holt, Rinehart, and Winston.

Blos, P. (1941). *The adolescent personality: A study of individual behavior.* New York: D. Appleton-Century.

———. (1979). Character formation in adolescence. In *The adolescent passage: Developmental issues,* pp. 171–191. New York: New York University Press. (Reprinted from *The Psychoanalytic Study of the Child, 1974, 29,* 162–186.)

Bordo, S. (1990). Feminism, postmodernism, and gender-scepticism. In L. Nicholson, ed., *Feminism/postmodernism,* pp. 133–156. New York: Routledge.

Bronfenbrenner, U. (1977). Toward an experimental ecology of human development. *American Psychologist, 32,* 513–531.

———. (1979). *The ecology of human development.* Cambridge, MA: Harvard University Press.

Brown, L. M., Argyris, D., Attanucci, J., Bardige, B., Gilligan, C., Johnston, K., Miller, B., Osbourne, R., Ward, J., Wiggins, G., & Wilcox, D. (1988). *A guide to reading narratives of moral conflict and choice for self and moral voice.* Cambridge, MA: Center for the Study of Gender, Education, and Human Development, Harvard University, Monograph #2.

Brown, L. M., & Gilligan, C. (1990). Listening for self and relational voices: A responsive/resisting reader's guide. In M. Franklin, Chair, *Literary theory as a guide to psychological analysis.* Symposium conducted at the annual meeting of the American Psychological Association, Boston.

———. (1992). *Meeting at the crossroads: Women's psychology and girls' development.* Cambridge, MA: Harvard University Press.

Buhrmester, D., & Furman, W. (1987). The development of companionship and intimacy. *Child Development, 58,* 1101–1113.

Burton, L. M., Allison, K. W., & Obeidallah, D. (1995). Social context and adolescence: Perspectives on development among inner-city African American teens. In L. J. Crockett and A. C. Crouter, eds., *Pathways through adolescence: Individual development in relation to social contexts.* Mahwah, NJ: Lawrence Erlbaum Associates.

Caldwell, M. A., & Peplau, L. A. (1982). Sex differences in same-sex friendships. *Sex Roles, 8,* 721–733.

Camarena, P. M., Sarigiani, P. A., & Petersen, A. C. (1990). Gender-specific pathways to intimacy in early adolescence. *Journal of Youth and Adolescence, 19,* 19–32.

Campbell, A. (1984). *The girls in the gang.* Cambridge, MA: Basil Blackwell.

Children's Defense Fund. (1991). *Preventing adolescent pregnancy: What schools can do.* Washington, DC.

Clark, M. S., & Reis, H. T. (1988). Interpersonal process in close relationships. *Annual Review of Psychology, 39,* 609–672.

Collins, P. H. (1987). The meaning of motherhood in black culture and black mother-daughter relationships. *Sage, 4,* 3–10.

DaCosta, K. (1996). *Urban black adolescents' appraisals of social and academic concerns.* Poster presented at the Sixth Biennial Meeting of the Society for Research on Adolescence, Boston.

Damon, W. (1979). *The social world of the child.* San Francisco: Jossey Bass.

Dash, L. (1989). *When children want children: The urban crisis of teenage childbearing.* New York: William Morrow.

Deaux, K. (1977). Sex differences. In T. Blass, ed., *Personality variables in social behavior.* New York: Wiley.

Debold, E. (1991). The body at play. *Women and Therapy, 11,* 169–183.

Douvan, E., & Adelson, J. (1966). *The adolescent experience.* New York: Wiley.

DuBois, D. L., & Hirsch, B. J. (1990). School and neighborhood friendship patterns of blacks and whites in early adolescence. *Child Development, 61,* 524–536.

Dunn, L. M. (1987). *Bilingual Hispanic children in the U.S. mainland: A review of research on their cognitive, linguistic, and scholastic development.* Circle Pines, MN: American Guidance Service.

Earls, F. (1993). Health promotion for minority adolescents: Cultural considerations. In S. G. Millstein, A. C. Petersen, & E. O. Nightingale, eds., *Promoting adolescent health.* New York: Oxford University Press.

East, R. L., and Rook, K. S. (1992). Compensatory patterns of support among children's peer relationships: A test using school friends, nonschool friends, and siblings. *Developmental Psychology, 28*(1), 163–172.

Eccles, J. (1997). Personal communication.

Eder, D., & Hallinan, M. T. (1978). Sex differences in children's friendships. *American Sociological Review, 43,* 237–250.

Eichenbaum, L., & Orbach, S. (1988). *Between women: Love, envy, and competition in women's friendships.* New York: Viking.

Epstein, J. L., & Karweit, N. (1983). *Friends in school: Patterns of selection and influence in secondary schools.* New York: Academic Press.

Erikson, E. H. (1958). *Young man Luther.* New York: Norton.

———. (1963). *Childhood and society.* 2d ed. New York: Norton.

———. (1968). *Identity: Youth and crisis.* New York: Norton.

Feldman, S., & Elliot, G. R. (1990). *At the threshold: The developing adolescent.* Cambridge, MA: Harvard University Press.

Fine, M. (1991). *Framing dropouts: Notes on the politics of an urban high school.* Albany: State University of New York Press.

Fine, M., & Macpherson, P. (1995). Hungry for an us. *Feminism and Psychology*, 5(2), 181–200.

Fine, M., & Weis, L. (1996). Writing the "wrongs" of field work: Confronting our own research/writing dilemmas in urban ethnographies. *Qualitative Inquiry*, 2(3), 251–274.

Fine, M., & Zane, N. (1989). Bein' wrapped too tight: When low-income women drop out of high school. In L. Weis & H. Petrie, eds., *Dropouts from school*, pp. 23–43. Albany: State University of New York Press.

Flax, J. (1990). Postmodernism and gender relations in feminist theory. In L. Nicholson, ed., *Feminism/postmodernism*, pp. 39–62. New York: Routledge.

Fordham, S. (1993). "Those loud black girls:" (Black) women, silence, and gender "passing" in the academy. *Anthropology and Education Quarterly, 24*, 3–32.

Frankenberg, R. (1994). *The social construction of whiteness: White women, race matters*. Minneapolis: University of Minnesota Press.

Freire, P. (1970). *The pedagogy of the oppressed*. New York: Seabury Press.

Furman, W., & Buhrmester, D. (1985). Children's perceptions of the personal relationships in their social networks. *Developmental Psychology, 21*, 1016–1024.

Gadamer, H. G. (1979). The problem of historical consciousness. In P. Rabinow & W. Sullivan, eds., *Interpretive social science*. Berkeley: University of California Press.

———. (1984). *Truth and method*. New York: Crossroad.

Gallagher, C., & Busch-Rossnagel, N. A. (1991). *Self-disclosure and social support in the relationships of black and white female adolescents*. Poster presented at the Society for Research on Child Development, March 25–29, Seattle.

Garcia Coll, C., Lanberty, G., Jenkins, R., McAdoo, H. P., Crnic, K., Wasik, B. H., & Garcia, H. V. (1996). An integrative model for the study of developmental competencies in minority children. *Child Development, 67*, 1891–1914.

Gergen, K. J. (1985). The social constructivist movement in modern psychology. *American Psychologist, 40*, 266–275.

Gibbs, J. T. (1985). City girls: Psychosocial adjustment of urban black adolescent females. *Sage, 2*(2), 28–36.

Gilligan, C. (1982). *In a different voice: Psychological theory and women's development*. Cambridge, MA: Harvard University Press.

———. (1991). Joining the resistance: Psychology, politics, girls and women. *Michigan Quarterly Review, 29*(4), 501–536.

Gilligan, C., Brown, L., & Rogers, A. (1990). Psyche imbedded: A place for body, relationships, and culture in personality theory. In A. Rabin, R. Zucker, R. Emmons, & S. Frank, eds., *Studying persons and lives*, pp. 86–147. New York: Springer.

Glaser, B., & Strauss, A. (1967). *The discovery of grounded theory: Strategies for qualitative research*. New York: Aldine.

Gold, M., & Yanof, D. S. (1985). Mothers, daughters, and girlfriends. *Journal of Personality and Social Psychology, 49*(3), 654–659.

Gramsci, A. (1971). *Selections from prison notebooks*. New York: International Publishers.

Greenberg, M. T., Siegel, J. M., & Leitch, C. J. (1983). The nature and importance of attachment relationships to parents and peers during adolescence. *Journal of Youth and Adolescence, 12*(5), 373–385.

Greene, B. (1990). Sturdy bridges: The role of African-American mothers in the socialization of African-American children. *Women and Therapy, 10*, 205–225.

Harding, S. (1986). *The science question in feminism*. Ithaca, NY: Cornell University Press.

Hare-Mustin, R., & Marecek, J. (1988). The meaning of difference: Gender theory, postmodernism, and psychology. *American Psychologist, 43*(2), 455–464.

Harries, K. (1987). Truth and freedom. *Studies in Philosophy and the History of Philosophy, 18*, 131–155.

Hauser, S., & Kasendorf, E. (1983). *Black and white identity formation*. Malabar, FL: Kreiger Publishing Company.

Haynes, N., & Emmons, C. (1994). Lecture given at the Developmental Psychology Luncheon Series, Yale University, Department of Psychology, March 28, 1994.

Heidegger, M. (1927/1962). *Being and time*. New York: Harper and Row.

Hirschman, A. O. (1979). The search for paradigms as a hindrance for understanding. In P. Rabinow & W. Sullivan, eds., *Interpretive social science*. Berkeley: University of California Press.

hooks, b. (1989). *Talking back: Thinking feminist, thinking black*. Boston: South End Press.

Hoshmand, L., & Polkinghorne, D. E. (1992). Redefining the science-practice relationship and professional training. *American Psychologist, 47*(1), 55–66.

Jessor, R. (1992). Risk behavior in adolescence: A psychosocial framework for understanding and action. In D. E. Rogers & E. Ginzburg, eds., *Adolescents at risk: Medical and social perspectives*. Boulder, CO: Westview Press.

———. (1993). Successful adolescent development among youth in high-risk settings. *American Psychologist, 48*(2), 117–126.

Jones, D. C., Costin, S. E., & Ricard, R. J. (1994). Ethnic and sex differences in best friendship characteristics among African-American, Mexican-American, & European-American adolescents. Poster presented at Society for Research on Adolescence, San Diego, February 10, 1994.

Jones, R., ed. (1989). *Black adolescents*. Berkeley: Cobb and Henry.

Joseph, G. (1984). Black mothers and daughters: Traditional and new populations. *Sage, 1*(2), 17–21.

———. (1991). Black mothers and daughters: Traditional and new perspectives. In P. Bell-Scott et al., eds., *Double stitch: Black women write about mothers and daughters*, pp. 94–106. Boston: Beacon Press.

Kandel, D. (1974). Race, maternal authority and adolescent aspiration. *American Journal of Sociology, 76*, 999–1020.

Kerns, K. A., & Barth, J. M. (1995). Attachment and play: Convergence across components of parent-child relationships and their relations to peer competence. *Journal of Social and Personal Relationships, 12*(2), 243–260.

Kohlberg, L. (1981). *The philosophy of moral development: Moral stages and the idea of justice.* San Francisco: Harper and Row.

Kotlowitz, A. (1991). *There are no children here.* New York: Anchor Books.

Kozol, J. (1995). *Amazing grace.* New York: Harper Perennial.

Ladner, J. (1971). *Tomorrow's tomorrow.* New York: Anchor Books.

———. (1979). *Labeling black children: Some mental health implications.* Vol. 5. Washington, DC: Institute for Urban Affairs and Research, Howard University.

Lakoff, R. (1975). Language and woman's place. *Language in Society, 2,* 45–80.

Lamm, H., Schmidt, R. W., & Trommsdorff, G. (1976). Sex and social class as determinants of future orientation (time perspective) in adolescents. *Journal of Personality and Social Psychology, 34*(3), 317–326.

Lather, P. (1988). Feminist perspectives on empowering research methodologies. *Women's Studies International Forum, 11*(6), 569–581.

———. (1991). *Getting smart: Feminist research and pedagogy with/in the postmodern.* New York: Routledge.

Laursen, B., ed. (1993). *Close friendships in adolescence.* San Francisco: Jossey Bass.

Leadbeater, B. J., Batgos, J., & Lin, J. T. (1992). Gender differences in same- and cross-sex friendships: What counts as intimacy? Unpublished document, Yale University, New Haven, CT.

Leadbeater, B. J., & Way, N. (1996). *Urban girls: Resisting stereotypes, creating identities.* New York: New York University Press.

Lehne, G. (1989). Homophobia among men: Supporting and defining the male role. In M. S. Kimmel & M. A. Messner, eds., *Men's lives,* pp. 420–440. New York: Macmillan.

Lewin, K. (1951). *Field theory in social science.* New York: Harper.

Lewis, O. (1961). *The children of Sanchez.* New York: Random House.

Liebow, E. (1967). *Tally's corner.* Boston: Little, Brown.

Lyotard, J. F. (1984). *The postmodern condition: A report on knowledge.* Minneapolis: University of Minnesota Press.

Mac an Ghaill, M. (1994). *The making of men: Masculinities, Sexualities and Schooling.* Philadelphia: Open University Press.

MacLeod, J. (1987/1995). *Ain't no makin' it.* Boulder, CO: Westview Press.

Mann, J. (1994). *The difference.* New York: Warner Books.

Massing, M. (1995). Ghetto Blasting. *New Yorker,* Jan. 16, 32–38.

Marcia, J. E. (1980). Identity in adolescence. In J. Adleson, ed., *Handbook of adolescent psychology,* pp. 159–187. New York: Wiley.

McKenry, P. C., Everett, J. E., Ramseur, H. P., & Carter, C. J. (1989). Research on black adolescents: A legacy of cultural bias. *Journal of Adolescent Research, 4*(2), 254–264.

Messer, S., Sass, L., & Woolfolk, R. (1984). *Hermeneutics and psychological theory: Interpretive perspectives on personality, psychotherapy, and psychopathology*. New Brunswick, NJ: Rutgers University Press.

Miles, M., & Huberman, A. M. (1984). *Qualitative data analysis: A sourcebook of new methods*. Beverly Hills, CA: Sage.

Miller, B. (1988). Adolescent friendships: A pilot study. Unpublished qualifying paper, Harvard Graduate School of Education, Cambridge, MA.

———. (1991). Adolescents' relationships with their friends. Ph.D. diss., Harvard Graduate School of Education: Cambridge, MA.

Miller, J. B. (1976). *Toward a new psychology of women*. Boston: Beacon Press.

Morrison, T. (1987). *Beloved: A novel*. New York: Knopf. (Distributed by Random House.)

Nobles, W. W. (1980). Extended self: Rethinking the so-called negro self-concept. In R. L. Jones, ed., *Black psychology*. New York: Harper and Row.

Orenstein, P. (1994). *Schoolgirls: Young women, self-esteem, and the confidence gap*. New York: Doubleday.

Passow, H. A., ed. (1963). *Education in depressed areas*. New York: Teacher's College, Columbia University.

Pastor, J., McCormick, J., & Fine, M. (1996). Makin' homes: An urban girl thing. In B. J. Leadbeater & N. Way, eds., *Urban girls: Resisting stereotypes, creating identities*. New York: New York University Press.

Pipher, M. (1994). *Reviving Ophelia*. New York: Ballantine Books.

Price, L. N., & Clarke-McLean, J. G. (1997). Beyond stereotypes: Configurations and competence among African American inner city youth. Poster presented at the biennial meeting of SRCD, Washington, DC, April.

Rabinow, P., & Sullivan, W. (1979). *Interpretive social science*. Berkeley: University of California Press.

Raymond, D. (1994). Homophobia, identity, and the meanings of desire: Reflections on the cultural construction of gay and lesbian adolescent sexuality. In J. M. Irvine, ed., *Sexual cultures and the construction of adolescent identities*. Philadelphia: Temple University Press.

Reid, P. (1993). Poor women in psychological research: Shut up and shut out. *Psychology of Women Quarterly, 17*, 133–150.

Reisman, J. M. (1990). Intimacy in same-sex friendships. *Sex Roles, 23*, 65–82.

Riley, K. (1985). Black girls speak for themselves. In G. Weiner, ed., *Just a bunch of girls*. Philadelphia: Open University Press.

Robinson, T., & Ward, J. (1991). "A belief in a self far greater than anyone's disbelief": Cultivating resistance among African-American adolescents. *Women and Therapy, 11*, 3(4), 87–103.

Rogers, A. (1990). Black girls speak for themselves. In G. Weiner, ed., *Just a bunch of girls*. Cambridge, MA: Harvard University, Project on the Psychology of Women and the Development of Girls.

————. (1993). Voice, play, and a practice of ordinary courage in girls' and women's lives. *Harvard Educational Review, 63*(3).

Rorty, R. (1979). *Philosophy and the mirror of nature.* Princeton, NJ: Princeton University Press.

Rose, S. M. (1985). Same- and cross-sex friendships. *Sex Roles, 23,* 65–82.

Sadker, M., & Sadker, D. (1994). *Failing at fairness: How America's schools cheat girls.* New York: Charles Scribner's Sons.

Salguero, C., & McCusker, W. (1996). Symptom expression in inner-city Latinas: Psychopathology or help-seeking? In B. R. Leadbeater & N. Way, eds., *Urban girls: Resisting stereotypes, creating identities.* New York: New York University Press.

Sass, L. A. (1988). Humanism, hermeneutics, and the concept of the human subject. In S. Messer, L. Sass, & R. Woolfolk, eds., *Hermeneutics and psychological theory: Interpretive perspectives on personality, psychotherapy, and psychopathology.* New Brunswick, NJ: Rutgers University Press.

Savin-Williams, R. C., & Berndt, T. J. (1990). Friendship and peer relations. In S. Feldman & G. R. Elliot, eds., *At the threshold: The developing adolescent.* Cambridge, MA: Harvard University Press.

Segal, L. (1986). *The dream of reality: Heinz von Foerster's contructivism.* New York: Norton.

Seidman, E. (1991). Growing up the hard way: Pathways of urban adolescents. *American Journal of Community Psychology, 19,* 173–206.

Selman, R. (1980). *The growth of interpersonal understanding: Developmental and clinical analyses.* New York: Academic Press.

Shade, B. (1983). The social success of black youth: The impact of significant others. *Journal of Black Studies, 14*(2), 137–150.

Sharabany, R., Gershoni, R., & Hofman, J. (1981). Girlfriend, boyfriend: Age and sex differences in intimate friendship. *Developmental Psychology, 17*(6), 800–808.

Shorris, E. (1992). *Latinos.* New York: Norton.

Shulman, S. (1993). Close friendships in early and mid adolescence: Typology and friendship reasoning. In B. Laursen, ed., *Close friendships in adolescence.* San Francisco: Jossey Bass.

Simpson, J., & Weiner, E. (1989). *The Oxford English dictionary.* 2d ed., vol. 3. Oxford: Clarendon Press.

Spencer, M. B., Brookins, G. K., & Allen, W. R. (1985). *Beginnings: The social and affective development of black children.* Hillsdale, NJ: Erlbaum.

Spencer, M., & Dornbusch, S. (1990). Challenges in studying minority youth. In S. S. Feldman and G. R. Elliott, eds., *At the threshold: The developing adolescent.* Cambridge, MA: Harvard University Press.

Stacey, J. (1988). Can there be a feminist ethnography? *Women's Studies International Forum, 11*(1), 21–27.

Stack, C. (1974). *All our kin: Strategies for survival in a black community.* New York: Harper and Row.

Steinitz, V. A., & Solomon, E. R. (1986). *Starting out: Class and community in the lives of working-class youth.* Philadelphia: Temple University Press.

Strauss, A. (1987). *Qualitative analysis for social scientists.* New York: Cambridge University Press.

Strauss, C. (1990). Who gets ahead? Cognitive responses to heteroglossia in American political culture. *American Ethnologist,* May.

Sullivan, H. S. (1953). *The interpersonal theory of psychiatry.* New York: Norton.

Sum, A. M., & Fogg, W. N. (1991). The adolescent poor and the transition to early adulthood. In P. B. Edelman & J. Ladner, eds., *Adolescence and poverty: Challenge for the 1990's.* Washington, DC: Center for National Policy Press.

Taylor, J. M., Gilligan, C., & Sullivan, A. M. (1995). *Between voice and silence: Women and girls, race and relationship.* Cambridge, MA: Harvard University Press.

Taylor, R. L. (1995). In R. L. Taylor, ed., *African-American youth: Their social and economic status in the United States.* Westport, CT: Praeger.

Thomas, M. (1996). Diversity in women's friendships. Talk given at Association for Women in Psychology, Portland, Oregon, March 14–17.

Torres, L. (1992). Women's narratives in a New York Puerto Rican community. In L. L. F. Rakow, *Women making meaning: New feminist directions in communication.* New York: Routledge.

Turner, R., Irwin, C., Tschann, J., & Millstein, S. (1994). *Autonomous-relatedness and changes in self-esteem during early adolescence.* Paper delivered at the Society for Research Adolescence, San Diego, February 13.

Wade-Gayles, G. (1984). The truths of our mothers' lives: Mother-daughter relationships in black women's fiction. *Sage, 1*(2), 8–12.

Ward, J. V. (1988). Urban adolescents' conceptions of violence. In C. Gilligan, J. V. Ward., & J. M. Taylor, eds., *Mapping the moral domain.* Cambridge, MA: Center for the Study of Gender, Education, and Human Development.

———. (1990). Racial identity formation and transformation. In C. Gilligan, N. Lyons, & T. Hanmer, eds., *Making connections: The relational worlds of adolescent girls at Emma Willard School.* Cambridge, MA: Harvard University Press.

———. (1996). Raising resisters: The role of truth telling in the psychological development of African American girls. In B. J. Leadbeater & N. Way, eds., *Urban girls,* pp. 85–99. New York: New York University Press.

Way, N. (1990). Social class and time perspective: A review and critique of the literature. Unpublished qualifying paper, Harvard Graduate School of Education, Cambridge, MA.

———. (1995). "Can't you see the courage, the strength that I have?": Listening to urban adolescent girls speak about their relationships. *Psychology of Women Quarterly, 19,* 107–128.

———. (1996). Between experiences of betrayal and desire: Close friendships among urban adolescents. In B. J. Leadbeater & N. Way, eds., *Urban girls*, pp. 173–192. New York: New York University Press.

———. (In press). Using feminist research methods to understand the friendships of adolescent boys. *Journal of Social Issues.*

Way, N., & Stauber, H. (1996). Are "absent fathers" really absent? Urban adolescent girls speak out about their fathers. In B. J. Leadbeater & N. Way, eds., *Urban girls*. New York: New York University Press.

Way, N., Stauber, H., Nakkula, M., & London, P. (1994). Depression and substance abuse in two divergent high school cultures: A quantitative and qualitative analysis. *Journal of Youth and Adolescence, 23,* 331–357.

Weiner, B., Russell, D., & Lerman, D. (1978). Affective consequences of causal ascriptions. In J. H. Harvey, W. J. Ickes, & R. F. Kidd, eds., *New directions in attribution research*, vol. 2. Hillsdale, NJ: Erlbaum.

Weininger, O. (1975). Personality and the subjective experience of time. *Journal of Personality Assessment, 37,* 103–114.

Weis, L., & Fine, M. (1996). Narrating the 1980s and 1990s: Voices of the poor and working class. Unpublished manuscript.

White, R. (1952). *Lives in progress: A study of the natural growth of personality.* New York: Dryden Press.

Willis, P. E. (1977). *Learning to labor.* Aldershot: Gower.

Winfield, L. F. (1995). The knowledge base on resilience in African-American adolescents. In L. J. Crockett & A. C. Crouter, eds., *Pathways through adolescence: Individual development in relation to social contexts.* Mahwah, NJ: Erlbaum.

Wong, M. (1997). Women on welfare. Ph.D. diss. CUNY Graduate Center, Department of Social and Personality Psychology, New York.

Wortham, S. (1997). Identity development among culturally isolated Latino adolescents: Evidence from life-history narratives. Paper presented at the Society for Research in Child Development Biennial Meeting, Washington, DC.

Youniss, J., & Smollar, J. (1985). *Adolescent relations with mothers, fathers, and friends,* Chicago: University of Chicago Press.

Index

Death: attitude toward, 49–50, 62; and depending on others, 70; fear of, 164–84, 266
Debold, Elizabeth, 109
Decenteredness of experience, 22–23
Deficit model of minorities, 13
Dependency, attitudes toward, 70
Development, human, importance of context in study of, 24–25
Developmental metanarratives, 18–19
Developmental psychology: biases in, 16–21; challenging theories of, 19; limited perspective of, 4; new methods needed in, 265; privileged metaphors in, 25; sexism in, 21
Developmental theory, definition of, 16*n*
Discovery research, neglect of, in social science research, 17
Discrimination: experiences of, 205–17; strategies for overcoming, 212–16. *See also* Racism
Dropping out of school: poor opinion of school as cause of, 197; rate of, among poor youth, 5; rate of, at studied school, 30; risk for, 201
Drug use: attitudes toward, 48, 71–72, 232–33, 243; interview protocol on, 275
DuBois, D. L., 143

Eichenbaum, Luise, 104
Emmons, Christine, 142
Epstein, Joyce, 142
Erikson, Erik, 16, 20
Ethnography, definition of, 10*n*
Eva (case study), 227–59; background of, 40; on effect of interviewer's sex and race, 219; on experiences with sexism, 212; junior year of, 236–46; on laziness in school, 188; on overcoming discrimination, 214; physical description of, 227, 246; self-description of, 254; senior year of, 246–58; sophomore year of, 228–36; on speaking out, 2, 78, 88, 110
Expectations, learning to challenge in research, 13–16

Extended self: among African Americans, 264; among Latinos, 264

Failure, fear of, 164–84
Family: interview protocol on, 271; sense of commitment to, 44, 145–63
Family members: loss of, 164, 165–66
Father(s): abusive, 93; Eva's relationship with, 227, 228–29, 237, 249–51; interview protocol on, 272; Malcolm's relationship with, 43, 53–54, 71; as negative example, 149; as negative force, 155–56, 192; relationship with, 146, 157, 158, 159; as role models, 90–91; willingness to challenge, 84–86, 87, 94, 102. *See also* Parents
Father figure(s): child as, 54–55; mother as, 43–44. *See also* Male role model(s)
Fatherhood, among urban youth, 47–48, 64, 65, 70
Fear: of failure, 164–84; of harm, reaction to, 64–65. *See also* Danger; Death, fear of
Felicia (case study): on experiences with racism, 210; on friends, 134–35; on problems with school, 196–97
Fine, Michelle, 24, 40–41, 110
Flax, Jane, 22
Florence (case study), on speaking out, 89
Focus of this study, 8–9
Frankenberg, Ruth, 220
Freud, Sigmund, 16
Friends: abandonment by, 125–27; vs. associates, 45, 114–16; attitudes toward, 45, 55, 66–68, 238–39; best, vs. close, 116; danger of being outspoken with, 96; desire for, 261; difficulty of finding, 112; improving relations with, 88; inability to trust, 97–99, 113–23, 123–29; intimacy among, 118–19, 120–21, 123–25; lack of, 86; loss of, in adolescence, 67, 113–14, 120, 122–23, 134–38; loyalty among, 132. *See also* Relationships
Friendship(s): among boys, 112–29, 133–44; among girls, 129–44, 239, 240; betrayal in, 118, 121–23, 127–37, 168,

Romantic relationships. *See* Boyfriend(s); Girlfriend(s); Relationships

Rorty, Richard, 24

Safety. *See* Danger

Sample analyzed in this study, characteristics of, 29–30, 32

Samuel (case study): on effect of interviewer's sex and race, 218; on experiences with racism, 208; on fears of the future, 167–68; on laziness in school, 188–90

Schleiermacher, Friedrich, 12

School(s): attitude toward, 49, 60, 68–69, 185–204, 233; blame for decline in quality of, 30; interview protocol on, 275–76; lack of challenge/interest in, 190, 192–94, 195, 198–202; poor conditions in, 187–88, 196–97, 200, 201–2. *See also* Academic performance; Academic standards, low; Setting for this study

Self: blaming, for poor academic performance, 185–96; sense of, among African Americans, 43, 264; sense of, in urban youth, 22; unitary, feminist questioning of, 22

Self-description, 59, 69, 71, 78–111, 254; interview protocol on, 274–75

Selman, Robert, 20

Setting for this study, 30–32, 142, 187–88

Sex: attitude toward, 47–48, 94, 230, 241; as conquest, 46, 47; interview protocol on, 274. *See also* Birth control; Children, attitudes toward

Sexism: in developmental theory, 21; in encouragement of leaders, 103; as excuse, 214; interview protocol on, 275–76; perceptions of, 211–12, 221–22, 267; and silencing of women, 104–11; in social science, 4

Shakira (case study): on effect of interviewer's sex and race, 218–19; on overcoming discrimination, 214; on speaking out, 81–83, 92

Shawn (case study), on friends, 119, 143

Shorris, Earl, 162

Sibling(s): Eva's relationship with, 227, 229, 237–38; interview protocol on, 272–73; Malcolm's relationships with, 45, 52, 62, 64; Mary's relationships with, 80

Social science: bias in methodology of, 6; exclusion of poor and minorities from, 4–6; importance of theoretical framework in, 16–17; neglect of discovery research in, 17; racism of, 13; sexism of, 4; validity of, 12–13

Society: attitudes toward, 72; interview protocol on, 275–76. *See also* Culture, American

Solomon, Ellen, 182

Sonia (case study): on defeating stereotypes, 2; on experiences of racism, 211; on fears of the future, 177–78; on friends, 131–33; on laziness in school, 194–96; on mother, 158; on overcoming racism, 216

Speaking out. *See* Outspokenness

Steinitz, Victoria, 182

Stereotypes: dangers of, 10; racist, affirmation of, 216; of urban youth, 1, 2, 5–6, 203, 260, 269

Study, details of: analysis of data, 26–27, 34–38, 76–77, 277–78; effect of researcher on study participants, 26–28, 223; interview protocol, 33–38, 271–76; purpose, 8–9, 24, 268–69; researcher background, 29–30; sample analyzed, 29–30, 32; setting, physical, 30–32, 142, 187–88

Success: attitudes toward, 59–60, 61–63, 68–69, 72, 254–55; competition as motivation for, 234–35; and mothers, 146–47, 149, 162–63; and racism, 62–63, 205–6, 222

Suleiman, Susan, 22

Sullivan, Harry Stack, 16, 20

Sullivan, W., 12

Suspension rate, at school studied, 30–31

Talking Back (hooks), 110

Taylor, Ronald L., 5